Natural Health and Nutrition For Dogs
Revised Edition 2

About The Author
Debbie Daniel is certified in Natural Pet Care and has studied extensively in Canine Arthritis and Joint issues. Her approach is to educate pet parents on how to avoid many toxins in your pets lives along with keeping the joints healthy even into the senior years, and to help extend your dog's life and reduce illness overall. Her mission is to help Pet Parents learn about Holistic Integrative Remedies and Nutrition.

Copyright © Debbie Daniel
9781793817389
Revised Edition 2 - January 9th, 2019
All rights reserved.
No part of this book may be reproduced, scanned, or distributed in any printed or electronic form without permission.
Printed in the USA
Cover Designed by Debbie Daniel

*I would like to acknowledge my 5 dogs Diamond, Stormy, Sydney, Callie and Carley that have taught me so much just from the many illnesses and joint problems along the way. My life changed when I adopted these girls. They are my life and every day I continue to learn from them. How they interact with one another, how they deal with pain and anxiety and when they need me the most. And most of all, bring me joy and make me laugh every day! These girls are work but it's worth it because they deserve a terrific life compared to the life they had before me. I owe it to them to make up for the past abuse they may have suffered throughout. And this is why I have learned to provide the best diet and protect them from our own environmental toxins in today's world.
RIP to Molly and Sassy!*

Intro

This book is about making changes in your dog's life to help them thrive and live a long healthy life instead of just surviving. Learning to feed a proper diet and reduce many illnesses and exposure to toxins.

This is a 2nd revised edition as I keep finding and thinking of more things to add. I feel passionate about providing you the correct important information that I may run across or learn.

This is my recommendations and solutions using holistic and natural health care, nutrition, and herbal remedies.

Remember: *Always know what's ahead instead of waiting for what's to come. Prevention has always been the best medicine. Be proactive instead of reactive!*

Contents

Ch. 1-Kibble and Pet Foods..4

Ch. 2-Allergies, Leaky Gut and Acid Reflux............10

Ch. 3-Homemade Diets for Dogs................................28

Ch. 4-Supplementation...87

Ch. 5-Canine Arthritis & Joint Pain........................102

Ch. 6-Lawn Care with Weeds, Fleas, and Ticks......146

Ch. 7-Heartworm Treatment/Prevention.................155

Ch. 8-Heart Disease..163

Ch. 9-Storm Anxiety..178

Ch. 10-Cancer-Prevention, Treatment, and Diet....184

Ch. 11-Healing Herbs...228

Ch. 12-How to Prepare for the Rabies Vaccine.......256

Ch. 13-Leaving Your Pet At The Vet........................262

Ch. 14-Dog Parks: How Safe Are They?..................266

Ch. 15-Safety Precautions Walking Your Dog........268

Chapter 1
Kibble and Pet Foods

Carnivores cannot digest properly when eating foods like corn, wheat, rice, or potatoes without stressing out the digestive system and yet these are the ingredients in the most pet foods that the manufacturers use as primary ingredients in their formulas. Fortunately, most dogs are tough. Not only do they not die immediately eating inappropriate foods, but it often takes years before the significant physical destruction that occurs from a lifetime of eating the wrong foods before it becomes noticeable.

One of the reasons we're able to deceive ourselves into believing convenience pet foods are good for pets is because the changes to a pet's health and vitality brought on by a processed diet are usually not immediate or acute. The pet foods today have created dozens of generations of animals that suffer from degenerative diseases linked to nutritional deficiencies.

Many pet food companies use the cheapest ingredients they can find. Whether it comes from dead, diseased, road kill, or euthanized pets from shelters. These ingredients are not suitable for human consumption. If you won't eat it, why should your dog! Most pet foods contain 4-D ingredients. 4-D is meat and by-products that have been derived from animals that were rejected by food inspectors who classified the animals as not fit for human consumption because they were "Dead, Dying, Disabled or Diseased" at the time of inspection. Any chemicals that existed within that animal would still be inside of it when dead. Meat by-products are nothing more than slaughterhouse waste; waste that's been banned for use in human food and then sold to the pet food industry. It's what's left over after the slaughter and classified as inedible waste, unfit for human consumption.

With dry foods, the ingredients are cooked twice. First during rendering and again in the extruder. Altered proteins may contribute to food intolerances, food allergies, and inflammatory bowel disease.

High-heat processing of pet food creates potent carcinogens like acrylamide and heterocyclic amine. Needless to say, these cancer-causing by-products won't be listed on any pet food ingredient list. But they are extremely dangerous, even in small amounts, when fed day in and day out. There's a connection between these carcinogens and the rising rates of cancer in today's pets. Proteins, antioxidants, fats, enzymes, minerals, vitamins, and beneficial bacteria are all damaged or destroyed during the heating process. Grains and legumes contain mold and even through extrusion (400 degree temps), it does not remove or kill the mold. Mold can cause cancer and/or organ failure. Your dog has 10 times higher risk of getting cancer by feeding kibble foods than any other foods. Stay away from grains and fillers such as peas and potatoes. Also, even though it isn't listed on the bag, pet foods are loaded with sugar. Nearly half of the bag is pure sugar although you won't find that on the label. The carbs break down into sugars. Do you really want to feed your dog this? Learn to read ingredients. Feeding these foods will shorten the life of your dog, because many horrible diseases like allergies, autoimmune disease, cancer, seizures, diabetes, arthritis/joint issues, gastrointestinal disorders, heart disease, kidney & liver failure, obesity, skin and coat disorders, and/or urinary tract disorders and you will be spending hard earned dollars on trying to save or care for your sick furry family member.

During extrusion, this is what occurs;

- Starch gelatinization
- Inactivation of nutritionally active factors
- Protein denaturation
- Vitamin loss

Mycotoxin ("Myco" stands for "fungus") is still a big risk in dry pet foods even after the manufacturing process is complete. Before you start moistening your pet's food to try to replace the missing moisture, you should know about mycotoxins, another potential side effect of the use of grains in pet food. Mycotoxins are naturally occurring fungal by-products that can cause disease and death in pets. When grains are improperly stored, mycotoxins can develop. Two of the most common forms have been found in pet foods are aflatoxin and vomitoxin. Although mycotoxins are found all over the world they only become toxic in temperatures above 82 degrees and over 80 percent humidity at which point they interfere with cellular function, and are extremely carcinogenic and immuno-suppressive. Aflatoxin B1 is the most toxic of the aflatoxins and is the most potent liver carcinogen known.

We know that dogs and cats are carnivores, so why do we continue to feed these foods? Not only are the ingredients extremely questionable, pet food companies have no obligation to provide the details of the ingredients. In fact, they go out of their way to try to change the names on contents to throw you off as well as leaving off vital information.

Pet food companies will switch one preservative with some unpronounceable name for another. Even if the foods are processed here in the United States, doesn't mean it wasn't sourced from China. And if you ask them, they may tell you they are made and sourced in the USA, but that may not be true at all. And they can even change the source at anytime without notifying its buyers. Most all vitamins are sourced from China - even human vitamins, so it's best to buy from a reputable company. Do your research.

These large companies are hiding so much of the truth of what is truly in these foods; it's terrifying. Corn is a cheap filler ingredient, loaded with GMOs, non-nutritious for pets, and a known allergenic. Wheat is a big source of food allergies as well and can cause intestinal upset. Wheat is covered in Glyphosate (found in Round Up weed killer) as most all of our foods are coated in it. Soy (GMO) is estrogenic and wreaks havoc on your pet's endocrine system. Even when people say they cannot digest gluten, it's more than likely not the gluten but the pesticides it's coated in. So many chemicals are causing our bodies to react and fight but when there are so many chemicals, your body just can't fight off the toxic effects day in and day out. I am certain dogs are going through the same thing on much higher levels.

Pet food companies are famous for using the **cheapest grains** they can find that are by-products of the human food waste industry. Why? How many recalls have we seen in the past several years? And it's apparent it will only get worse. Bags of dry pet foods have been filled with mold, rodents, worms, and moths to name a few. And how many bags have made humans sick from salmonella? Tons! And to top this off, studies found that the bag itself is leeching toxins into the foods.

Don't forget your 4-Ds:
4-Ds: Road kill, slaughter house rejects, animals that die on their way to meat packing plants - all are acceptable ingredients for pet food under the "4D" rule. Steroids, growth hormones and chemicals (yes there really is) used to treat cattle including insecticide patches end up mixed into the final product.

Feeding kibble to your pet has almost always some irreversible damage. Kibble dehydrates the system leaving it lacking in moisture which therefore causes kidney and bladder stones/crystals. Pets have to drink over 5 times the amount of water to stay hydrated throughout the day. Kibble also causes periodontal disease from buildup of chemicals, addicting additives and preservatives. Kibble is also loaded with sugar although you won't find that on the label. The bags are almost half sugar of the actual food in the bag. Unbelievable. Kibble almost always causes cancer and/or some form of kidney and liver failure as well as arthritis and food allergies. It may not occur immediately but over a period of time, it will take its toll on your pet. People think a dog living 10-15 years is great. It's not. Our pets should live almost double that time and they can if we change the diet and remove toxins, chemicals and the low quality ingredients in pet foods. When pets try to digest the kibble, the body has a very difficult time breaking down all the chemicals and additives, which overworks the entire digestive system causing other issues like vomiting, diarrhea, Irritable Bowel Syndrome (IBS), bloody stools, and colon cancer. To have a healthy gut, you must feed a species appropriate diet. This does not include feeding bagged, pouched, or canned pet foods.

All pet foods (canned, bagged etc) including prescription diet foods recommended by your vet, are extremely deadly. Vets did not take a course in nutrition. Large pet food manufacturers like Purina and Hills come into clinics/colleges and give a 3-4 hour lecture of why these foods are much better than others and how they can help heal your pet. It's a ploy to sell more pet foods. Veterinarians do not know any better. And the ones that do are most likely your holistic veterinarians. Don't be totally trusting in your vet. He/She may not know how to read the ingredients and don't know what harm they can do. You, as a pet parent need to be vigilante and know what's best for your pets when it comes to diet, vaccines, and medications. If you stand your ground, and still your vet will not accept the way you are feeding or your denial of vaccines, FIND A NEW VET THAT WILL! No one should tell you what you can and can't do on how to take better care of your pet. I hope this book will help you a lot in answering those questions. It doesn't cost a fortune to feed a super good food to your pets. Even if you buy **expensive high quality kibble** (or canned), you're still buying junk and paying a fortune. Why pay for hamburger at a high price when you can buy steak for the same or lower price. Make a change today. You won't regret it! And remember, not only are these pet foods killing pets, so are the deadly tainted toxic treats. If you must buy treats, buy homemade from small mom and pop shops. Check ingredients. Search out organic ingredients.

DO NOT BUY grocery store or pet store treats!! There have been many deaths from these! As I always say, **"Better Safe Than Sorry."**

Stop buying these foods and supporting these companies or they will continue to sell them and more animals will die.

Most all of your gastrointestinal disorders are caused by diet and lack of nutrients and enzymes. Commercial pet foods are the hardest on the digestive system. Kibble takes a long time breaking down in the GI tract that puts the digestive system into an overly stressed situation and causing a slight dehydration at all times. Homemade is easier to digest and provides little to no stress on the digestive tract and provides extra moisture that is needed. It's time to make a change now so your dog can live a long healthy pain-free life and this book will tell you how to do just that.

"Running to the store to buy a bag of pet food is nothing more than a convenience to the human. But it is a slow death to your pet."

All disease begins in the gut. - Hippocrates

Throughout this book, I am going to sound like a broken record. It is so that you will understand the importance of what I am saying and how it applies to every ailment or daily activity. And I hope it will come naturally to you by the time you finish so that you won't second-guess yourself when making changes.

Chapter 2
Allergies, Leaky Gut and Acid Reflux

Normally allergies are caused from the overly processed same diet fed for years. Diet is crucial as to what creates these allergies. Changing of the diet fixes allergy symptoms 80% of the time.

If you suspect or have had issues for awhile with your pets skin including hot spots, black gunk in the ears, yeasty ears and feet, frito feet (feet smell like corn chips), scratching, skin redness and/or bumps, flaky skin, sneezing, coughing and/or watery eyes, regurgitation or loose stools then read further on how to help your pet become allergy-free.

First off, eliminate all chemicals around the house. This includes laundry soaps, shampoos, lotions, medications, floor cleaners, glass cleaners, air fresheners and anything you use that contains chemicals including burning candles. Get a diffuser instead (if you don't have cats). Learn about essential oils before using. Use chemical-free fabric softener sheets (Seventh Generation) or better yet, purchase organic wool dryer balls. Dryer sheets are hard on your dryer sensors and may cause your dryer to fail. Use organic all-natural lawn fertilizers, no weed killers or bug sprays. There are many products available that do not contain chemicals and work just as well, if not better. Most all of your popular name brand products contain a lot of chemicals. Think about your sheets, blankets, clothes, towels that are being washed in chemicals and you are lying on or wearing on your body. Your dog is right there with you. And your carpets, rugs, and even your couch that may contain Scotchguard. What about in your vehicle? Oh my, all those chemicals. Isn't it overwhelming?

Do not use ANY flea and tick medications you buy from your vet or from a pharmacy. Even the OTC (Over-The-Counter) junk you buy in stores is extremely toxic. I have seen/heard of many deaths from using these as well. Use all-natural treatments. Do not vaccinate your pets yearly. It is not needed. Rabies (by law) is to be given every 3 years. Make sure your vet is on the same page as this and offers the 3-year Rabies vaccine and doesn't force pet parents to do the 1-year vaccine. If he/she does, FIND A NEW VET. Ask for the Thimerosal-Free Rabies vaccine. I recommend titer testing for the core vaccines (Distemper, Parvo, and Adenovirus) and including Rabies. If your vet charges outrageous prices for titers, have him/her look into Vaccicheck or check with Kansas State University and/or Dr. John Robb at ProtectThePets.com for titers on vaccines for all 4 for a much cheaper price. Or order the titers direct through KSU. Do not let your vet take your dog to the back without you watching the vaccine being drawn up and injected if you decide on a vaccine. You will probably have to pay for an office visit this way but at least you KNOW what's taking place.

Some vets want to charge for both titers and vaccines. Don't get sucked into this. They should not ask you to pay for a vaccine if you paid for a titer.

For heartworm treatments or preventatives, use the all-natural solutions (see chapter on Heartworm Prevention and Treatment). Also add fragrant grasses in and around your yard that deter mosquitoes and insects. (Lavender, Lemongrass, Peppermint, Eucalyptus, etc.) For applications for your yard and to be added into foods, use Diatomaceous Earth (FOOD GRADE). Also, D.E. kills and repels insects in your yard and home. It's a great dewormer as well. It does not kill tapeworms or heartworms. Pumpkin Seeds (can use raw powder as well) will kill tapeworms along with other parasites excluding heartworms. Give 1/4 teaspoon of pumpkin seed powder per 10 pounds of your dog's weight. It has also been said that Chamomile can work to prevent/expel both roundworms and whipworms.

If you would like to check for food allergies only using saliva, you can do this through Dr. Jean Dodds at Nutriscan.org. The test is around $300 at this time. I've spoke with several people using this test and they come back with allergic reactions to many things. So expect a lot of positive allergy reactions. In my opinion, I feel your dog will not be allergic to all the ones that test positive. Overall, it's best to do an elimination diet but it may give you direction.

There is also another company now doing testing and can be found on my website. It is done through Modern Allergy Management. They test for foods and environmental allergies for a much lower price ($75) using hair testing. If you are not sure if it's just food, you can use this one to also test for environmental.

Also, make sure you have a thyroid check (T-4) as well. Stay completely away from grocery store or dept store pet treats and foods. These are made with lots of preservatives and chemicals. Learn to read ingredients when shopping. And when it comes to commercial pet foods; these are the number one problem in skin allergies and intolerances. These foods and treats contain so many chemicals including food dyes, preservatives, synthetic vitamins, and the 4-Ds (Dead, Disabled, Dying, Diseased animals), all of which can make your pet very sick. Maybe not for a while but eventually. Look into feeding a species-appropriate diet (raw). If you want results, you must make these changes.

Commercial pet foods are the lowest quality ingredients on our planet as you read in Chapter one. So your best bet is to steer completely away from pet foods. Feed a homemade diet with the much recommended supplements to help protect your dog's joints, organs, and skin. If you want your pet to live a longer healthier life, this is the only way to go. Some commercial pet foods have also reported to even have killed pets or made them deathly sick and it took thousands of dollars to save that pet if at all. It's like playing Russian Roulette with these commercial pet foods and treats.

There are many dogs that have had allergies to pet foods; let's say chicken, and the pet parent was unable to feed chicken flavored dog foods to their dog due to reactions. But many times when fed a raw diet, these allergies do not show up at all and therefore it means the dog is not and never was allergic to chicken. It was the commercial pet food; the way it is processed and the chemicals used and including the ingredients that actually have caused the issues. In fact, pet foods really do not contain much meat at all and what's in it is disgusting. Kibble is sprayed with rancid grease for taste as well. Who knows what's in that mix! If for some reason, there is still a reaction to chicken in the raw diet, try organic. Regular chicken contains hormones, antibiotics and chemicals and that could be the problem. Yes, it does; no matter what the package says. Organic chicken does not.

Giving dogs steroids constantly WILL shorten your dog's life. It is slowly damaging the kidneys and liver. Do **not** use these long term (over 2-3 weeks max) or regularly.

Steroids are a band-aid in a pill or injection form. They are not the solution! Neither is Apoquel. It's the new medication being handed out like candy by vets for allergies. This suppresses the immune system; not allowing it to do its job. You must remove the culprit that's causing the itching. This is not the solution, this is a big toxic band-aid. Throw away the band-aid and allow the body to heal from within. Apoquel is killing dogs and making them very sick. Why put your dog through this when it isn't necessary? Yes, you want to make your dog comfortable from all that scratching and sores, but you can do the same thing by changing the food you are feeding. Yes it takes some work, but isn't the end result worth it? Why allow both you and your dog to continue to be miserable!

Many allergies either cause a buildup of yeast or are created from a buildup of yeast. Either way, ridding the yeast is a must to resolve allergies. Many times yeast is diagnosed as allergies to other things. Candida lives off of the sugar buildup within the body coming from sugar and carbohydrates in the diet. All commercial pet foods contain sugar and carbs even though it isn't listed on the package. Antibiotics can cause a yeast build up due to antibiotics breaking down and destroying the good bacteria in the body. It is important to replenish the body with good bacteria by adding in probiotics daily.

How do you know if your dog has yeast? Yeast has a very obvious odor to it. Some people think it smells like molded bread; others think it smells like cheese popcorn or corn chips. I myself smelled corn chips on my dog's feet. Ears can have a foul odor as well when there is a buildup of yeast. Yeast infections also cause a lot of bacteria build up and lots of scratching, as it is very itchy. First thing to do is avoid all sugars even in a good natural form like raw honey or blackstrap molasses. While these may work for some illnesses and are beneficial, it only feeds the yeast and creates more scratching and redness. So avoid all foods and products containing sugars and yeast additives at this time.

Many times vets will give you medications for treatment but these are only band-aids. You MUST address the diet or you will continue on this long battle of never ending scratching, stinky feet, ears, and skin rashes.

You can help fight off yeast of the skin and ears by using Apple Cider Vinegar on them daily until all symptoms have dissipated. Applying ACV to open sores may burn so you may try diluting it at first until sores start to go way or heal. Daily dunking of the feet in ACV and water will help reduce yeast. Simply wiping the feet down won't help as it won't cover in-between the toes and cracks and crevices. Check sweaty areas of the body or creases and folds in the skin for yeast build up as well. If the entire body/skin is affected, try povidone iodine baths (dark tea color) followed with a rinsing of apple cider vinegar daily. When you start to see progress, you can do this every other day until symptoms are completely gone. Do not rinse after the bath. Pat dry. Do not get this in your dog's eyes. You can use a rung out washcloth for helping to wipe down the face.

Make sure you add apple cider vinegar into the dog's diet as well daily. This will work internally on the yeast and balance the PH levels in the body. For future baths, use a good chemical-free shampoo. Oatmeal is not one of those options as believed in the past. There are some descent ones on the market for your pets. Mercola.com makes several for pets. Yeast tends to rear its ugly head in summer months when there is more heat and humidity but can also be a year round issue in weakened immune systems. You may also rinse with apple cider vinegar after a shampooing.

Supplements and herbs to fight off Candida are listed below. Use these in very small amounts in the beginning as to not have a huge reaction to them and have more scratching going on and a miserable dog. Introduce these a little at a time to help combat yeast internally as well. Use several at a time and use for 30 days then alternate with the other ones. Do this for several months or until your dog has been symptom free for 30 days.

Candida/Yeast:
Pau D'Arco
Golden Seal (do not give to puppies)
Garlic
Oregano Oil (short-term use-2 weeks)
Apple Cider Vinegar (raw, unfiltered)
Probiotics/Digestive Enzymes (daily from here on out)
Organic Coconut Oil
Grapefruit Seed Extract
Olive Leaf
Saccharomyces boulardii (found in some probiotics)

Leaky Gut Syndrome
Many times when there is so much havoc going on in the body, it can also be blamed on Leaky Gut. Leaky Gut Syndrome is the inability of the intestinal lining to prevent undigested food or potentially toxic organisms from passing into the bloodstream. Leaky Gut is caused by damage to the gut lining which allows abnormal absorption of bacteria, toxins and gut proteins, and leads to a large number of chronic conditions. Diseases that are said to be initiated or worsened by a leaky gut include environmental and food allergies, arthritis, inflammatory bowel disease (IBD), pancreatic disease and overgrowth of yeast.

It has been determined by holistic drs that leaky gut is one of the causes of cancer. A connection has been found between the two. Leaky gut causes inflammation throughout the entire body wreaking havoc and causing different symptoms. This inflames all of the organs including weakening the immune system and allowing more disease and illness to attack.

Leaky gut starts out as allergy symptoms and progresses to malnutrition, and then it can create higher liver enzymes or other organ irregularities. Leaky gut should not be taken lightly and is one of the main causes in allergies. Chemicals and preservatives in foods can also contribute to leaky gut.

When leaky gut occurs, nutrients from foods do not get absorbed into the body. It leaks throughout holes in the digestive lining causing the body to react. Therefore, you get your allergy symptoms.

Some of the symptoms of Leaky Gut may include:

- Gas, Bloating, Diarrhea
- Vomiting
- Immune System Disorders
- Ear infections
- Bad breath
- Gum disease
- Dry eye
- Liver, Gallbladder and pancreatic disorders

- Joint pain
- Cancer
- Seizures
- Nutritional deficiencies
- Inflamed bladder
- Hyperactivity
- Skin rash, hot spots

NSAIDs and steroids are also known to cause Leaky Gut Syndrome as well as antibiotics. Remember, 70-80% of the immune system lives in the large intestine.

Once you make a diet change, you will need to help detox the body. You will need to use supplements to help it complete the detox process. Add in these recommended supplements:

- Probiotics
- Digestive Enzymes (higher doses)
- Fish oils (high quality sardine/anchovy, squid, or green lipped mussel)
- Vitamin E (non-soy) three times a week
- Organic Greens Powder or raw juiced/finely chopped leafy green veggies
- Humic/Fulvic Acid
- Calcium (if not feeding raw bone daily)
- B-Complex
- Magnesium
- Quercetin* (it acts like Benadryl-not to be given longer than 3 months)
- Slippery Elm* (not to be given longer than 3 months)
- Milk Thistle* (not to be given longer than 30 days)
- Glutamine / L-Glutamine (can be used for ulcers also)

Take a 30 day break after time given to use.

If your dog has a sensitive stomach or intestinal tract issue, add Slippery Elm daily to help coat the lining of the tract. Slippery Elm along with Probiotics and Digestive Enzymes will help many allergies and tummy issues as well as Leaky Gut and diarrhea. Use Slippery Elm for 3 months at most, and then take it out of the daily diet. If several months down the road you feel your dog needs it, it's ok to add it back in for a little while but do not give Slippery Elm daily long term. Occasional use is acceptable.

To help remove heavy metals from the body that have been acquired through vaccines, unfiltered water, non-organic foods etc, you can use any or all of these:

- Activated Charcoal
- Chlorella
- Wheatgrass
- Moringa
- Dandelion Root
- Burdock Root
- Milk Thistle
- Diatomaceous Earth (Food Grade)
- Calcium Bentonite Clay

Dark leafy greens in general help remove these toxins.

Just add these in with wet foods. Activated Charcoal is well...black. So putting into food will turn it black and everything it touches. You may have better luck using capsules. I use the powder in my doggie cookies I make. Add coconut oil to the diet as well. You can also use it externally.

For immediate relief from itching and hot spots: Give a bath in Povidone Iodine and water. Dilute it to resemble a darker tea color. It's safe, non-toxic, antifungal, antibacterial, and anti-yeast. Soak for 2-5 minutes. Do not rinse off. Do this daily until itching stops or sores have subsided. Great for washing irritants off gathered from the lawn or other public places on those paws. You can find Povidone Iodine at any Pharmacy. You can also follow up with a diluted apple cider vinegar rinse in worse cases.

Until you make these changes, your dog will only become worse. It is inevitable that when all of these toxins enter the body that it eventually will no longer be able to fight off all the chemicals. So start immediately and make these changes not only for your dog but for your health as well. And also if you smoke, do NOT smoke anywhere around your pets at all. Take it outside and away from your pets. They cannot tell you that so I will.

Raw goat's milk is good for allergies. Pasteurized dairy of any kind is not. In fact, pasteurization contributes to leaky gut as well. Fermented dairy is acceptable and tolerated.

Colloidal Silver
For ear infections, you can place 3 to 5 drops of Colloidal Silver into the ear canal 2 to 3 times a day. Gently rub/massage the ear in a circular motion till ear is saturated. Do not use any of this treatment if your dog's eardrums are perforated/punctured. Apply to hot spots or insect bites 3 times daily with cotton ball or purchase the Colloidal Silver spray.

The best way to detox your dog is feed a homemade diet using as much organic foods as possible, filtering the water including the removal of fluoride and chlorine and a HEPA air filtration system in the home. You can get several air purifiers to put in your home especially at night where everyone sleeps. Diffusing certain essential oils will help as well. You can also diffuse colloidal silver as well.

Once you have changed the diet and added in probiotics and digestive enzymes, fish oils, vitamin E, filtered water, and cleared the house and yard of chemicals, you can then begin another form of detox. You add in your greens, milk thistle and other items listed. Do all of this slowly. Add in one or two into the diet, then after 7 days; if there is no reaction; add in one or two more. Also, start with lower dose and work up. Do not add everything in all at once or you may create a huge mess with the entire immune system. Your dog may get cannon butt and become one big ball of ITCH. It takes awhile to detox the body and you cannot hurry this. You must take it slow.

Signs of detox include:

- Mucous in poop
- Loose stools
- More scratching
- More hot spots
- Sneezing/watery eyes
- Itchy ears

You actually may experience numerous symptoms related to what you have already experienced with allergies and they may become more intense before it gets better. This is why we must detox the body slowly. So again, change the food, filter the water, remove chemicals inside and outside the house, remove toxins like flea and tick medications. Anything medication related for preventing heartworm, flea and tick and so on. All of these are chemicals in which can create reactions in the body.

Once you have done all of this and you are not having any intense reactions, this is when to add in your added supplements to finish cleansing the immune system. For severe conditions, I would detox for 6 months then off for 6 months then back on for 30 days. Do this every 6 months. Don't give up on getting through the detox part. It will be difficult especially the first time but if you take it slow, the symptoms will not be so severe. And next time it will be much easier and milder.

Pure Mangosteen Rind Juice
Mangosteen Juice has shown great promise in treating allergies in humans; it can also work just as well in treating animal diseases and symptoms of dog's allergies. The best way to help your dog with allergies is adding in Mangosteen Juice to your dog's diet. It's worth a try.

Approximate Dosage:
Small dogs: 1 tsp
Medium dogs: 1 1/2 tsp
Large dogs: 2 tsp

Acid Reflux or Gastroesophageal reflux (GERD)
Acid Reflux happens when the sphincter muscle of the lower esophagus is weak or has been damaged. Stomach acids can come up into the esophagus causing more damage and irritation. This condition can be mild or severe. Some breeds with flat faces are more prone to Acid Reflux/GERD as well. Smaller and more frequent meals work better for these dogs. Limit treats. Avoid fatty meats such as pork, lamb, duck, and beef. My dog Carley that has Acid Reflux doesn't do well with beef or turkey even. She does great on rabbit and goat in which are very lean meats. Carley is on a raw diet and gets limited treats. Smaller meals have worked better for her but supplements added have really helped a lot as well.

L-Glutamine, Collagen and Amla has helped quite a bit along with stronger human digestive enzymes, probiotics, Slippery Elm and Apple Cider Vinegar daily in her meal. Her symptoms usually occur at night and last all night long although on occasion during the day with no reason at all.

Acid Reflux can occur when your dog is given anesthesia that can cause the esophageal sphincter to relax and creates an opening between the stomach and the esophagus. This happens when a patient is not properly positioned while undergoing anesthesia on the surgery table, or when the dog hasn't been fasted properly before anesthesia when having surgery. To diagnose Acid Reflux, make sure your dog does not have an ulcer. Have your veterinarian check. Ulcers may require different treatment not listed here.

Signs and Symptoms of Acid Reflux/GERD are:

- Regurgitation
- Vomiting up meal hours later
- Eating grass
- Licking front legs/feet
- Smacking lips
- Constant swallowing
- Gagging/hacking sound
- Sleepy or laying down after eating

Dogs with Acid Reflux should not exercise before or after meals for at least one hour. Chiropractic and Acupuncture has been known to help these dogs with Acid Reflux.

There is also another known condition called Megaesphagus. This condition is caused by improper functioning of the esophagus muscles in your pet. Usually an x-ray of the esophagus can diagnose this condition. Megaesophagus is usually misdiagnosed as a gastrointestinal disorder. There is much more to this illness and it's best to do your research on it before knowing how to handle this completely.

Some Symptoms of Megaesophagus are:

- Weight loss
- Difficulty swallowing, exaggerated swallowing and frequent swallowing
- Refuse to eat
- Chronic bad breath
- Regurgitation (passive vomiting without retching) of food, mucus or water
- Clearing the throat with a hacking sound
- Loss of appetite

Many dogs can live with this disease under very close management and using a Bailey Chair for eating and for up to 20 minutes after eating. A Bailey Chair is where a dog is in a cushioned box similar to a high chair and they eat with their bodies in an upright position. Dogs can adjust to these and do well using them. Megaesphagus should be closely monitored and taken very seriously if you are to have a good outcome. Many times dogs need a higher calorie intake to keep weight on them so monitoring the weight is critical as well. Some dogs may do better on a liquid diet such as blended foods. These dogs also do better with smaller meals and fed more often throughout the day. Aspiration pneumonia is common in dogs with Megaesophagus and is usually the cause of death.

These supplements can be used for such issues:

Leaky Gut/ GI Tract Issues/Allergies/Acid Reflux/GERD

L-Glutamine/Glutamine
Powder Dosage:
Small dogs: 1/8 - 1/4 scoop
Medium dogs: 1/4 - 1/2 scoop
Large dogs: 1/2 scoop - 3/4 scoop

Slippery Elm (use up to 3 months)
Powder Dosage:
Small dogs: 1/4 scoop
Medium dogs: 1/2 scoop
Large dogs: 1/2 scoop - 3/4 scoop

Calcium Bentonite Clay/ Calcium Montmorillonite Clay
Small dogs: 1/4 tsp
Medium dogs: 3/4 tsp
Large dogs: 1 tsp
Daily for 14-30 days then take a break for a bit. Give plenty of water along with this as well.

Colostrum
Dosage:
Small dogs: 1/4 - 1/2 teaspoon daily
Medium dogs: 1/2 - 1 teaspoon
Large dogs: 1 - 2 teaspoon

Probiotics (10 billion+)
Dosage as directed in pet products or human caps:

If using human supplement:
Dosage:
Small dogs: 1/4 - 1/2 capsule
Medium dogs: 1 capsule
Large dogs: 1 - 2 capsules
Giant dogs: Human dose

Digestive Enzymes (higher doses-human or pet supplement)
Dosage:
Small dogs: 1/2 - 1 capsule
Medium dogs: 1 - 2 capsules
Large dogs: 2 capsules

L-Histidine (amino acid)
Dosage:
Small dogs: 25mg
Medium dogs: 50mg
Large dogs: 75mg

N-acetylcysteine (amino acid) (also used for Tylenol toxicity)
Dosage:
Small dogs: 25mg
Medium dogs: 50mg
Large dogs: 75mg

Bee Pollen
Dosage:
1 teaspoon for every 50 lbs of body weight

Licorice (do not use with heart disease) or Deglycrrhizinated Licorice (DGL) (small amounts or short term use)
Dosage:
Small dogs: 1/4 - 1/2 capsule
Medium dogs: 1/2 - 3/4 capsule
Large dogs: 3/4 - 1 capsule

Make sure there is NO Xylitol in the human brand you purchase.

Cat's Claw
Follow herb chart in this book
Do not use Cat's Claw if your dog has Leukemia, bleeding disorders, Autoimmune disease or low blood pressure.

Oregon Grape
Follow herb chart in this book

If dosage isn't listed above for capsules, follow the label on amounts. If it says one capsule per human, give based off of a 150lb human. if your dog is 20 lbs, give 1/8-1/4 capsule contents. If your dog is 60 lbs, give 1/2 capsule. These are approximate but you will adjust accordingly.

Calcium Carbonate/Eggshells (natural antacid and calcium supplement)
Dosage:
Follow dose on container or 1/2 teaspoon of ground eggshell yields about 1,000mg of calcium

Apple Cider Vinegar
Dosage:
0-25 lbs: 1 teaspoon
25-50 lbs: 2 teaspoon
50-75 lbs: 1 TBSP
75+ lbs: 1 1/2 - 2 TBSP

Collagen
Collagen works on nails, coat, joints, and digestive tract to name a few. Collagen peptide is another term for hydrolyzed collagen. If purchasing human products, start with a low dose and work up in dosing over a few weeks time. Adjust accordingly. Not all Collagens are created equal. Some do not contain amino acids. Collagen is a tasteless and odorless powder so easy to use and mix into wet foods. There are 9 essential amino acids: histidine, isoleucine, leucine, lysine, methionine, phenylalanine, threonine, tryptophan, and valine. And 20 amino acids in total. These amino acids play a key role in our health as well as our pets. The body cannot make amino acids so they must come from the diet.

Approximate Dosage:
Small dogs: 1/4 scoop
Medium dogs: 1/2 scoop
Large dogs: 1 scoop

Amla
Amla fruit (Emblica officinalis), also known as Indian Gooseberry or Amalaki, is one of the richest sources of bioflavonoids and vitamin C. This plum-sized fruit is admired for its anti-aging and immune system-enhancing properties. Each Amla fruit contains up to 700mg of vitamin C. Amla also acts as an antacid and anti-tumorigenic agent. In addition, it increases protein synthesis and is useful in cases of hypoglycemia. Amla powder is also rich in fiber, which helps support digestion and prevents constipation. *Amla may also help reduce acidity in the gut*, protect from gallbladder infections, treat diabetes, and reduce the risk for gastrointestinal cancer and cancer of the respiratory tract.

Dosage:
Small dogs: 500mg
Medium dogs: 750mg
Large dogs: 1000mg

This is the beginning of your mission in helping your dog heal. A strict diet can heal much more than just leaky gut. It can work wonders for your dog. With a dog that has many issues such as listed above, everything will need to be taken very slow. We must avoid all chemicals, vaccines, medications, flea and tick and heartworm preventatives, unfiltered water, chemical ridden homes and lawns. All of this can be changed. Just a fabric softener sheet such as Bounce can wreak havoc on the body. It's loaded with toxic chemicals. Also your laundry soaps, shampoos, carpet cleaners, floor-cleaning products, air fresheners, cleaning products such as Windex etc.

You can use diffusers for air fresheners using safe essential oils (such as peppermint or sweet orange), organic dryer balls and chemical-free fabric softener sheets, organic laundry soaps, chemical-free lawn fertilizers and products. You can use Heartworm nosodes or other safe products for heartworm preventative, natural products for fleas and ticks. Vinegar (white) and water for floors and carpets. A mix of rubbing alcohol and vinegar to clean windows. Think how much you can save using these cheap products. Baking soda and vinegar is a great cleaner for garbage disposals. You want to avoid toxic fumes from using chemical products. The mix of vinegar and baking soda will create a foaming action without chemicals. Use the internet to your advantage to find safe products. I have numerous lists on my website for many things. There is one non aerosol spray that is used for air freshener and it is made from oranges called 'Pure Citrus'. I love this stuff. They also make one that's lemon scented.

If dosage isn't listed under each supplement, use this chart for dosing:

Herb Dosage

Weight	Tincture	0 Capsule	Tea	Powder
5-10 lbs	2 drops	1/2 cap	1 tsp	1/4 tsp
10-20 lbs	4 drops	1 cap	2 tsp	1/4-1/2 tsp
20-30 lbs	6 drops	1 cap	1 TBSP	1/2 tsp
30-50 lbs	6 drops	2 caps	4 tsp	1/2-1 tsp
50-70 lbs	6-10 drops	2 caps	5 tsp	1 tsp
70-90 lbs	14-18 drops	3 caps	2 TBSP	1 1/2 tsp
90-110 lbs	18-22 drops	4 caps	3 TBSP	2 tsp
110-150 lbs	22-26 drops	4 caps	4 TBSP	2 1/2 tsp
150-180 lbs	26-30 drops	5 caps	5 TBSP	3 tsp

All herbs should be given 5 days on and 2 days off.

If your pet experiences unusual side effects, substitute with something else. Adverse reactions to the herbs recommended are unusual. But just like people, allergic reactions are possible. Do not give your dog softgels. They do not dissolve. Poke a hole and squeeze out for best results.

Some herbs can be toxic in higher doses and should be used under a holistic vet's supervision. The ones listed here are safe unless a note with it says otherwise.

Chapter 3
Homemade Diets for Dogs

Starting a new diet change for your dog is exciting and nerve-racking, not knowing if you are ready or have all the information you need. Let me reassure you, it isn't as difficult as it may seem, nor is it as expensive as you may think. If you do your homework, you can have a workable budget and a happy, healthy dog. This article will be about my experiences with feeding raw; the transition of detoxing, and all the research I have done along the way.

First off, sit down with a pen and paper and do the math. How much a month do you spend on dog food, vet bills, vaccines, medications and anything else that pertain to caring for your dog? That includes prescription meds, heartworm preventatives, flea and tick meds etc.

To start off, you need to make a decision; are you going to fast your dog for 24 hours then jump right into raw or are you going to slowly transition? I know you may hear it's best to do it one way or the other. Honestly, I think you need to do what works best for you and your dog. (Puppies shouldn't fast. Just feed raw next meal). Always remember, anytime there is a change in diet, there will be a change in poop.

Poop
Poop plays a huge role here in knowing what's going on, so learn to read the poop.

- Large stinky poop - kibble fed dogs
- Loose poop - detoxing, too many quick changes in diet
- Diarrhea - overloaded by all the changes in diet and supplements, slow down or fast for 24 hours then start again very slowly.
- White poop - too much bone or calcium, reduce calcium intake
- Small firm (uniformed) poop (with less odor) - just right

Mucus In Poop
Mucus means an irritated colon. The problem can be from mild to severe, and is caused by bacteria, parasites, viruses, foreign objects, etc. If it doesn't clear up after a bowel movement or two, a trip to the vet may be in order.

No Poop For A Day Or Two
This can be caused by numerous things such as dehydration, stress, infected anal glands, blockage and more. Exercise can help get the digestive tract moving along with giving extra fish oil for a day or so, canned pumpkin, raw chopped leafy greens, coconut oil, and apple cider vinegar should help clear the tract. If no poop for two or more days, see a veterinarian right away.

Red or Black Poop
Red (blood) or black tarry looking poop resembling coffee grounds is an emergency. See a vet right away.

Diarrhea (may or may not include blood)
This is a different category than what I listed earlier in defining poop. Diarrhea is scary and can be serious. As mentioned under mucus in poop, the same applies. The problem can be from mild to severe, and is caused by Parasites (Giardia, hookworms, roundworms, and whipworms), bacterial and viral (a.k.a Parvovirus) infections, diet change, stress, Inflammatory disorders (Irritable Bowel Syndrome), Cancer, metabolic diseases (which may include disorders of the pancreas, liver or thyroid), medications, poisons, and obstructions.

Puppies, small dogs, and seniors are at higher risk of dehydration from just one round of explosive diarrhea. Seek vet immediately.

If your dog seems fine after an episode of diarrhea - meaning he/she is acting normal, it's best to keep an eye on him/her in case behavior changes.

If your dog seems fine but is experiencing recurrent bouts of diarrhea, you should make an appointment with vet. If it doesn't clear up after a bowel movement or two, a trip to the vet is recommended.

If your pet is an adult, healthy, and acting normal except for the diarrhea, I recommend you withhold food for 12 hours. Drinking water is fine. After 12 hours, feed a bland diet such as cooked turkey or chicken (no fat/skin) and organic pumpkin, sweet potatoes or squash. Avoid hamburger as beef contains too much fat, and rice in the colon with diarrhea tends to increase gassiness. Rice also goes right through the GI tract and causing the next bout of explosive diarrhea and undigested. Feed small meals several times a day for several days until stool is back to normal. You may also offer bone broth or chicken broth. Colostrum, digestive enzymes, probiotics, and a clay base (absorbs) called Kaolin as well as pectin (found in fruits and causes thickening) will provide relief. Also add in Slippery Elm for a few weeks.

Slippery elm is safe for puppies, adults, and senior dogs and it is safe mixed in with other medications. Give up to half teaspoon for each 10 lbs of body weight, mixed in with the bland diet twice a day.

You can give activated charcoal as this absorbs toxins in case there has been exposure.

While Imodium isn't always what we want to give, but in extreme cases of serious diarrhea and you have nothing else, you can give 1-2 caplets per bowel movement. Kaopectate works also. But stock up in your emergency kit with the items listed above. They also make specific products OTC you can keep in your kit. These will contain some preservatives and sugars but I feel it's acceptable for emergency purposes. Such products are called Toxiban or Pro-Pectalin. Toxiban contains activated charcoal as well. Pro-Pectalin contains Kaolin. For deworming, use pumpkin seed powder (does not work on heartworm).

For moderate to severe diarrhea (making your own):
Using a **food grade** Calcium bentonite clay/Calcium Montmorillonite Clay mix. Make sure it is a clean form and sold by a reputable company.

- 1 tsp Slippery Elm
- 1/2 tsp Calcium Bentonite Clay (food grade)
- 1/2 tsp Probiotics (or one capsule emptied into mix)
- 1/4 tsp Activated charcoal (absorbs most poisons and toxins)
- Up to 1 cup purified water

You want to form a paste. It may be easier to load into a large syringe specifically for thicker substances and squirt into back of mouth every 6-8 hours.

Approximate dosing (or 1cc per 10 lbs):
Small dogs: 1/2 - 1 tsp paste
Medium dogs: 1 - 1 1/2 tsp paste
Large dogs: 1 1/2 - 2 tsp paste

Make sure your dog has access to water during this time. Continue use until you have 1-2 consecutive firm stools.

Note: There is also a sodium-based clay not recommended for internal use. It swells much more internally and could cause swelling in the stomach and intestines. Used externally, Bentonite clay has been found to work well on bruises, bee stings, bug bites, and minor burns and wounds. The cool mud offers pain relief, and its absorptive properties help draw out toxins and other things can cause irritation in the skin.

Keep the clay away from metal and use a stainless steel or glass bowl and wooden spoon when mixing clay with water to keep the clay's electrical charge intact. Calcium Bentonite Clay consists of 60 trace mineral element. It is absorbed best when given on an empty stomach.

Seek a veterinarian right away, if severe diarrhea contains blood, mucus or last longer than 24 hours. Puppies should see vet right away.

FYI- Charcoal is not what you use in the grill for cooking food. It is activated charcoal and is specially made for consumption removing any impurities and making it ingestible.

Antibiotics are not needed unless it is a bacterial infection. I have seen vets prescribe steroids, menstrual bleeding injections, and other off the wall medications for diarrhea. I know Flagyl (rx) is used as my dog got this medication when she had severe diarrhea along with Pro-Pectalin but all medications have serious side effects as well. Research it before you give it and try the safe options first at onset of diarrhea.

When to take diarrhea serious:

- Loss of appetite or thirst
- Lethargy/depression
- Pain/discomfort
- Fever
- Blood in the stool
- Associated vomiting
- Reduced or absent urinations

Also, consider chiropractic adjustments especially in the lumbar section. (X-ray for any lumbar injuries). Chiropractic can do wonders for all types of illnesses and disease. Not just for joints.

Severe Constipation (2-3 days with no poop)
Do not give laxatives made for humans. Make appointment to see vet.

Storing Meat
Look for a small freezer (used or new) to store raw foods in especially if you have large or multiple dogs. You will need the space.

Once you have decided how and when you will start, be prepared. First, you will need supplements. You may hear many raw feeders say that dogs do not need added supplements when feeding a raw diet. This would be further from the truth. In the wild, when a wolf is eating its prey, they are gathering the needed nutrients. A wild rabbit to a wolf will be fresh meat that hasn't been laced with antibiotics and toxins. A cow when raised for slaughter is raised in very inhumane conditions. Yes, this is what we humans are eating. So buying food from the grocery store is NOT your best selection for clean meats. Only when you run out of food at home or can't get your hands on other better raw foods is grocery store food acceptable. Another decision to make here is what sort of raw will you feed? Whole prey (whole carcass), pieces of raw (chunks of meat fit for your size of dog) or ground raw. This book isn't about feeding dehydrated or commercial raw pet foods you buy in pet stores because most all contain synthetic vitamins and who knows where all of it is sourced from. Nor is this book about whole prey diets. This is about gathering ingredients for a home-prepared raw diet. You have raw meats that you can purchase in chubs from the stores (without added vitamins-meat only) or from suppliers from farms. Most store bought pet foods come with some (synthetic) vitamins but I can tell you, you will STILL need to add supplements, so why not know exactly what you are putting into your dog's food and adding in whole food forms of nutrients? You will spend more up front for supplements to gather a stock of what is needed but you get to pick them. Also, know that commercial foods are much more costly. You may find meats from local butchers and farmers. Find out what they feed to their cows, goats, etc before purchasing. An ideal meat would be grass-fed or organic-fed grains to the slaughter animals. Before starting your transition, I recommend a probiotic and digestive enzyme combo at least 7-30 days before changing foods. The longer the better on starting probiotics and digestive enzymes before making the diet change to help with the transition. If you have a puppy or a dog with allergies, add Colostrum into the daily diet as well. Once you have started your probiotics and digestive enzymes, try to see if your dog likes coconut oil. Put some on a spoon or finger and see if she/ he will eat it. Some dogs love it, some don't. You can always mix some in with the food. Start with a very small amount and increase a little bit as you go. Buy coconut oil that is unrefined extra virgin cold-pressed and in a glass jar. Normal amounts are 1/2 teaspoon per 20 lbs. If your dog doesn't seem to like the coconut oil at all and absolutely refuses to eat the food with it in it, try the **refined** coconut oil. It doesn't have that smell or flavor like unrefined although unrefined is much better but getting it in your dog is better than none at all. Also, there is an MCT oil available. No smell or taste. Stay away from plastics and cans of all foods as much as possible. Look for glass! Start with a very small amount and work up or you may get some loose stools.

I find the most confused novice pet parents trying to learn to feed a better diet for their dogs are the ones that don't have something to look at (like a menu) to go by. It seems to make more sense when it is written down in a recipe you would use for baking or cooking. It's like, I have this in my frig, can I feed this to my dog? Great question, let's find out. Starting out it seems extremely scary and overwhelming but don't let it be. It's not as difficult or confusing as it sounds. Plus you will have this book to refer back to.

*DO NOT continue a long-term diet of kibble and raw. It confuses the digestive system. *Do NOT feed kibble and raw together at the same meal although I am seeing holistic vets recommend this. Not sure why as they know how the two digest differently. I believe their reasoning is, if they can't get people to take their dog off of kibble, the next best thing is ok. While it may be true in that sense, I can't see where this will help the dog long term as it could do more damage with a messed up digestive system. So I am going to have to disagree with this recommendation at this time until I can further research this. But overall common sense tells me it's not a good idea. To me it gives an excuse to the pet owner to continue to feed kibble and lessen the guilt by throwing in some leafy greens.

GMO versus Non-GMO
GMO grains (and animal feed) contain genetically modified organisms. GMO crops have been engineered in laboratories. These GMO crops are not required in the USA or Canada to be labeled as GMO. Approximately 64 countries around the world like Australia, Europe, and Japan require GMO labels. Anyone can claim Non-GMO but the verified "Non-GMO project label" is required for true Non-GMO products. The FDA does **not** test products so anyone can make these claims. Look for the verified project label.

Non-GMO is grown from a natural source and has not been modified in a laboratory in any form. This also means it probably has had pesticides and chemicals sprayed all over it. So while you think Non-GMO is better, it actually isn't. It just hasn't been genetically modified but it still caries all the cancer-causing agents with it.

Grass -Fed/Pasture -Fed versus Organic
There are many products out there that may say these words. What are the differences? Grass-fed or pasture-fed means animals foraging on grasses in the pastures. They will consume some grains but the finished diet (2 - 4 weeks before slaughter) is an important element. So if in doubt, feel free to ask the seller or manufacturer of these meats.

Organic will be fed both pasture and organic grains. These also will **not** contain antibiotics or hormones or certain drugs allowed in feeding animals. Organic food and supplements will **not** contain any harmful pesticides, hormones etc of any sorts. They can and do use natural pesticides that do **not** cause harm. When you see a label that says, Organic pasture-fed, that's the best food you can get. It's as clean as you can find and your very best option. Now there is a catch, 95% of the ingredients must be organic to be labeled as such. So 5% still may not be. So look for 100% organic. Even in organic, you will find carrageenan, canola oil, soybean oil, safflower oil and sunflower oil. These should **not** be in our foods due to contamination as well. They are also high in omega-6, which causes inflammation in the body and creates vitamin deficiencies. And anything that has natural flavors can contain hundreds of different chemicals to create a flavor or smell. These are called "Trade Secrets". No one can find out. It is protected by the government. Also, look for the USDA organic label. I have seen claims of being organic but no label is present. Meaning it may say it's organic but it hasn't been approved by the USDA.

First time feeding:
Use only one protein, chicken is normally the preferred protein to start but if your dog has been eating chicken for years, don't start with chicken. Feed a bland diet of chicken with bone or rabbit with bone for a couple of weeks. These can be ground up. After a couple weeks, you can add in organ meats. **Bone will make the poop firm; the organ meat will soften it.**

If your dog is allergic to chicken or poultry, start with rabbit or goat. Stick to one protein source for as long as needed (usually a couple of weeks) and monitor poops. If the first meal the dog gets with raw is chicken for example, feed chicken until poops return to normal: small and firm.

Percentages to feed per meal:
10% Bone
10% Organ (Offal) (no more than 5% liver)
80% Meat
Liver - 1 oz per 10 lbs at least once a week. (part of organ diet)

*Meats are high in phosphorus, bones are high in calcium.
*Muscle meat also includes heart, lung, gizzard, and tongue.
*Organ meats: liver, kidney, spleen, brain, pancreas, thymus, ovaries, and testicles.

Fruits/Veggies: 5% - 8% can be added daily on average.

> *While I do not specialize in kidney and liver disease, I did find this recommendation for feeding a raw diet with kidney and liver issues:*
>
> *For kidney and liver disease (low phosphorous):*
> 12-15% bone
> 10-30% organ
> 30-50% muscle meat
> 5% fish

Feeding times:
- Young adults (over 6 months old) and mature adults –1-2 meals per day. If 2 meals, then split daily amount.
- 4-6 months old - split into 3 meals per day.
- Less than 4 months old - split into 4 meals per day.

While two meals a day have been recommended for as long as I can remember, now it is being said to feed one meal a day. I think you know your dog and what is possible and works for you. So it's your choice. My dogs would eat my arm off if I fed them only once a day. Other dogs could care less.

Here is the break down in the amounts of food (for ex: 2.0 % of body weight):

1.5% – Overweight
2.0% – Average Activity (little outdoor time/2 or fewer walks a day)
2.5% – Above Average Activity (a few hours of activity per day)
3.0% – Average Activity with Weight Gain Goals
3.5 % – High Activity or Weight Gain Goals (working dogs)
4%+ – Puppies and Nursing or Pregnant bitches

The amounts vary and can always be adjusted up or down. It will be up to you to watch his/her weight and adjust it as needed. Some dogs will act as though they are starving. Just up the meat content a little. You can also add in veggies cooked or raw (juiced, steamed, or finely chopped). Raw chunks of veggies don't digest so well so you will need to help the dog out by juicing or chopping down into small fine pieces. Dogs have shorter digestive systems than us humans. Raw is best because they get the most nutrients. Buy organic if you can possibly afford it. Veggies and fruits have a high amount of GMOs along with pesticides so it is best to buy organic or you may be dealing with some issues with chemical reactions and even cancer, so buy organic if possible. This applies to EVERYTHING including eggs and supplements. Always buy organic and pasture-fed if you can. I have found some good prices even with organic supplements, and when adding supplements into the diet; don't just throw in the whole list of supplements and not expect issues with the poop or tummy upsets. Take it slow. Add supplements in a little at a time. A couple for one week and if all goes well, add in a couple more the next week or so. Do these until you get them all going in. And start with low amounts and work up to recommended amounts. But don't start a bunch of these in the beginning; introduce them over a 30-45 day process.

Safe Protein Sources for Dogs

Muscle Meat
Beef
Lamb
Pork *(Never feed your dog **'fresh'** raw pork as doing so can cause trichinosis - a parasitic disease caused by eating raw or undercooked*

pork. Make sure you freeze it 3 weeks prior to serving it raw. This also applies to wild game you may have hunted/killed or received from a friend).

Rabbit
Goat
Alpaca
Chicken
Turkey
Goose
Bison
Ox
Llama
Kangaroo
Ostrich
Duck
Pheasant
Quail
Venison
Buffalo
Moose
Elk

Meats high in fat: *Lamb/ Mutton/Veal, Pork and Duck. Beef, Buffalo and Bison vary so use caution in pancreatic dogs. Cooked animal fat is dangerous for pancreatic dogs as well. Lean meats are great to use for losing some weight, for digestive and stomach issues, acid reflux, and pancreatitis.*

*Meat cooked with a lot of fat is dangerous to a dog and should not be fed. This can cause pancreatitis.

Leaner meats may include: *Chicken without skin, Turkey without skin, Moose, Elk, Goat, Alpaca,* **Rabbit,** *Kangaroo, Ostrich, and Venison.*

Organ Meats

Organ meats such as spleen, pancreas, brain, kidney, thymus, eyeballs, ovaries, testicles, liver (especially liver), or any other secreting organ should also be included. Organs such as heart, lungs, or other **non-secreting** organs are recognized as muscle meat. Organ meats are low in fat. Ten percent (10%) of organ meats recommended daily once your dog has adjusted to the muscle meat.

Green tripe (NOT bleached tripe found in grocery stores) is a great addition. It can be used to add weight gain and for added probiotics as well. Warning: It stinks! Put a clothespin on your nose and keep going. Your dogs will love you for it.

If for some reason you run out of organ meat, they make a grass-fed organ mix in a capsule. It's called Ancestral Beef Organs. Nice product. This comes in capsules but you can open and sprinkle into food. Label recommends 6 capsules for human. I can't say exactly where the right amount for a dog would be, but 1-2 capsules will probably work just fine depending on your dog's size. Don't give too much as it could cause more issues such as diarrhea. This contains bovine liver, heart, kidney, pancreas, and spleen. (FYI-Heart is a muscle meat, not considered an organ meat). If your dog gets diarrhea after giving this, back off on the amount given.

I try to give you options. Everyone has different work schedules and life styles and sometimes in a pinch, you can't carry around all these food/ supplements and sometimes you may not feel like it. I hope most days you can have time though to prepare your dogs food, as it is as important as it is for your children. But having something to fall back on or make life a little simpler on some days is what we need to be ready for. So this is why I mention these alternative products.

Calf Liver:
Giving your dog raw calf liver once a week will supply it with all the vitamin A that it needs. Calf liver is one of the safest ways to give your dog vitamins A and B, B-12, iron, trace elements such as copper, zinc, chromium, and COQ10. One ounce per 10 lbs at least once a week. (Twice at most) or 5% daily.

Avoid giving daily liver treats as this can cause an excess of vitamin A toxicity.

Fish (cooked or canned in water) *buy low sodium*:
Anchovies
Salmon-Wild Pacific
Sardines
Shad
Smelt
Mackerel
Herring
Krill
Squid
Green Lipped Mussel oil

I use Iceland Pure sardine/anchovy oil because at this time it's the only one I trust. If you can afford it, you may try Calamari oil from Dr. Peter Dobias which is another trustworthy product. The rest I pretty much do not trust at this time.

Raw Fish
To feed or not to feed? Your decision. If you feed raw fish make sure it is wild caught. Farmed fisheries are not safe as it may contain flukes - a parasite that infests the liver. If you feed raw fish, freeze it for at least 3 weeks prior to feeding. I like feeding skinless/boneless sardines packed in water that contains a low amount of sodium. Sodium is important to search out when buying all store-bought meats. Keep amounts minimal. Read the label. Look for under
110 milligrams (mg) of sodium in meats. Small fish are best. Larger fish contain more mercury.

You can add a pinch of Himalayan Pink Sea Salt to food a couple times a week for minerals. *Avoid if there is heart disease.*

Fish oil vs. Flaxseed Oil
Technically flaxseed oil has omega-3, however, it doesn't have the DHA and EPA which is sorely missing from most diets and is crucial for your dog's health. Plus, it can be difficult for your dog to convert the ALA into needed DHA and EPA. You can make it easier for your dog to get these necessary omega-3 fatty acids with high quality fish oil for dogs. Calamari and Green Lipped Mussel oils work as well.

Fish oils (Which kind is best?)
Cod Liver Oil:
High in vitamin A and D. Use caution. I do not recommend due to vitamin A toxicity especially if you are feeding liver.

Salmon Oil (wild caught):
High in vitamin D. Does not contain vitamin A. High in omega-3.

Sardines/Anchovy:
High in omega-3s, vitamin B-12, Selenium, vitamin D and Calcium.

Krill Oil:
High in vitamin A, D, E, and Astaxanthin. Lower in omega-3s than other fish oils. Not recommended due to overfishing.

Marine Phytoplankton:
High in omega-3s and also contains trace minerals, Superoxide Dismutase (SOD), Selenium, Iron, Magnesium, vitamin E, A, C, D and B-12.

Green Lipped Mussel Oil:
Contains EPA, DHA, and ETA (Eicosatetraenoic acid-omega-6 and omega-3) and minerals.

Seeds (always buy organic with nuts and seeds)

Flax Seeds
While Flax seeds are fine to give, I do not recommend them for omega-3 purposes or daily use without also using fish oils. Flax must be converted into omega-3s. It makes the body work harder to convert so why not use fish oils instead. These do not replace your fish oils as fish oil is always needed. Do **not** give any Macadamia nuts. These are toxic to your dog. You can find more on this further down as you read. Nuts and seeds contain molds and mycotoxins unless organic. Is it really worth all that trouble? Just use high quality fish oil.

Chia Seeds (organic only)
Two tablespoons of Chia seeds provide a 3-to-1 ratio of Omega-3 to Omega-6. Chia is non-allergenic. Look for milled and organic Chia

seeds if possible. Chia seeds contain10 grams of fiber per two tablespoons. You can use these when baking treats. Remember, these seeds will soak up a lot of water and create a gelatin effect so soak before feeding or serve up a smaller amount in wet foods so there isn't any possible choking when the moisture is absorbed. They also will need to be converted from ALA to DHA and EPA. All nuts and seeds must be converted. This again is why I am partial to fish oils. While seeds are nutritious, I wouldn't use unless baked in a treat.

Amount to use: 1/4 teaspoon for every 10 pounds of your dog's body weight. High amounts of omega-6 can cause diseases like arthritis so keep these amounts low. Keep all nuts to a minimum. A couple of organic raw pecans are fine but don't give any more than that at a time. Nuts can cause intestinal upset. My dogs like a few organic pecans on occasion.

Dairy Products
Limit all dairy to no more than twice a week. Pasteurized milk is not good for your dog. Raw milk helps with weakened immune systems and Kefir is a good source of protein and also a source of acidophilus which helps to prevent the overgrowth of bad bacteria in the digestive tract. You can make your own at home using either coconut milk or purified water grains. Look for organic grains. Homemade has stronger properties for healing and a much higher amount of probiotics. Plain organic yogurt is fine but Kefir is better.

Kefir or yogurt sweetened with sugar from tore bought products is not ideal for your dog. Kefir or yogurt sweetened with artificial sweeteners should be avoided AT ALL COSTS! Xylitol is especially dangerous for dogs and can result in liver damage and death even in small amounts. Making your own is 10 times better and higher in probiotics.

*(Dairy products **do not replace** your probiotics and digestive enzymes supplements with exception of homemade organic kefir grains using raw goat's milk).*

Digestive enzymes also do much more than aid in digestion. They purify and cleanse the blood and remove toxins, parasites, and fungus. Digestive enzymes also help boost the immune system. Cooking also destroys digestive enzymes, so it is important that your dog gets extra digestive enzymes and probiotics to help aid digestion especially with sensitive tummies, leaky gut, or allergy issues.

Acceptable Dairy (organic):
Plain Cottage Cheese
Plain Yogurt
Plain Kefir or homemade Kefir milk
Raw goats milk (pasture-fed)

(Yes, it's ok to give them a bite of raw/organic cheese now and then- wink. It's a great treat.)

I do **not** recommend canned foods due to the BPA lining in the cans. Even if it says BPA Free, it will contain BPS (bisphenol S). It is 10 times as toxic as BPA. There is no winning with the cans. So avoid if at all possible. Use frozen or fresh organic.

I recommend veggies (raw preferably-juiced/finely chopped) to gather as many nutrients as possible. A small amount can be added to each diet. If you don't want to spend much time in the kitchen preparing veggies, you can add in an organic greens powder. It is full of nutrients and it's easy to add into ground raw foods. Starwest Botanicals brand does have a strong flavor and smell so you may need to mask it using something your dog likes. Some dogs are not bothered by this powder and others are. There is an alternative powder that contains more than greens made by Amazing Grass-The Original). Some of these are safe for your dogs. These have less of a strong smell than the Starwest Botanical brand. Get to know your dog's new likes with this new diet. You can try organic Chlorella, Moringa, or Kale powders instead. Also, a good mineral supplement is Humic/Fulvic Acid. It's all-natural. Find what works for you and your schedule. Some people have plenty of time to prepare an entire meal, others work full-time, and the last thing they want to do is be in the kitchen all night. So to make it simple, add the greens powder and supplements and that will help keep it balanced. Also, try preparing meals that will last for a week so that on your busy days, you can just plop it on a plate and feed. I like to add in my powders and also throw in a tablespoon of raw organic chopped kale into the mix when serving.

If you choose to cook the veggies, that's ok just make sure they get their supplements for the day. Cooked foods do not need to be juiced. You can also steam the veggies as more nutrients are retained that way.

Fruits (organic):
Apples
Apricots *(Apricot seeds are great to be used for a cancer treatment and preventative). (See Cancer Prevention/Treatment Chapter)*
Avocado is safe for dogs. *The pit and skin of the avocado is toxic and should never be consumed by dogs.*
Bananas
Blackberries
Blueberries *(antioxidant -great for cancer prevention and treatment, and an immune system builder)*
Cantaloupe
Cherries (remove the pit)
Cranberries
Coconut
Kiwi
Mango
Peaches (remove the pit)
Pears
Pineapple
Plums
Raspberries
Strawberries
Watermelon
Citrus (such as lemon, lime, oranges, grapefruit) in small amounts.

When buying fruits, buy organic only. I am hearing some brands of organic strawberries are not organic. Sometimes we just need to research this stuff. Try frozen organic if you like. Some people may think that giving a dog fruit and/or vegetables will give the dog diarrhea. They actually provide high quality soluble fiber and help prevent diarrhea and constipation.

Soluble fibers attract water and form a gel, which slows down digestion thereby delaying the emptying of the stomach and makes a dog feel full, which helps to control a hungry pooch and keep the weight down.

Slower stomach emptying can also have a beneficial effect on controlling blood sugar levels and insulin sensitivity, which helps control diabetes. Keep fruits to a minimum though. I find blueberries or any of your berries to be some of the best fruits to add. They are loaded with antioxidants and are great immune boosters. In the summer, make some frozen treats using berries. Yogurt and blueberry frozen in ice cube trays or alike. If your dog doesn't like cold treats, serve up some room temp berries mixed in cottage cheese, kefir or yogurt or serve alone. You can even add into their foods. For treats, make some dehydrated fruit snacks.

Vegetables (organic-raw chopped, cooked or raw pureed):
Alfalfa Sprouts
Asparagus
Broccoli
Brussels Sprouts
Carrots *(raw carrot juice has been used in cancer patients as well)*
Cauliflower
Celery
Cucumber
Green Beans *(Limit amount. Can cause stones in higher amounts for dogs prone to stone formation).*
Green Peas
Kale *(can reduce bladder cancer by 90%)*
Squash
Spinach *(while spinach is safe to feed, too much spinach can cause kidney/bladder stones)*
Sugar Snap Peas (in the pod or out)
Sweet Potatoes (high in carbs - limit amounts)
Yams (high in carbs - limit amounts)
Zucchini

- Finely chop fruits/vegetables - either by hand or with a food processor/blender/juicer
- Lightly steam vegetables

*Spinach is included in the Starwest Botanicals Greens Power that I recommend so if your dog has a history of kidney or bladder stones, try using Organic Kale, Organic Chlorella, or Organic Moringa.

Grains:
Grains are not part of a dog's natural diet; here are some important points to note. I recommend removing all grains from your dog's diet.

If you must keep grain in your dog's diet:
Make sure that you only provide your dog with human quality grains and ONLY organic in small amounts! Otherwise, grains contain aflatoxins and can cause liver cancer. Grains absorb liquid, so ingesting uncooked grains that have not been pre-soaked can lead to swelling and bursting of the stomach; dangerous at the least, lethal at worst.

I do **not** recommend grains in diets at all. They cause too many serious problems especially in larger dogs. So do not feed grains or high carbs like white potatoes, or rice. Grains can be completely replaced by substituting a combination of sweet potato, chickpeas, and lentils.

Calcium (Important)
One of the most common mistakes that people make when feeding a home-cooked diet is not adding in calcium. You **must** add calcium when you feed a diet that does not include bones. Adult dogs need around 800 to 1,000 mg of calcium per pound of food fed.
The ideal Calcium: Phosphorus ratio in the canine diet is between 1:1 and 2:1. Meat contains a lot of phosphorus, so the more meat a diet contains, the more calcium will be required to reach the correct calcium: phosphorus ratio. Adding 800 to 1,000 mg of calcium will provide the correct calcium: phosphorus ratio even for a high-meat diet, unless you use a calcium supplement that also contains phosphorus. In that case, moderately higher amounts of calcium may be needed to balance out the additional phosphorus contained in the supplement.

Ground eggshell can be used as a calcium supplement. Rinse eggshells and dry them on a counter overnight, or in the oven, then grind them in a clean coffee grinder. One large eggshell provides one teaspoon of ground eggshell, which contains approximately 2,000mg of calcium. Don't use eggshells that haven't been ground to powder, as they may not be absorbed as well. I recommend powdered calcium you can use in place of above - powdered seaweed calcium or powdered eggshell calcium is acceptable.

Calcium and phosphorus must be in balance. Calcium deficiencies sometimes brought on by high meat diets and no bone, as meat contains phosphorus can result in nervousness, lameness, muscle spasms, heart palpitations, eczema, decrease in bone density, osteoporosis, gum erosion, increased cholesterol levels, seizures, hemorrhages, arthritis, and bone fractures. For dogs, supplement high amounts of calcium only in the first year of life, or during pregnancy and nursing, as too much can cause kidney stones (use vitamin C along with calcium to help prevent this). Also, add in Magnesium Citrate to avoid all types of stones and to treat oxalate stones. Dog's deficient in magnesium has been known to cause stone formation.

Calcium-eggshell or seaweed
Approximate dosage or follow label and/or see above under calcium:
0-25 lbs: 1/4 - 1/2 teaspoon
25-50 lbs: 1/2 - 1 teaspoon
50-75 lbs: 1 - 1 1/2 teaspoon
75+ lbs: 1 1/2 - 2 teaspoon

Raw Eggs
Make sure you wash the eggshell before cracking open if fresh off the farm. Some people advise that dogs should not be given raw eggs due to the chance of salmonella poisoning. It is also true that a dog's stomach acids are stronger than a humans and a dog produces more bile than a human does. While dogs are better at fighting salmonella than humans, dogs still can get salmonella poisoning, but they can tolerate higher levels of salmonella than we can. If you want to be on the safe side you can cook your dog's egg (poached, scrambled, boiled). Feed the whole egg. Feeding the white of the egg only can cause a vitamin deficiency.
Organic and pasture-fed; no more than twice a week if you choose to feed these. Once a week is preferred especially if raw. If you have access to farmed eggs, make sure the chickens are pasture-fed and/or organic grains only and not fed grains such as GMO corn.

NOTE: Garlic is safe in lesser amounts and not to be given daily.
In large doses, Garlic (like onions) can cause oxidative damage to red blood cells, creating Heinz bodies and making the body reject these

cells from the bloodstream. If large doses are ingested on a regular basis, the process can lead to Heinz-body anemia and even death.

Most dogs adjust to a quick transition, one night its kibble for dinner, the next day they have a raw breakfast. Others need a fasting period of 24 hours and never do this longer than one meal with puppies. Do not mix kibble and raw, as the time it takes to digest kibble is far longer than it takes to digest raw sometimes resulting in a stomach upset. Canned organic 100% pumpkin is great to have on hand to help any upset tummies and great for constipation and diarrhea. (You can use pumpkin from other sources that do not come in a can if you like).

Has your dog been eating kibble all of its life? Kibble is full of a lot of unnatural ingredients like preservatives, artificial flavors, sugars, food colorings, chemical toxins, synthetic vitamins, and minerals. When switching to a healthy diet, the body may begin to detox causing allergic symptoms. Don't panic, it's all part of nature. The body is cleansing itself. Give it a couple of weeks to adjust and cleanse. Once you have gotten through this process, add in organic Milk Thistle powder to this (5 days on, 2 days off weekly for 1 month). This will help cleanse the liver (See Chapter 2 - Allergies, Leaky Gut and Acid Reflux).

Detox every 6 months for 2 - 4 weeks to rid the toxins your dog is still getting. Toxins come from breathing in air, drinking water if not filtered, medications (all types), vaccines, chemicals in yard(s) and house. (Wash off feet after walking on neighbors grass or other public areas. Use apple cider vinegar and water or povidone iodine and water). You can't avoid everything but you can reduce the exposure so start looking into making changes in these areas as well for the future to reduce the amount of exposure.

While your dog is transitioning, you may see excess shedding, dry skin, runny eyes, and mucus in the poop, or perhaps dried up white poop a day or so later. The white is the bone content in the diet. You can reduce calcium if you are giving it. Keep bones at the recommended dosage. White poop (dried a day or so old) is a sign your dog is getting enough calcium and you can reduce the intake of calcium. You may see the poop becoming smaller in size and less of it. The smell will become less. Your dog may not drink as much water as normal. Raw diets are full of water content so your dog won't require as much water as the dehydrating cardboard kibble. Cooked diets have less water. Also during the transition, you may see your dog showing some skin conditions. If it is mild, apply coconut oil onto the dog's skin and/or half (water) and half Apple Cider Vinegar. You will want to use raw unfiltered with "mother" ACV. If there is itching involved, bathe your dog in Povidone Iodine and water (dark tea color). Do not rinse off; pat dry. Colloidal Silver works as well for a topical for skin lesions after povidone iodine or ACV treatments.

Unrefined virgin organic coconut oil is a wonderful addition to any diet. You can use internally and externally. Internally don't go overboard; start off with a smaller amount, 1/4-1/2 teaspoon and work your way up depending on your dog's size. Less for tiny/small dogs. The situation will resolve itself with time, (generally a week or two, but up to a couple months in some cases) as new cells must replace older ones in order for the detox process to be completed. If your dog can't stand the taste, try using the "refined" organic coconut oil.

If all is going well after a couple of weeks, try a new protein like goat, venison, beef, or rabbit. You can feed chicken necks no more than once a week.

Also skinless/boneless low sodium sardines in water, low sodium salmon (Trader Joe's has a very low sodium pink salmon and they also have some low sodium sardines although I found some lower made by Season Brand and Wild Planet. (Wal-Mart and Costco's carry the Season Brand in some of their stores). Look for below 100mg of sodium. You can feed organic cottage cheese once a week or add a little bit of organic plain kefir to the food or serve alone for an additive. Cottage cheese is like a dessert for my dogs. It's not a necessity. It's more for adding in something different and tasty. You can do so many things. Keep it interesting for your dog. Change up the meals. Do NOT feed the same protein day in and day out once you establish the transition, which may take a couple of months. Your dog WILL get sick. This is unhealthy.
Feeding the same type of food every day will make your dog unhealthy. We need to balance the diet so rotate at least 4 proteins over a period of

a month. Your dog will probably stop drinking as much water as raw meats contain a lot of moisture. This doesn't apply to a cooked diet so much.

Do not feed pits of fruits and no grapes (grape seeds are safe), raisins, onions, or chocolate. (Carob in place of chocolate is safe and acceptable). Learn what is safe to feed and what isn't. Watch out for Xylitol in peanut butters and other human foods. It's in toothpastes as well so do not use human toothpastes on your dog. Xylitol is very toxic even in small amounts. It's being added to candies, sweeteners, breads, gum and sugar-free diet products.

For fighting gum disease, I have created a special recipe for brushing your dog's teeth and providing an oral rinse to fight bacteria.

- 1 teaspoon of Coconut oil
- 1 teaspoon of Baking soda (can substitute with Diatomaceous Earth-Food Grade)
- 1/2 teaspoon of filtered Chlorine and Fluoride-free water to help form a paste (if needed)

Brush using your dog's own toothbrush. Soft bristled. Or use a finger brush. You can also use an electric toothbrush with your dog's own brush, whatever your preference.

After brushing

Mix one capsule (or 1/2 teaspoon of powder) of probiotics with filtered Chlorine and Fluoride-free water. Pour into a syringe for oral administration. Squirt this liquid around your pet's teeth and gums. This will also help fight bacteria and any yeasty problems in the mouth. Do this with each brushing. Following these steps will reduce your build up of tartar and bacteria. You may also follow up with some Colloidal Silver spray and spray onto gums and teeth. You can brush the teeth using Colloidal Silver as it helps to prevent tarter build up as well. No need to dilute when brushing. Get yearly teeth cleanings as well if needed. Keep the teeth clean and free from tarter build up and bacteria.

Give probiotics to your dogs (add into food) weeks before, during and after a teeth cleaning to help reduce bacteria from spreading.

As for raw bones, they are wonderful for cleaning teeth. A raw rib bone 2-3 times a week will keep the teeth fairly clean. Although you may need a teeth cleaning eventually depending on your dog. Just keep an eye on the teeth and brush as often as possible. Daily is recommended. Some dogs have more teeth issues than others, certain breeds like Chihuahuas, Dachshunds, Yorkies etc. Clean teeth are important to your dog's health. If you have rotten, loose, tarter buildup or failing teeth, these can cause more bacteria in which can spread throughout the body causing organ failure so a clean mouth is very important to your dog's health. Just ask your vet to skip the fluoride with the cleaning. Yep vets use this on our pets too.

Do not feed cooked bones at all. Cooked bones are dangerous. Also, stay away from the weight-bearing bones. They can break teeth. Marrow bones can also be dangerous like getting stuck on the snout or bottom jaw. Always supervise your dog when they have bones. Chicken necks are soft and easily to chew and digest. Only feed once or twice a week at most on the necks. They are soft so they don't clean the teeth as well since the bones are smaller. Chicken feet are good as well and loaded with glucosamine. Turkey necks are _much_ larger and may cause an issue with smaller dogs or fast-eating dogs when swallowing. (Feed with caution until you get to know your dog). I recommend chicken necks until you get better acquainted with feeding raw bones. I do **not** recommend pork bones of any kind. Only finely ground in raw foods.

As for feeding pork, there is a lot of debate on whether to feed pork or not. Pork is fine to feed but make sure it has been frozen for 3 weeks prior to feeding it to your dog. Same goes for wild game that you may have killed in the wild. This also includes raw fish. I myself don't recommend feeding raw fish but if you do, freeze it for 3 weeks prior to feeding. Pork is higher in fat so if your dog has a history of pancreatic inflammation, don't feed pork, lamb or duck and limit your beef. Can also cause weight gain.
Clean up is easy. Clean as you would after you prepare to cook your meats for yourself. You handle raw chicken, fish, hamburger, steak,

pork, prime rib etc. You clean up after your family so the same applies to raw dog food diets.

Make sure you use digestive enzymes and probiotics if your dog has pancreatic inflammation. (Give anti-inflammatory herbs as well for the inflammation.) You may need to triple the amount of probiotics and digestive enzymes if a normal dose isn't working. Make sure you feed small meals and limit treats. Feed lean meats only.

While you are transitioning, don't lose hope if your dog isn't taking to it as well as you think she/he should. Sometimes it can take a couple months to get your dog accustomed to eating a different diet but eventually they will get the hang of it. It is always the pet parent that gives up before they should. Give it some time. If something isn't working, try something different. Add a little cooked chicken or chicken broth or bone broth on top of the raw food. For newly fed raw diets, you can try searing small bite size pieces of meat before feeding. This may also help your dog transition. Add some sardines in the mix.

The thing for you to do is to look for a nearby co-op or buy from a source online or local. Go to the Farmers Market for great deals. I myself buy from an online supplier and the shipping is low considering it is being shipped with ice and it is delivered right to my doorstep so no heavy loading and unloading my vehicle of meats. And they sell the meat/bone/organ ratio (80/10/10) so it makes it much simpler for me.

According to the size of your dog or how many mouths you have to feed as to what it will cost you per month.

Doing The Math

Quality Kibble - 50 lbs of dog food ($120 for a 25lb bag) = $240
Quality Canned - (almost 10 lbs (9.75) per case-13 oz cans), 5 cases ($50 each) = $250, (some go up to $120 per case)
Raw/cooked - 50 lbs of a variety of standard proteins = $216. Standard proteins are lowest in cost (Beef, Turkey, Chicken, Pork). Exotic meats run higher.
I buy from an online source and most all of it I buy is a (meat/bone/organ ground mix). Many of you may find better deals on

raw from local farmers or co-ops. So tell me, what's the reason you still feed kibble?

Raw diet is controlled by you. You know what's going into your pet. Kibble is crap, canned is crap with water. Make changes today and do it right! Your pets will love you for it.

I have a dog; pickiest dog on the planet. Her and I struggled and fought over food every single day for years (kibble to canned then raw). NOW since she finally caught onto the homemade thing (and it took her awhile), now I can't keep her out of the kitchen. They show you what they love. Maybe not right away but eventually they finally catch on and love it. I love a happy dog!

You are probably wondering why I like to add veggies when you may have heard raw diets do not need them. I do consider dogs carnivores, but if you can add a few raw veggies to add whole food nutrients, then that's why I recommend them. But some pet parents don't want to puree or chop up raw veggies so I recommend the greens powders. You can buy pre-chopped organic frozen veggies in stores if you look. I may even add a little organic carrot juice at times and Fulvic/Humic acid. You can always take an afternoon one day and make all the veggie servings needed for the week and freeze/store them until time to feed. And to back up my recommendations, these comments come from some of the top holistic vets out there.

"It is no longer a question if a diet without supplements is complete. The question is what is missing. No matter what diet you feed, it is likely to be depleted of some nutrients because of worldwide mineral and nutrient soil depletion. ~ Dr. Dobias"

"The best of diets – even a raw, species-specific diet – can come from soils that are depleted or from lower quality food sources. Sometimes the food simply loses many of its nutrients through processing and storage. And most commercially available pet foods, even if they're "fortified" to meet AAFCO standards, contain synthetic, lab-concocted vitamins and minerals which don't provide optimum nutrition."~ Dr. Karen Becker

And when it comes to fur and feathers, here is what Dr. Becker has to say:
"*Protein quality is extremely variable. There are highly assimilable and digestible proteins (proteins your pet's body can easily absorb and make use of), and there are proteins that are wholly indigestible. For example: beaks, feet, hides, tails, and snouts are 100 percent protein, but all 100 percent is indigestible. All protein has a biologic value, which is its usable amino acid content. Eggs have the highest biologic value at 100 percent. Fish is a close second at 92 percent. Feathers, as you might guess, have zero biologic value. They are all protein, but they are neither digestible nor assimilable.*" ~ Dr. K. Becker

All of us including dogs lack in vitamin D. Humans can get vitamin D from sunshine. Dogs not so much. Foods high in vitamin D are: salmon, sardines, cod liver oil, egg yolks, and mushrooms.

Bone Content (Helpful extra info)

Chicken
Whole bird – 27-32% bone
Breast – 15-20% bone
Back – 44% bone
Thigh – 21% bone
Drumstick – 33-34% bone
Wing – 46% bone
Leg quarter – 27-30% bone
Neck – 36% bone
Cornish game hen – 39% bone

Turkey
Whole bird – 21-29% bone
Neck – 42% bone
Breast – 14% bone
Back – 50% bone
Thigh – 19-21% bone
Wing – 44% bone
Drumstick – 38% bone

Quail
Whole – 10% bone

Duck
Whole – 28% bone -gutted and plucked
Whole wild – 38% bone
Leg– 34% bone
Breast– 15% bone
Wing – 39% bone
Frame – 75% bone
Neck– 50% bone
Foot – 60% bone

Goose
Whole – 19% bone

Pheasant
Whole – 14% bone

Guinea
Whole – 17% bone

Rabbit
Whole – 10% bone
Dressed (skinned and gutted) – 28% bone

Lamb
Neck – 32% bone
Ribs – 27% bone
Shank – 28-36% bone
Shoulder – 21-25% bone
Chop – 15% bone

Veal
Ribs – 35% bone
Shoulder – 21% bone
Shank – 48% bone
Loin – 30% bone

Goat
Whole – 33% bone

Beef
Ribs – 52% bone
Tail – 45-65% bone

Pork
Shoulder – 16-25% bone
Ribs – 21-30% bone

Let's Get Started

Day One Feeding Raw:

Day 1 of starting (after you have already started probiotics and digestive enzymes preferably at least a week before):
(If allergic to poultry, try rabbit or goat. If your dog has allergies to chicken, it may be best to avoid all poultry for several months)

- Chicken with bone (ground or small bites-no skin)
- Pureed or finely chopped raw veggies with some fruits (fruits are optional)
- Apple Cider Vinegar (1 teaspoon-1 TBSP depending on size of dog)
- Fish oil /Calamari oil and/or low-sodium sardines in water (Wild Planet and Season Brand has the lowest sodium content. Trader Joe's also has a low sodium one).
- Probiotics/Digestive Enzymes
- Add Calcium (if not 10% bone in diet)

Day 2:
- Chicken with bone (ground or small bites-no skin)
- Pureed or finely chopped raw veggies
- Apple Cider Vinegar (1 teaspoon - 1 TBSP depending on size of dog)
- Fish oil/ Calamari oil and/or low-sodium sardines in water
- Coconut oil (1/4 - 1/2 teaspoon per 20 lbs)

- Probiotics/Digestive Enzymes
- Add Calcium (if not 10% bone in diet)

You will need to add in Vitamin E (non-soy) three times a week along with fish oils. This is important. Soy can be hidden in labels (mixed tocopherols).

Alternate these days for 14 days. If all is going well the first week still using same protein, add in organ meats for another 7 days. This may cause some loose stools. Keep an eye on the poop. Loose stools or even mucus in stools is not a bad thing; it's adjusting and releasing toxins. But if you ever have runny diarrhea, stop organs immediately. This isn't normal for diarrhea but loose stools are. This shouldn't last more than a couple of days. Add in some 100% organic pumpkin to the diet or you may have to fast your dog for a day to resume back to feeding meat and bone only if diarrhea occurs. If it does, wait till poop returns to normal then add in tiny bits of organ meat and gradually work up over a 7-day period. Some systems are more delicate than others so you have to go much slower than normal. You will get there, just be patient. You can also double the amount of digestive enzymes and probiotics for a while until the system adjusts and calms down and is doing beautifully. I would also add in Slippery Elm at this time.

If your dog is doing wonderful and not having any issues at all, try a new protein for example like beef or rabbit.

Feed:
Beef (80%)/organs (10%)/bones (10%) for 7 days along with the recommended supplements you have been using from day one.
If everything is going well (nice firm poop), after 7 days switch to another protein like Turkey (80%)/organs (10%)/bones (10%).
After 7 days of doing well, you can try a new protein. If all 4 have worked well with only minor bumps in the road, time to start adding in some things.
If loose stools occur, cut out organ meat until poop is firm again, then slowly add organs back in. You can also cook/sear the meat.

Permanent Menu/Recipe:
Your protein choice (4 different proteins per month) with bone and organ meats (see feeding schedule - once or twice a day for adult dogs). Pureed or finely chopped raw veggies with some fruits (or greens powder) daily or every other day. *(See Chapter on Supplements and dosing if not listed below).*

Add in or continue with these added nutrients:
- Humic/Fulvic Acid (daily or every other day)
- Probiotics/Digestive enzymes daily
- Fish oil/Calamari oil and/or low sodium sardines in water daily
- Calf Liver (1 oz per 10 lbs) once a week
- Add Calcium (daily if you don't have 10% bone)
- Vitamin E (non-soy) three times a week

Optional or can be given once or twice a week or alternated. These are just extras for variety.

- Plain Kefir (1 teaspoon - 1 TBSP depending on size of dog) couple times a week
- Plain Cottage Cheese once a week (for added flavor to a meal)
- Raw or cooked egg 1 - 2 times a week
- Chicken feet (full of glucosamine) once a week
- Chicken necks once a week
- Low sodium sardines in water-twice a week
- Canned low-sodium pink salmon (Check Trader Joe's for best) once a week or less. Most are high in sodium so use sparingly. *(avoid salmon if your dog has heart disease)*

Foods dogs cannot/should not have or are toxic:
- Chocolate
- Green Tomatoes
- Grapes (skins and meat) (seeds are fine)
- Raisins
- Xylitol (found also in some peanut butters and other foods)
- Rhubarb
- Onions/onion powder

- Yeast dough
- Sugar
- Salt (Himalayan pink sea salt is acceptable-a pinch) NO table salt!
- Cinnamon-Cassia (Acceptable is **Ceylon** Cinnamon)
- Macadamia nuts - can cause bladder stones if you give to your dog regularly. They also can affect the muscular and skeletal systems and cause hindquarter paralysis in some dogs if fed long-term.

All nuts that are given to dogs should be ORGANIC ONLY due to mycotoxins and kept in low quantities.

For Treats: You can make your own dehydrated chicken or beef (any type of meats you would normally feed) jerky strips or bake some grain free organic cookies for your dog. I make my own treats and use organic buckwheat (fruit and contains all 9 essential amino acids) flour and add in some carob, greens powder, herbs, and ginger. You can also mix coconut flour or quinoa with buckwheat flour for a good mix. I throw in different flavored things to keep it interesting for my dogs. You can also buy some that are organic from small mom and pop shops. See a good list on my website of the Top Best Dog Treats for ordering. Watch out for food coloring. Avoid non-organic products.

Here is a quick reference chart

Week One	Week Two	Week Three
Chicken with bone/no skin/ground or small bites. Add Calcium supplement (if not 10% bone in diet)	Chicken with bone/no skin/ground or small bites. Add Calcium supplement (if not 10% bone in diet)	Goat with bone - ground or small bites. Add Calcium supplement (if not 10% bone in diet) Alternate proteins every week.
Finely chopped raw veggies (pick 1-2 at a time) (kale, broccoli)	Finely chopped raw veggies (pick 1-2 different ones at a time)	Finely chopped raw veggies (your preference) 5-8% veggies
Apple Cider Vinegar (1 teaspoon-1 TBSP depending on size of dog)	Apple Cider Vinegar (1 teaspoon-1 TBSP depending on size of dog)	Apple Cider Vinegar (1 teaspoon-1 TBSP depending on size of dog)

Fish oil/Calamari oil and/or low-sodium sardines in water	Fish oil/Calamari oil and/or low-sodium sardines in water	Fish oil/Calamari oil and/or low-sodium sardines in water
Probiotics/Digestive Enzymes (Double dose enzymes for 30 days)	Probiotics/Digestive Enzymes (Double dose enzymes for 30 days)	Probiotics/Digestive Enzymes (Double dose enzymes for 30 days)
Coconut oil (1/4 teaspoon per 20 lbs) Alternate every other day	Coconut oil (1/4-1/2 teaspoon per 20 lbs) Alternate every other day	Coconut oil (1/4-1/2 teaspoon per 20 lbs) Can alternate every other day or daily
Do not feed cooked bones ever!	Add Vitamin E (soy free) - 3 times a week	Add Vitamin E (soy free) - 3 times a week
Cooked egg 1-2 times a week (boiled, poached, or scrambled)	Cooked egg 1-2 times a week (boiled, poached, or scrambled)	Cooked egg 1-2 times a week (boiled, poached, or scrambled)
No organ meat at this time	No organ meat at this time	Add organ meats if poop is normal. (Spleen, brain, kidney, eyeballs, ovaries, testicles, calf liver (1 oz per 10 lbs) once a week) 10% total
Chicken necks and chicken feet 1-2 times a week. Chicken hearts for added Taurine.	Chicken necks and chicken feet 1-2 times a week. Chicken hearts for added Taurine.	Chicken necks and chicken feet 1-2 times a week. Chicken hearts for added Taurine.
If allergic to chicken, start with goat or rabbit (meat and bone only)	Himalayan Pink Sea Salt couple times a week for minerals (a dash)	Himalayan Pink Sea Salt couple times a week for minerals (a dash)
No added supplements at this time	Add in Fulvic/Humic Acid	Add in supplements (2 at a time for 3 days at least) Then two more and so on.
Feed raw bones such as rib bones for chewing 2-3 times a week	Add Colostrum for sensitive or weak immune systems. RAW goat's milk is also good.	Can add an organic dairy listed from book at this time once a week

Week Four	Week Five	Week Six
Beef with bone and organs (80/10/10) - ground or small bites. Add Calcium supplement (if not 10% bone in diet)	Rabbit with bone and organs (80/10/10) - ground or small bites. Add Calcium supplement (if not 10% bone in diet)	Turkey with bone and organs (80/10/10) - ground or small bites. Add Calcium supplement (if not 10% bone in diet)
Finely chopped raw veggies (pick 1-2 at a time) (kale, broccoli)	Finely chopped raw veggies (pick 1-2 different ones at a time)	Finely chopped raw veggies (pick 1-2 different ones at a time)
Apple Cider Vinegar (1 teaspoon-1 TBSP depending on size of dog)	Apple Cider Vinegar (1 teaspoon-1 TBSP depending on size of dog)	Apple Cider Vinegar (1 teaspoon-1 TBSP depending on size of dog)
Fish oil/Calamari oil and/or low-sodium sardines in water	Fish oil/Calamari oil and/or low-sodium sardines in water	Fish oil/Calamari oil and/or low-sodium sardines in water
Probiotics/Digestive Enzymes	Probiotics/Digestive Enzymes	Probiotics/Digestive Enzymes
Coconut oil (1/4 teaspoon per 20 lbs) Alternate every other day	Coconut oil (1/4 teaspoon per 20 lbs) Alternate every other day	Coconut oil (1/4 teaspoon per 20 lbs) Alternate every other day
Vitamin E (soy free)- 3 times a week	Vitamin E (soy free)- 3 times a week	Vitamin E (soy free)- 3 times a week
Cooked egg 1-2 times a week (boiled/poached/scrambled)	Cooked egg 1-2 times a week (boiled/poached/scrambled)	Cooked egg 1-2 times a week (boiled/poached/scrambled)
ORGAN MEATS: (Spleen, brain, kidney, eyeballs, ovaries, testicles, calf liver (1 oz per 10 lbs) 1-2 times a week) 10% total	ORGAN MEATS: (Spleen, brain, kidney, eyeballs, ovaries, testicles, calf liver (1 oz per 10 lbs) 1-2 times a week) 10% total	ORGAN MEATS: (Spleen, brain, kidney, eyeballs, ovaries, testicles, calf liver (1 oz per 10 lbs) 1-2 times a week) 10% total
Chicken necks and chicken feet 1-2 times a week. Chicken hearts for added Taurine.	Chicken necks and chicken feet 1-2 times a week. Chicken hearts for added Taurine.	Chicken necks and chicken feet 1-2 times a week. Chicken hearts for added Taurine.

Supplements: Colostrum-immune builder; Camu Camu or Rosehips-natural Vit C. Magnesium-to replenish magnesium that we all are missing in our diet; B-complex to build immunity and restore energy.	Supplements: Colostrum-immune builder; Camu Camu or Rosehips-natural Vit C. Magnesium-to replenish magnesium that we all are missing in our diet; B-complex to build immunity and restore energy.	Supplements: Colostrum-immune builder; Camu Camu or Rosehips-natural Vit C. Magnesium-to replenish magnesium that we all are missing in our diet; B-complex to build immunity and restore energy.
Milk Thistle for stressed systems making changes to diet, feeding kibble/canned foods, on medications, recently vaccinated, or had surgery. Give for 30 days	Slippery Elm for sensitive tummies and digestive tracts. (give separately from medications and supplements) Give up to 90 days	
Feed raw bones such as rib bones for chewing 2-3 times a week. Can do this weekly.	Add Colostrum for sensitive or weak immune systems. RAW goat's milk is also good.	Can add an organic dairy listed from book at this time once a week if you like.

If your dog has allergies, overweight, leaky gut, yeast build up, pancreatitis, or any other illness, start with rabbit as your first protein. It is lean and easy to digest. Goat is another good one.

For problems in transitioning:
While this is extremely rare, if your dog's body goes into complete chaos, then stop the diet, fast the dog for 24 hours, then start again by cooking the food first. (Actually, you may want to start with bone broth for a day to ease back into the diet.) Cook the food for a couple of weeks, then as your dog gets use to cooked foods, start slowly backing away from it being completely cooked. Cook it half way. Cut into small pieces if needed. Feed for a couple weeks like that. Then try cooking it less each time until you are able to get to raw only. Some dogs may transition this way much easier as well. Sometimes you have to trick the dog because they are smart little critters. Most all dogs love cooked

foods but they will obtain more nutrients from raw so try to get to that point if possible. Even if you sear them from now on, at least they are getting some form of raw.

If any loose stools, diarrhea or constipation, add some canned 100% pumpkin to the diet (1/2 teaspoon per 10 lbs). If any occasional vomiting (no more than 2-3 times overall), you can add in Slippery Elm daily for a month or so for sensitive tummies. Slippery Elm also works for diarrhea.

Bully Sticks
Some say these are bad and some say good. Let me explain this. I recently read where a well-known holistic vet mentioned to their followers not to feed bully sticks due to the bacteria. My mouth dropped and I had to laugh. Really? Ok, you have bacteria in raw meats; you have bacteria in kibble foods and canned foods. In fact, most contaminated food is commercial pet foods. Just always remember, anytime you handle any type of foods, human foods, pet foods, raw foods, bully sticks, treats and alike, always wash your hands with soap and water after handling. That's it. It's that simple.

Some bully sticks are hard and may break or chip teeth. Use with caution.

Do not give store bought rawhide bones or alike. These are dangerous and there are many horrible gut-wrenching reports of deaths from these. Also, antler chew bones have been known to break teeth.

Now for supplements, I have created a list of what you will need. See next chapter on supplements and dosage amounts as well. These supplements can be tweaked along the way. But for now, it's a great list to start with and provide with daily meals.

Calcium-eggshell or seaweed (if not feeding 10% bone)
Approximate dosage or follow label:
0-25 lbs: 1/4 - 1/2 teaspoon
25-50 lbs: 1/2 - 1 teaspoon
50-75 lbs: 1 - 1 1/2 teaspoon
75+ lbs: 1 1/2 - 2 teaspoon

Fish oils (needed): (Squid or Anchovy/ Sardine) I no longer recommend krill oil due to the overfishing of krill in our oceans. Always buy high quality fish oils. You will find many oils out there but not of good quality and therefore are rancid or loaded with mercury. Follow dosing on bottle. Buy in glass or metal containers. NO plastic due to BPA/BPS. Calamari (squid) oil is a great oil as well.

Stop fish oil and Vitamin E approximately seven days before surgery.

The areas with the highest contamination levels include most of the Atlantic Ocean, the Gulf of Mexico, the Chesapeake Bay, the waters around Northern Europe and China. These are areas that have been industrialized for many years. The waters surrounding New Zealand are some of the cleanest on the planet. Industrialization is mostly limited to the North Island. The waters are far away from major shipping lanes. The government has many regulations in place that help to protect the environment, prevent pollution, and ensure that the fish populations are sustainable.

Krill and Wild Salmon oil contains some form of Astaxanthin. Astaxanthin is a powerful antioxidant. Antioxidants help protect your dog's cells from free radical damage. Needed especially in older dogs.

I recommend adding an Astaxanthin supplement instead of feeding Krill oil.

Follow label or:
Daily Dose:
Small dogs (up to 30 lbs): 250 - 500mg
Medium dogs (31-50 lbs): 750 - 1000mg
Large dogs (51-80 lbs): 125 - 1500mg
Giant dogs (81+ lbs): 1700 - 2000mg

Greens Powder (if not adding in veggies)
Ingredients in Starwest Botanicals Greens Powder:
Organic barley grass, organic wheat grass, organic spirulina, organic spinach, organic alfalfa leaf, organic kelp, organic dulse leaf, organic barley grass juice, organic orange peel, organic beet root, organic

dandelion leaf, organic lemon peel, organic ginkgo leaf, and organic wheat grass juice.

Dosage:
Small dogs: 1/4 - 1/2 teaspoon
Medium/Large dogs: 1/2 - 1 teaspoon
Giant dogs: 1 - 1 1/2 teaspoons

Greens contain some of your highest amount of vitamins. In today's world even the best-grown organic veggies and fruits are lacking in higher content of vitamins and minerals due to our depleted soils. Same for our meats. In a perfect world we wouldn't need extra supplementation but because of our meats lacking due to over-use of antibiotics and medications and poor diets fed to the cows and chickens and other animals we consume, we must add extra food sources. Although dogs are carnivores, giving a small amount of veggies or greens powder can have huge benefits for your dog due to what is lacking in our foods and especially our meats. Greens (leafy) have your best sources for vitamins. If your dog doesn't want to eat the organic mixed greens blend, I recommend trying organic Kale, Moringa, Spirulina, or Chlorella powders. "Amazing Grass - The Original" is a good brand and doesn't have as strong of a smell and is well tolerated.

ORGANIC BARLEY GRASS: Rich in SOD, Calcium, Iron, and trace minerals. Barley has been reported to relieve arthritis, gastrointestinal disorders, chronic fatigue, constipation, poor circulation, and Psoriasis, Acne, and body odor.

ORGANIC WHEAT GRASS: Wheat grass is rich in Choline and Chlorophyll. It has good amounts of vitamin A, C, and E, with small amounts of Thiamine, Riboflavin, Niacin, Pantothenic Acid, and vitamin B6 and B12. Wheat grass is rich in Potassium and Phosphorus. It has good amounts of Calcium, Sodium, and Magnesium with small amounts of Iron, Folic Acid, Selenium, and Zinc.

ORGANIC SPIRULINA: It is rich in B vitamins, particularly B-1, B-2, B-3, and B-6. Spirulina is the richest source of vitamin B-12 found in nature!

ORGANIC SPINACH: An excellent source of minerals like Calcium, Phosphorus, Iron, Potassium, and Zinc as well as antioxidants like Carotenoids, vitamin C and vitamin E.

If your pet has had oxalate stones previously, do not give spinach to them. It does have a tendency to cause oxalate stones in some.

ORGANIC ALFALFA: Alfalfa has roots that reach up to 60 feet into the soil to absorb trace minerals. Its lightweight proteins stimulate the rebuilding of tissues and strengthen hair, skin, and nails. Also good for digestive system support and to stimulate the appetite. The leaves are a source of chlorophyll. Also a source of carotene (vitamin A) and vitamin K, vitamin C, Niacin, and vitamin B-1.

Avoid while taking blood-thinning agents. Because alfalfa has an estrogenic effect, patients with hormone-sensitive cancers should avoid alfalfa. You have hormone-sensitive cancer such as breast, prostate, cervical, or uterine cancers.

ORGANIC KELP, DULSE: Known to contain over 96 different minerals and trace minerals. These foods represent the most potent mineral-rich whole foods. The little known red kelp called Dulse has been reported to restore kidney function, while the iodine in green kelp is helpful for thyroid problems. **Iodine in small amounts is needed in every diet.**

Note: Dogs low in iodine can have signs of aggression, fear of noises and weight gain. Kelp has a high amount of iodine so be very careful with it. Dulse is a much lower content of iodine and is much safer to use even in higher amounts. Dulse also contains manganese.

ORGANIC ORANGE PEEL: Orange peel contains higher amounts of certain nutrients than its flesh. For instance, 3.5 ounces of orange peel provides 136mg of vitamin C, while the flesh contains about 71mg. Orange peel also contains considerable amounts of Calcium, Copper, Magnesium, vitamin A, Folate and other B vitamins, and dietary fiber.

ORGANIC BEET ROOT POWDER: Beet Root Powder provides a wide range of nutrients, but its most significant phytochemical is

Betaine. Betaine is found in digestive enzymes as well. This plant chemical may support liver and kidney health by recycling the amino acid Methionine to maintain the body's stores of S-Adenosyl-Methionine, more commonly known as SAM-e. Betaine may also support the liver's ability to process fat. This may possibly prevent the accumulation of fatty tissues in the liver. Beet roots are sources of Potassium, Phosphorus, Iron, Magnesium and Calcium as well as vitamin A, B and C. Beets have been shown to provide antioxidant, anti-inflammatory, and detoxification.

ORGANIC DANDELION LEAF: An excellent digestive aid and diuretic. Full of vitamins A, B, C, and D as well as minerals such as Iron, Potassium, and Zinc. Aids in detoxifying.

ORGANIC LEMON PEEL: Lemon peels contain as much as 5 to 10 times more vitamins than the lemon juice itself. To name a few: vitamin C, vitamin A, Beta-carotene, Folate, Calcium, Magnesium, and Potassium.

ORGANIC GINKGO LEAF: Ginkgo leaf is often referred to as a brain herb because of its rich nutrient content and health benefits. Ginkgo leaf is packed with plant-based antioxidants called Flavonoids, which protect cells and reduce the risk for developing age-related diseases. It is also rich in Terpenoids that researchers believe improve blood flow to the brain.

ORGANIC WHEAT GRASS: Wheat grass is loaded with Beta-carotene, Calcium, Chlorophyll, fiber, Iron, and vitamin K. Wheat grass contains an abundance of Chlorophyll, which helps detoxify and cleanse the body while eliminating harmful toxins. Chlorophyll is also the reason wheat grass has an alkalizing effect on the body, balancing pH levels and correcting a build-up of acids, which can inhibit the body's ability to absorb nutrients. Wheat grass contains immune-boosting nutrients like beta-carotene and vitamin C.

Other good greens:

ORGANIC KALE: Kale is also a good source of dietary fiber and an excellent source of vitamin A (in the form of Carotenoids), vitamin K, and Manganese. It is a very good source of Copper, Tryptophan, vitamin B-6, and Potassium; and a good source of Magnesium, vitamin E, vitamin B-2, protein, vitamin B-1, Folate, Phosphorous, and vitamin B-3. Also worth noting in Kale's nutritional profile is its vitamin K content. Kale contains nearly twice the amount of vitamin K as most of its fellow cruciferous vegetables.

ORGANIC CHLORELLA: It has the highest concentration of Chlorophyll of any plant known in the world. Chlorella contains protein, carbohydrates, the whole range of B vitamins, vitamin C, and E, amino acids and trace minerals. It contains more vitamin B-12 than calf liver does. Chlorella is a great supplement to help boost the immune system and to help the body detoxify as well. It aids in cleansing of the bloodstream.

ORGANIC BROCCOLI: Broccoli contains phytochemicals shown to benefit the immune system, blood pressure, eyes, skin, blood sugar disorders such as diabetes, cancer, bladder and kidney and heart health. Broccoli is full of vitamin A, vitamin C, Vitamin K, Choline and Calcium. Assists in leaky gut and digestion due to high in fiber.

ORGANIC MORINGA: Moringa is a nutrient rich food that contains 46 antioxidants, 90 nutrients including high quality protein, Calcium, trace minerals, Iron, and all 9 essential amino acids.
Not only does Moringa provide all that nutrition, it also contains powerful antioxidants, and has anti-fungal, antibacterial, and anti-inflammatory properties.

I also like Amazing Grass Green Superfood brand for a green mix and alternate with the Starwest Botanical brand. Once diet is established, when giving supplements, take at least 1-2 days off a week. I pick Sunday for nothing but meats on that day. I however have two dogs with joint issues so I watch them and if I feel they need joint supplements at that time, I will add those in. Stop supplements at least 1-7 days before having surgery of any type. If joint supplements are important, do not use the day before surgery. Stop vitamin E and fish oils about 7 days prior to having surgery.

Raw Unfiltered Apple Cider Vinegar with "Mother"
Dosage:
0-25 lbs: 1 teaspoon
25-50 lbs: 2 teaspoon
50-75 lbs: 1 TBSP
75+ lbs: 1 1/2 - 2 TBSP

ACV is known for maintaining the acid/alkaline balance of the digestive tract. If you have a dog that has clear, watery discharge from the eyes, runny noses, or coughs with a liquid sound, use ACV in his or her food. ACV works well against yeast. If your dog has the itchies, add into food. You can use a few drops in his or her ears after cleaning them to avoid ear infections. Apple cider vinegar is also known for its antibacterial and anti-fungal properties. Works well for yeast in the body and adjusting the pH levels as well. Add to diet for cancer patients. This has worked well in dogs that have unknown type allergies or skin issues and leaky gut or with acid reflux.

Vitamin E (needed 3 times a week): Vitamin E is a powerful antioxidant that plays a crucial role in supporting pet health. Pet food alone does not contain enough vitamin E to meet your dog's needs. Supplementing your dog's diet with natural vitamin E three times a week can help prevent serious health problems created by vitamin E deficiency. It is a must especially when giving fish oils. Most of your vitamin E supplements contain soy. Avoid soy in all products. I found Dry E Succinate doesn't contain it in most incidences and comes recommended by holistic drs. Do not give softgels to dogs. They go in one end and out the other without dissolving. Poke holes in them and squirt into the foods.

Dosage:
Vitamin E amounts:
Small dogs: 200IU three times a week
Med/Large dogs: 300 - 400IU three times a week
Giant dogs: 600IU three times a week
(Do not go over this dosage)

Water
Next, we will look at your water. If you don't have a water filter, get one! It is a thousand times better having one. I can't say this enough. It is crucial to you and your dog's health. A Chlorine-free and Fluoride-free multi-stage filter or reverse osmosis and a fluoride filter added. You can get one pretty cheap. Check out my website for affordable water filters. I myself have one on my refrigerator for my water/ice dispenser (not the one that comes with the refrigerator inside) and one on my kitchen sink (under counter) as well as my shower. A whole house filter is ideal but much more costly. So for a fast solution, get one smaller for at least drinking and cooking water for a price as low as $100-$200.

Fluoride and Chlorine have been classified as a neurotoxin. Our waters are contaminated with pesticides and medications. These are not removed when treatment plants filter the waters. Some city waters are even in much worst shape depending on where you live. Test your water with affordable test kits ($40+) available in stores and online. Find what is in your water and make sure you pick a filter that removes high amounts of these toxins and chemicals. Chlorine and Fluoride are known to cause Hypothyroidism also. Do not think your city water is safe. Our waters are **not** safe, even the cleanest isn't clean. Provide water (and food) in high quality stainless steel, glass, or ceramic bowls. Keep the bowls clean, chip/crack free, wash with soap and water daily and provide fresh filtered chemical-free, chlorine and fluoride-free water to your pets.

Distilled water is not acceptable. Distilled water has had all the minerals removed. The body needs minerals. In most cases, distilled water that you find at a store was produced using drinking water, so it is fine to drink. But distilled water from different sources may not be safe to drink. For example, if you take non-potable water from an industrial source and then distill it, the distilled water may contain enough pollutants that are hazardous for drinking. Due to the demineralization done during the evaporation process, when consumed, distilled water increases urine output. It also eliminates electrolytes such as the potassium level which is critical in making the muscles function correctly. Distilled water takes away all minerals and nutrients due to the process of distillation. So then, your body is forced to give electrolytes to the mineral and nutrient-free water. Because of this, the electrolyte level will slowly decrease and eventually cause electrolyte imbalance in the body. Electrolytes are important for the body because it helps to eliminate waste and function properly. So if you drink distilled water consistently, you are putting you and your dog's health at risk. It has no sufficient amount of minerals and nutrients that can protect the body against disease and illness. It can also potentially lead to certain health problems such as bone deformities, digestive tract disorders, and even blood-related sickness. So that's why filtered only!

Tip: Cooking with fluoridated water simply concentrates fluoride in the food, a point that all pet food manufacturers must consider in addition to the ingredients they use in their manufactured pet foods. Water from lakes, ponds, rivers etc is also not a good source of water. Your dog can contract many water borne diseases and some are life threatening. Waters are polluted with pesticides and chemicals including waste from unknown sources so it is always best to give your dog water from your home that has been filtered.

Air
While the outside air may contain pollutants and do harm, inside your home make sure you have a good filtration system. Adding HEPA room air purifiers is a huge plus. Buy several and use in main rooms and bedrooms. You will probably need more than one in your home depending on size of rooms.

Vaccines
Reduce vaccines. Do not give yearly vaccines, as these are not necessary. Do not give on the same day of surgery or when your dog is ill. After getting puppy shots, you can do titer testing in the future. You will need another Rabies one year after puppy vaccines. The second one can be the 3-year vaccine. You may want to skip the Leptospirosis vaccine. Rabies is the only vaccine required by law so get with a vet that offers a Thimerosal-Free 3-year vaccine. This is a law in the USA although some towns will push the one-year. Check with your city ordinance and find a vet that offers the 3-year vaccine. According to whether you live in the country or city will determine what you may need to give for the other vaccines. There are Rattlesnake vaccines, Flu vaccines; you name it. They are coming up with different vaccines on a

daily basis for the pharmaceutical companies and vets to be able to make more money. And most of these do not work at all. Choose wisely and avoid vaccines if unnecessary or that don't really work like the Flu and Bordetella vaccine. Titering is always recommended so you don't subject your dog to more disease-causing vaccines. ***Distemper and Rabies given together have been known to cause aggression in dogs.***

Flu vaccines will not keep your dog from getting the flu, just like human flu vaccines. They are also loaded with metals and toxins. Same applies for the Bordetella. It will not stop or fix your dog from getting kennel cough. Avoid!

Bordetella is a vaccine I wouldn't recommend either. If you must, use the nasal medication only. It does not contain the adjuvants found in the vaccine so it is much safer. Do **not** use the injectable and don't give it on the same day as any other vaccine. For dogs less than 12 lbs, ask for a partial amount of the vaccine. You have to use the full Rabies vaccine due to laws but the others you should use only partial or adjusted dosage for your size of dog. It also has been said that vaccines can be more harmful in white dogs.

Make sure your vet does not give one vaccine that is a combination of all. Each should be given in single doses and at least 2-4 weeks apart. I myself would wait a month in-between. This should apply to puppies and all dogs.

Vaccines are contaminated with mercury, aluminum, bacteria, and who knows what else. Many of these ingredients are also categorized as a neurotoxin. Vaccines can cause other diseases such as arthritis, autoimmune disease, lameness, cancer, seizures, and even death. It's best to avoid vaccines at all costs as much as possible. As for the Bordetella, you can treat kennel cough using natural remedies such as Mullein, Astragalus, and Echinacea. *See more later in this book.*

Give a small dose of Zinc for 3-5 days before vaccines. Zinc in high doses is toxic to humans and pets. (For example: Normally a human dose is 30-40mg, give your dog no more than 10mg.) Extra Magnesium works well too. Magnesium Malate or Citrate is recommended for vaccination periods. You can add in buffered vitamin C (Magnesium Ascorbate) to the diet. Adding in a little extra Selenium, Zinc, Curcumin, and Quercetin are great as well for combating vaccine reaction symptoms. Try to give these within an hour of getting the vaccine. Astaxanthin is good at protecting against the toxic effects of the vaccine also. You may add a little vitamin D3 into the food for these several days before, during, and after. A low dose depending on your dog's size is sufficient. Do not overdo this vitamin. It is a fat soluble meaning your dog's body does not excrete it. It goes straight to the liver. Do not give this on a regular daily basis as part of the diet. Seek out a holistic vet for guidance on this vitamin if you plan on doing so.

Core Vaccines
These are the only vaccines recommended:
- Rabies (Thimerosal-Free)
- Distemper
- Parvovirus

(For puppies, it's best to wait till 6 months of age for vaccines to reduce many unwanted reactions. This means keep your new dog inside and away from everyone and other animals and stay with your new pup at all times.)

Never get combo vaccines. Single dose only of each and wait 30 days in-between. It is recommended to do titers for canine distemper and parvovirus every three years up until age 10. Seniors do not need any more vaccines due to age or if any dog has a chronic illness. This includes new injuries, illness etc. Get a waiver if your dog has an illness or injury or wait until they are healthy and their immune system is strong again. It is stated by the manufacture of the vaccines to NOT give to an ill or diseased pet. Vaccines actually last 7-15 years but requesting titers every 3 years will help you find if your dog is protected. Also note; studies on severe reactions have **not** been done on vaccines.

Best to avoid these vaccines:
Most of these do not protect or are not the right strains. Moneymakers for manufactures and vets. Do your research thoroughly before feeling that it is necessary to give any of these. These vaccines can have serious consequences giving them to your dog. Know the risks.

Lyme (borelia)
Bordetella (kennel cough)
Parainfluenza (flu)
Leptospirosis
Adenovirus (hepatitis)
Rattlesnake
Coronavirus

The longer you wait to give a vaccine, the less of a chance of reactions or lifetime side effects (Seizures, Autoimmune disorders, etc.) **Do not vaccinate your dog if it has had a serious life-threatening vaccine reaction.**

For Vaccine Reactions (see Ch .12 also):
Use Thuja (200c preferably) for vaccines several days before, day of and several days after up to four weeks usually. Use Lyssin (200c preferably if found)-check Amazon or other websites) for Rabies vaccine for several days before, day of and after; up to four weeks. You can use the 30c if you can't get your hands on the 200c although I have found it on Amazon.

If your dog is experiencing any symptoms from reactions to the vaccines, continue the Lyssin and/or Thuja until symptoms are completely gone.

FOR DOGS 100 lbs TO 150 lbs: 5 pellets given at one time is one dose. Use one dose of 5 pellets daily for 3 days prior to rabies vaccination and continue on the day of vaccination and daily for at least one week following vaccination.

FOR DOGS 50 lbs up to 100 lbs: 4 pellets given at one time is one dose. Use one dose of 4 pellets daily for 3 days prior to rabies vaccination and continue on the day of vaccination and daily for at least one week following vaccination.

FOR DOGS 15 lbs up to 50 lbs: 3 pellets given at one time is one dose. Use one dose of 3 pellets daily for 3 days prior to Rabies vaccination and continue on the day of vaccination and daily for at least one week following vaccination.

FOR DOGS LESS THAN 15 lbs: 2 pellets given at one time are one dose. Use one dose of 2 pellets daily for 3 days prior to Rabies vaccination and continue on the day of vaccination and daily for at least one week following vaccination.

Do not touch the pellets. You may put pellets in the mouth or put into a glass bottle, add filtered water, shake vigorously, let dissolve then squirt into your dog's mouth using a syringe or dropper. Keep refrigerated for up to two weeks. You can also add into food although there is much controversy but it has been noted by holistic drs that it still works when putting into food.

If your dog is still showing reactions to a vaccine, you can give this dose twice a day for several weeks up to a month or as long as needed until you see improvement. You may give pellets every 2 hours with bad reactions.

Medications
When your dog is sick, you take them to the vet and the vet gives you meds and sends you home without any warning or warning label on these deadly medications and side effects. Depending on the illness, medications should be used only when absolutely necessary and sometimes shouldn't be used at all depending on the cause. You at least need a diagnosis. There are many other options to use that do not include medications. Always check out the insert for warnings and contraindications. NSAIDs, steroids, flea and tick meds (external, internal, collars) and even heartworm meds are highly dangerous and should be used with **extreme** caution and given only if absolutely necessary. There are dogs that die every day from using these medications. You can ask for Tramadol although Tramadol also has a list of side effects. All medications do. Some are just deadlier than

others. Tramadol doesn't work against inflammation so adding in anti-inflammatory herbs would work with Tramadol. If you need pain meds longer than 3 days, I highly recommend you check out a supplement called CanineActiv. It may replace the pain meds completely depending on what you need pain meds for. Do not just jump on the bandwagon and give medications prescribed by your vet until you do your research first. You may save your own dogs life.

Heartworm preventatives are not preventatives. But you can give Heartgard every 45 days which is by manufactures recommendations although I wouldn't use these chemicals. I myself live in the heart of mosquito country and it stays hot and humid here about 8-9 months out of the year. And I do not give heartworm preventatives that contain chemicals. I give once a week the Heartworm nosode. I do have my dogs tested every 6 months to make sure they are Heartworm negative. Nothing prevents heartworms. NOTHING! Most raw fed dogs have a smaller chance of infected mosquitoes biting them because raw fed dogs are healthier and mosquitoes prey on weakened immune systems. Heartworm preventatives are not needed if the temperature drops below 57 degrees and stays below that for at least 2 weeks. It kills off the mosquitoes. *(Read Chapter on Heartworms for more information).*

Flea and tick products including topicals (store bought or from the vet's office) are toxic and deadly and thousands of pets have died from these products. They make plenty of natural products that work just as well. Cedar oil works well. Use a carrier oil to dilute the cedar oil and apply to the coat lightly.

Immune Systems
Immune systems are weakened when you use medications, vaccines, poor diet, unfiltered water, and chemical laced environmental conditions. It is important to know when to use added supplements to rebuild the system if these conditions occur. A strong immune system will ward off fleas, ticks, mosquitoes and most of all, disease. It is vital that you keep your dog's immune system strong by doing all the things mentioned here.

Disease
Poor diet, vaccines, medications, unfiltered water, the air we breathe, and the ground we walk on are laced with pesticides and chemicals that are deadly to us and our pets. We have higher cancer rates in the USA than we did 20-30 years ago. More preservatives and additives have been added to our foods and waters. This includes our lawn fertilizers and medications. We must avoid all of these as much as possible. It is a critical time for all of us. Cancer, heart conditions, Diabetes, Cushing's, autoimmune disease, arthritis/lameness, and seizures/epilepsy just to name a few of what these toxins do to our bodies. Use organic all-natural fertilizers on your yard and pesticides that are not harmful to children or pets if you must use anything. Food Grade Diatomaceous Earth works for many things. Kills insects, fleas, great for cleaning, deworming, detoxing, added benefits for arthritis and over-all health. Too many to list here. Sprinkle D.E. all over your yard and add into your dog's food. Pumpkin seeds or organic pumpkin seed powder kills all parasites except heartworms.

Vet Visits
Vet visits should consist of wellness visits every 6 months for a senior or diseased dog and once a year for healthy dogs. Complete blood workup including checking calcium levels (I always check for these things along with any deficiencies that may show up with supplements), Heartworm test, thyroid test, and x-rays if needed in an aging dog or a dog prone to hip dysplasia or joint issues. Run a ProBNP blood test to check for early heart disease. If your dog shows early signs, get them on D-Ribose, Hawthorn, Dandelion Leaf, Taurine and Ubiquinol. Depending on your breed of dog and what they may be predisposed to, run tests for those genetic diseases as well as often as necessary. Veterinarian visits should not be determined by what your vet says is a must. If your vet tries to put your dog on a prescription pet food diet, refuse. You have other options. That is horrible food (corn) and actually makes things worse. Organic boiled chicken, organic scrambled eggs and a little added organic 100% pumpkin to the diet is always acceptable on a short-term for digestive problems like diarrhea and vomiting. Don't forget your organic bone broth. Refuse vaccines and receive only if needed on your terms.

Do your research. Speaking of doing your research, don't go to one website and believe what you read. Go to several ones that don't have the exact same wording. Seems websites follow other websites and you get the same wording. Find reputable websites you can trust. Most you can't completely trust will be coming from the medical profession.

Many pet owners who have made the switch to raw or a homemade diet have noticed drastic changes in their pets, including:

- Shinier, healthier skin and coats
- Cleaner teeth
- Improved digestion
- Improvement with allergy symptoms
- Anal gland problems cleared up
- Decreased shedding
- Firmer, smaller stools

This is a basic guide for raw diets. It's simple and it can be cheaper than any premium type of pet food out there. Your vet bills will decrease. It will be best to do yearly blood work. Yearly checkups are important. Every 6 months for seniors.

B-Complex, Magnesium, and Manganese vitamins are a great addition to the diet and will help joints as well (Pitties/Staffies) and large dogs need these always, as they are more apt for an ACL tear and other joint issues. If you want in-depth testing for allergies, vitamins or alike, there are several experts out there that offer this.

Dr. Peter Dobias offers hair testing for minerals and toxins and Dr. Jean Dodds offers blood work for thyroid and food sensitivities. Also, a place called Modern Allergy Management that you will find on my website. MAM tests for food intolerances at a much lower price and soon will be adding heavy metal level testing along with environmental.

After 6 months on a raw diet and you have been using the recommended supplements here, you can reduce the amount of some of these supplements if your dog isn't having any skin or allergy issues. I

sometimes give every other day except for fish oils and joint supplements. I give those daily unless I am feeding sardines too. Continue the vitamin E three times a week. If you miss a dose of these on any given day, don't panic. It takes awhile before the dog will start to show deficiencies and you would have to miss quite a few days. I also will skip at least one day on supplements per week except the joint supplements for the dogs with joint issues. You can also switch to a different brand of supplements. It's best to rotate brands so find some really good ones and rotate them about every 3-6 months or so.
Joint supplements should be given to all dogs of all ages starting at about 6-12 months of age. This will help to prevent future arthritis, hip dysplasia etc. More about joints later. The bigger the dog, the sooner to start them.

Tips:
Dogs prone to digestive upsets or vomiting immediately following a meal will benefit from using a bowl for fast eaters. Most you find are plastic but I have found some stainless steel ones out there. These dogs will definitely need to start on digestive enzymes and probiotics weeks before transitioning. I also like to add in a digestive enzyme with ox bile or something specific for pancreas as this helps with stomach issues as well. Also, try the ground-up meats instead so they can't gulp chunks and get food stuck in their throat. If your dog is experiencing runny/loose stools (soft stool is not diarrhea), constipation, or vomiting at times other than after meals, slow down the transition process and add 100% organic pumpkin (canned is ok) to their meal. Use 1-2 tablespoons per cup of food. Pumpkin is unique in that it helps with loose stools as well as constipation and upset tummies. Slippery Elm is great for diarrhea, digestive issues, and leaky gut. If you are adding organ meat in the beginning, stop these for a few days or until the system has adjusted to the change then slowly add back in using small amounts at a time. If these suggestions don't work, try fasting your dog for 24 hours. Let the digestive system rest. Feed smaller meals and more often. Start the diet back with feeding bone broth. Dogs with allergies/food intolerances; find a protein in the exotics to start with. Rabbit or goat is good. Exotic meats are higher in price so look for deals. Dogs that have been on steroids, antibiotics, or other long-term drugs, may experience longer detoxification periods. You should always consult with a holistic veterinarian if you believe your dog is

showing severe problems associated with the diet change. You can always start off cooking or searing the meats to avoid these types of reactions.

It is important to remember, never feed your dog one hour before and one hour after exercise; this will prevent bloat and life-threatening gastric torsion especially in larger dogs although in raw diets, this is less common.

Transitioning Picky Eaters and Older Dogs to a Raw Diet
These dogs may turn their noses up at the smell and texture of their new food. Don't worry, as this is a common occurrence and is usually easy to address by following these steps:

- Eliminate treats during the transition
- Fast your dog the night before starting the transition
- Partially cook/sear the meats
- Add cooked shredded chicken on top along with broth
- Add low sodium sardines in with the food

Let me tell you a story about my picky dog, Diamond. Actually, I have two dogs that are picky but Diamond took the longest to transition. When I first started the transition, I was feeding canned and I would put raw meat on one plate and canned dog food on another plate. I let her pick. Most of the time she picked raw. This went on over a week or two until she stopped going to the canned. Many times, she wouldn't touch her food. I would leave it for 20-30 minutes and if she didn't eat it by then, I picked it up. I would wait one hour and try again. Sometimes we even skipped that meal because she refused. I knew she liked it and would eat it but she seemed like she was hung up on something. I cannot tell you what. It may have been her smelling the greens powder or fish oil or something in it she didn't like. I don't really know. So this is when I started trying things. I found pouring a little chicken broth or adding some cooked chicken breast mixed in helped get her attention. To this day, I still use this tactic but not always. Her routine was, to go into her crate and wait for me to make her food, and then I would call her to come eat. I had to coax her to eat. This went on for the first 1-2 years after I had adopted her. It was always a battle to get her to eat.

After about 2-3 months of a raw diet and our daily battle of her not eating or being picky and me taking her food away; she finally got it. One day all of a sudden out of nowhere, she stopped fighting me. I finally won the battle. She still went to her crate and waited for me to call her but she would eat. Sometimes she wouldn't eat all of it but that was ok, she was eating enough. She has done this from day one but the past year, she now comes into the kitchen and sits and stares at me waiting for me to fix her food and she always cleans her plate, always. So it was a real struggle with her. Her habits could have come from her past as well as her pickiness, but now, she is not so picky about things anymore. She loves her raw foods, especially liver.

We had this same battle over her sleeping place at night. For two years, I left my bedroom door open and she would come and get in bed with me. As soon as I turned off the lights and crawled in, she was up and gone back to the couch. This was every single night for two years. I did not understand this at all. Well, one day I decided to just close the door after she came in and got in bed. She never tried to leave my bed again. To this day, this is our routine. So the point here is, change one thing of your routine and it may just work for you. As simple as just closing the door, remedied this problem. And for picking up her food and her not getting to eat, along with adding chicken in, fixed the problem. So if your dog is picky, you have to make a change, or they keep winning.

FYI - Most vets are unfamiliar with raw diets and do not support them due to their lack of knowledge and education in nutrition. Don't let your vet discourage you and if you get repeated lashings so to speak from your vet, FIND A NEW ONE! It's YOUR dog and YOUR money. You have the final say.

Once you have transitioned and all is going well, you can always do a full body cleanse. This is optional but you may give it a try if your dog had shown a lot of signs of detoxing throughout the diet transition. He/she may need a deeper cleanse. Your dog may also suffer from leaky gut. That's a dog that no matter what you try or do, the issues are still there. Like allergy symptoms or stomach and digestive issues, eye discharge, itchy ears etc.

Deeper cleansing may consist of Activated Charcoal, Milk Thistle, Burdock Root, Dandelion, Apple Cider Vinegar, and/or Colloidal Silver. Many things will cleanse the body. Even organic mushroom blends.

Since you have already added in the greens powder by this time, you can add in Rosehips. It is a diuretic and it is great for many things including joints. It contains high amounts of vitamin C. It is a great "go to" for adding vitamin C in a natural form to the diet. Although Camu Camu has the highest amount of vitamin C but costs more. Much healthier than synthetic vitamin C supplements. After a couple of weeks, you can add in the Milk Thistle. You don't want to add in supplements all at once. Meaning, don't start all new ones on the same day. Give it 5-7 days at least in-between each. Two at a time is a safe start. You may get some opposite reactions like rapid detox or digestive upset, which you don't want if you throw them all in at once. You want it to go slowly but you want to cleanse the entire body. And start with a smaller amount and work up to the recommended amount.

If your dog is ill or has a weakened immune system, try organic bone broth. It is great for an ill dog or one that needs a boost in their immune system, that doesn't want to eat, and/or has some aches and pains. This is high in Glucosamine so this will give a boost as well. Also, try feeding organic/pasture-fed scrambled eggs and some organic/pasture-fed cooked chicken breast meat. It's like when we get sick; we reach for the chicken soup. Bone Broth works the same way. It is a great soup for adding electrolytes back into the body as well.

Bone Broth
To make it, you will need:
- Organic Chicken with bone
- Raw unfiltered Apple Cider Vinegar with "mother"
- Filtered water (Chlorine and fluoride-free)

Put a whole chicken into the crock-pot. Pour in at least 1 tablespoon of Apple Cider Vinegar per gallon of water. It helps break the bones down and you may need to add more during the cooking process. Let it cook. This may take 24-48

> hours. Check it occasionally.
>
> You can feed the cooked chicken (not the bones) once it falls off the bone. Continue cooking bones until you can mash them with a fork. You can strain out any bigger pieces and feed the broth to your pets. Yum! Good for you too!

Additional Nutritional Foods in Powder Form (can also use organic frozen or fresh fruits)
These can be added if you choose for added nutrition. These help build the immune system, add in many minerals, vitamins, amino acids, and help build the immune system. It's a great way to alternate or add in on occasion or pick a mix of them and add into diet at anytime for added nutrients. Most fight cancer and are immune builders. Make sure they are not from China or India. It's much better than giving a multi-vitamin supplement made from synthetic vitamins. You can use the ones listed below if you aren't adding in any fruits in raw form to the diet. It's a great substitute. Only small amounts are really needed.

These include:

Organic Goji Berry Powder
Enhances the immune system, protects eyesight and supports the liver. High in vitamin C and A. Found on many sites including nuts.com, Amazon etc.

Organic Blueberry Powder
Such a wonderful fruit to add. It is an antioxidant. Great for heart disease, cancer, weakened immune systems, osteoporosis, memory loss, bladder infections and so much more. Full of fiber as well. Found on nuts.com. Easy to find anywhere in an organic form.

Organic Red/Black Raspberry Powder
Raspberries rank near the top of all fruits for antioxidant strength, due to their rich content of ellagic acid, quercetin, gallic acid, anthocyanins, cyanidins, pelargonidins, catechins, kaempferol and salicylic acid. Raspberries possess almost 50% higher antioxidant activity than strawberries, and three times that of kiwis. Znaturalfoods.com sells an organic red raspberry powder.

Organic Bitter Melon Extract
Shown multiple actions against pancreatic cancer cells. Helps to regulate blood glucose levels. It may help to maintain the body's defense mechanism in weather changes or air borne pathogen. Rich in iron and has twice the beta-carotene of broccoli. Has a bitter taste. Starwest Botanicals makes an organic form but found on many websites.

Organic Mangosteen Fruit Rind
The nutritional benefits of the mangosteen fruit are found in the **peel/rind,** which contains high levels of xanthanoids and other phytochemicals with strong antioxidant properties. Znaturalfoods.com sells an organic powder.

Organic Grape Seed Extract Powder
When purchasing grape seed extract supplements, make VERY certain that all ingredients including inactive ingredients do not contain grape skins or the meat of grapes. ONLY SEEDS. The seeds are very powerful and are considered a powerful antioxidant. Great for inflammation as well. Kills cancer cells. I found Organic Grape Seed Extract Powder called Biofinest Grape seed Extract Powder. It's 100% grape **seeds** and organic.

Organic Cranberry Powder
Cranberries are known for their use in the healing and prevention of urinary tract infections. Regular consumption has shown that cranberries can help boost memory, relieve stress, anxiety, or depression, and can help promote weight gain. Cranberries can help prevent cancer cells from multiplying or developing. Most all cranberry comes from the USA. Found all over in organic powder form but frozen can work as well. Blend them up and serve.

Organic Acai Berry Powder
Acai Berry is loaded with antioxidants, a combination of essential amino acids and is packed with monounsaturated and polyunsaturated fatty acids (omega-6 & omega-9). This berry is said to contain more antioxidants than blueberries, cranberries, and strawberries. Found at various websites including Amazon. You may also look for frozen

organic fruit to blend or feed as well. Frozen organic foods are just as good as these powders but better. Stay away from the 'spray freeze' method. This method uses high heat processing. You want freeze-dried or micro-dried in powder or frozen organic in stores.

Chapter 4:
Supplementation

Chapter 4
Supplementation

Digestive Enzymes (needed):
What happens when enzymes are depleted? When there are insufficient food enzymes for dogs, the full digestive burden will be placed on the dog's pancreas to produce digestive enzymes. An over-stressed digestive system can eventually lead to improper food digestion and nutrient malabsorption.

Signs of lacking in enzymes:
- Bloating
- Gas and/or diarrhea
- Bad breath
- Body odor
- Acid Reflux/GERD
- Sensitive tummies
- Allergies
- Skin issues
- Coprophagia (eating poop)
- Yeast infections
- Thyroid issues
- Leaky Gut

A lack of digestive enzymes is a major contributing factor at the root of cancer.

I have found some pretty good human digestive enzymes that I am using just for these issues listed above. For a dog with stomach issues, you may need a very high amount of enzymes with added probiotics along with something good for the pancreas such as ox bile.

Probiotics (needed):
Probiotics are most likely to be helpful in resolving or preventing canine diarrhea associated with diet, inflammatory bowel disease, medication, certain GI infections, stress, intestinal bacterial overgrowth, and malabsorption. Replaces bad bacteria in the body with good bacteria. Builds a stronger immune system. Using probiotics and digestive enzymes help keep the immune system strong and the digestive tract functioning like a well-oiled machine.

FYI - you cannot get enough of probiotics from dairy. You will need to use supplements to get the full benefits. *You may add them along with dairy.*

Fish oils (needed):
Always buy high quality fish oils. You will find many oils out there but not of good quality and therefore are rancid or loaded with mercury.

Follow dosing on bottle. Buy in glass or metal (with chemical-free liner) containers. NO plastic due to BPA and BPS (when it says BPA free, it usually contains BPS which is much worse). The smaller the fish, the less mercury exposure. Also, Calamari oil is a great oil as well as Green Lipped Mussel. Krill oil is **not** recommended due to the over fishing of krill and the decline of krill in oceans.

Stop fish oil and Vitamin E seven days before surgery due to its effects on thinning of the blood.

The areas with the highest contamination levels include most of the Atlantic Ocean, the Gulf of Mexico, the Chesapeake Bay, the waters around Northern Europe and China. These are areas that have been industrialized for many years. The waters surrounding New Zealand are some of the cleanest on the planet. Industrialization is mostly limited to the North Island. The waters are far away from major shipping lanes. The government has many regulations in place that help to protect the environment, prevent pollution, and ensure that the fish populations are sustainable.

Follow label or...
Daily Dose:
Small dogs (up to 30 lbs): 250 - 500mg
Medium dogs (31-50 lbs): 750 - 1000mg
Large dogs (51-80 lbs): 125 - 1500mg
Giant dogs (81+ lbs): 1700 - 2000mg

Vitamin E (needed 3 times a week): Vitamin E is a powerful antioxidant that plays a crucial role in supporting pet health. Pet food alone does not contain enough vitamin E to meet your dog's needs. Supplementing your dog's diet with natural vitamin E can help prevent serious health problems created by vitamin E deficiency. It is a must especially when giving fish oils. Most of your vitamin E supplements contain soy. Avoid soy in all products. Do not give softgels to dogs. They go in one end and out the other without dissolving even though I have found pet supplements in softgel form. Soy-free recommendations can be found on website as I am constantly updating as they are found.

Dosage:
Small dogs: 200IU three times a week
Med/Large: 300 - 400IU three times a week
Giant: 600IU three times a week

A diet high in carbohydrates can also deplete vitamin E. Add Vitamin E daily for dogs with seizures.

Stop Vitamin E seven days before surgery due to its effects on thinning of the blood.

Natural vitamin E is known as "**d**-alpha-tocopherol." This is the most biologically active form of vitamin E.

Synthetic vitamin E is known as "**dl**-alpha-tocopherol." You need "approximately 50% more IU of synthetic alpha tocopherol" to get the same nutritional effect.

Vitamin C (recommended but can be found in Rosehips, Camu Camu and Amla):
Vitamin C is highly recommended especially in healing any pets with a disease or illness. Give high amounts for illness until bowel tolerance. Synthetic vitamin C is still absorbed in smaller amounts and can still be beneficial to your dog, especially a sick dog. Ascorbic Acid is hard on the stomach so you should provide a buffered vitamin C, which is Sodium Ascorbate, Calcium Ascorbate, or Magnesium Ascorbate. Sodium Ascorbate contains sodium so our dogs don't really need that. Calcium Ascorbate contains calcium so if you are already giving calcium, more isn't needed. So I recommend Magnesium Ascorbate due to all diets lacking in Magnesium. I like to recommend a natural form of vitamin C. Rosehips and Camu Camu along with Amla have the highest vitamin C content. Camu Camu has the very highest. If you use the whole food forms of vitamin C, your side effects will be much less if any at all.

Dosage for synthetic vitamin C:
Adjust accordingly but a good place to work towards.
Small dogs: 500mg - 1500mg

Medium/Large dogs: 1000mg - 3000mg
Giant dogs: 2000mg - 4000mg

WARNING: *Avoid anything with Benzene, Benzoate, or Benzoic Acid;* **especially when combined with Ascorbic Acid, Citric Acid, and vitamin C ingredients.** *It becomes a toxic carcinogen.*

Magnesium (needed):
Dogs need to have Magnesium in their diet. Even with the best diet, your dog will probably be deficient. And if your dog is prone to ACL injuries, this is a **requirement** in the diet. Without the right level of magnesium, unabsorbed calcium can build up in your dog's body causing arthritis.

If you would like to add a Magnesium supplement to your dog's diet or your own:

Magnesium Citrate (for oxalate stones, can have laxative effect)
Magnesium Taurate (for low stomach acid, calming, heart, can make blood sugar fluctuate, no laxative effect)
Magnesium Glycinate (no laxative effect, high absorption, muscle pain, calming).
Magnesium Malate (for achy joints and/or muscles, fatigue, heart, can cause stomach upset, no laxative effect)
Magnesium Orotate (heart failure, high absorbing magnesium)
Magnesium L-Threonate (for brain, absorbs well, calming)
Magnesium Chloride (for cellular detoxification and tissue purification, sluggish metabolism)
Magnesium Lactate (for moderate absorption, avoid with kidney issues restoring red blood cell levels of magnesium)
Magnesium Carbonate (for indigestion and acid reflux, can have laxative effect)

***Magnesium Stearate, Magnesium Gluconate, Magnesium Glutamate, Magnesium Aspartate, Magnesium sulfate (also called Epsom salts), and Magnesium Oxide (hydroxide) should be avoided.*

Dosage:
Small dogs: 10mg - 20mg

Medium dogs: 20mg - 50mg
Large dogs: 50mg - 100mg
Giant dogs: 100mg - 150mg
Or when using powder 1/4 teaspoon up to 1/2 teaspoon depending on size of dog.

Ubiquinol/COQ10 (optional):
As your dog reaches middle age, his level of CoQ10 gradually diminishes. You may be wondering if your dog can get CoQ10 from his/her diet. Food sources of CoQ10 include oily fish like mackerel, salmon, and sardines, organ meats, and whole grains. If your pet *were* to consume a diet high in these sources every day, they would still be faced with their body's *decreased* ability to convert CoQ10 into the active form that they need as they age. This helps with many ailments such as heart disease, blood sugar and joints as well. Your dog's body requires this essential coenzyme to function properly. Your dog can benefit from an extra dose of Ubiquinol or CoQ10 especially in older dogs. Ubiquinol absorbs more easily so more effective and less needed.

Ubiquinol Dosage:
Small dogs: 50mg per day
Medium dogs: 100mg per day
Large dogs: 100mg twice per day
Giant dogs: 100 - 200mg twice per day

COQ10 Dosage:
Small dogs: 100 - 200mg daily
Medium dogs: 200 - 300mg daily
Large dogs: 300 - 400mg daily
Giant dogs: 400 - 500mg daily

Astaxanthin (recommended if not using COQ10/Ubiquinol)
Astaxanthin is a very powerful antioxidant and it is 800 times stronger than COQ10. Astaxanthin can play a crucial role in helping your dog's heart function properly. Wild caught Salmon is also contains Astaxanthin.

Astaxanthin is also 65 times more powerful than vitamin C. Dogs and humans do not make Astaxanthin themselves so we must get it from

other sources. When purchasing a supplement, make sure it is created from marine microalgae and not fungus. Look for oils and not powders. This supplement may make your dogs poop a reddish orange color.
Dosage:
1- 2mg per 20 lbs or follow directions if in a pet supplement form.

Colostrum (optional):
If you are giving your dog a Glucosamine supplement, add pasture-fed Colostrum to help the body to absorb the Glucosamine better. It helps to build immunity for a weakened immune system. Colostrum from pasture-fed cows is much higher in immune factors than a human mother's colostrum! Colostrum is one of the most important nutritional supplements available for enhancing the immune system and helping in tissue repair. Colostrum works well for dogs and cats with diarrhea and for weakened immune systems. Colostrum can be used in all animals and humans. It is also known for healing and sealing the gut. A great addition for leaky gut. It takes approximately 6 weeks to heal a leaky gut using Colostrum, sometimes longer.

Lactoferrin is another component of colostrum, which inhibits the growth of pathogenic organisms. Colostrum shows that it can be used to treat allergies, cancer, diarrhea, poor wound healing, hepatitis C, bacterial and viral infections, multiple sclerosis, obesity and peptic ulcers. Colostrum is useful in the treatment of ulcerative colitis, inflammatory bowel disease, and chemotherapy-induced mucositis. It's best if given at least 30 minutes before feeding time. The organic grass-fed is rather expensive but worth it for really sick animals. They also make a colostrum called Colostrum LD. It is liposomal Colostrum, meaning Liposomal Delivery (LD) system is an applied coating which allows colostrum to dissolve in liquids and ensures the colostrum will bypass digestion and will be transported through the bowel wall; circulate throughout the body and will reach the organs and cells to remain bioavailable at the cellular level. It comes from pasture-fed cows.

Dosage:
1/2 tsp per 25 lbs of body weight once per day.
You may notice changes as soon as one day to 2 months.

Calcium (needed):
One of the most common mistakes that people make when feeding a home-cooked diet is not adding in Calcium. You **must** add Calcium when you feed a diet that does not include bones. Adult dogs need around 800 to 1,000mg of Calcium per pound of food fed.

The ideal Calcium: Phosphorus ratio in the canine diet is between 1:1 and 2:1. Meat contains a lot of Phosphorus, so the more meat a diet contains, the more Calcium will be required to reach the correct Calcium: Phosphorus ratio. Adding 800 to 1,000mg of Calcium will provide the correct Calcium: Phosphorus ratio even for a high-meat diet, unless you use a Calcium supplement that also contains Phosphorus. In that case, moderately higher amounts of Calcium may be needed to balance out the additional Phosphorus contained in the supplement.

Ground eggshell can be used as a Calcium supplement. Rinse eggshells and dry them on a counter overnight, or in the oven, then grind them in a clean coffee grinder. One large eggshell provides one teaspoon of ground eggshell, which contains 2,000 mg of Calcium, so add 1/2-teaspoon ground eggshell per pound of food fed. Don't use eggshells that haven't been ground to powder, as they may not be absorbed as well. I recommend powdered Calcium you can use in place of above. A powdered seaweed Calcium or a powdered eggshell Calcium will work well adding into wet foods.

Your best source of calcium comes straight from raw bone so try to add in bone first and if that's just not possible, use the eggshell or seaweed calcium.

Bone meal is **not** recommended. Bone meal is sourced from other countries in most all cases. High heat processing is usually done by manufactures making it harder for your dog to digest. Bone meal may also contain high amounts of Fluoride and Lead and is no longer a recommended source of calcium for humans or pets. Bone meal in pet foods is 10 times more contaminated.

Taurine:
If you are cooking your dog's meats, you should add Taurine into the diet. *Taurine is found in raw heart muscle.* Taurine is best given on an empty stomach although not a must. Taurine is abundant in raw meat, particularly heart, but much is lost when the meat is cooked. Cooking reduces Taurine, so feed raw or cook lightly when feeding heart. Vitamin B6 is needed for the conversion of Taurine, so add a B-complex vitamin supplement as well if needed. A Taurine deficiency has also been found in pets that are known to have seizures and also may need higher amounts than normal, 1500-3000mg a day. Add Vitamin E daily for seizures as well.

Dosage for Taurine:
Small dog: Up to 250mg
Medium dog: Up to 500mg
Large dog: Up to 750mg

Coconut oil - (organic unrefined virgin):
Coconut oil aids allergies, skin issues such as dry skin and hair, ear infections, yeast buildup, healing wounds and sores. (Trader Joe's carries a good one in a glass jar as well as Simple Truth-organic). Look for glass jars. Remember, plastic contains BPA like cans.
Coconut oil is considered an antibacterial, antiviral, and anti-fungal agent. It's also considered a healthy fat.

Dose: 1/4 - 1/2 teaspoon per 10 lbs.

Start with smaller amounts and work up to recommended dosage.
I myself give it every other day and sometimes about 3 times a week. Depends on how much your dog needs it but you cannot go wrong with daily feeding.

TIP: If your dog doesn't like the taste or smell of coconut oil, you can try the REFINED coconut oil. It is said that it contains less MCT than unrefined but you will still benefit from it. They also make an MCT oil that can be added without taste. Giving both coconut oil and MCT oils can have huge benefits on cognitive dysfunction as well. Look for dark glass bottles in products that contain oils. Read label to make sure it is pure coconut oil. Some are mixed with other oils.

ACV (Raw, Organic and with "Mother") (recommended):
Apple Cider Vinegar has excellent antibacterial and antifungal properties. I truly love ACV and have seen it work wonders on dogs. Highly recommend this especially in dogs with cancer, allergies or leaky gut.

Internal use: Apple Cider Vinegar is good in maintaining the acid/alkaline balance of the digestive tract. ACV works well for all types of problems. Indigestion, allergies, yeast buildup, arthritis, recurrent UTI's, Cancer, and prevention of bladder and kidney stones.

Dosage:
0-25 lbs: 1 teaspoon
25-50 lbs: 2 teaspoons
50-75 lbs: 1 TBSP
75+ lbs: 1 1/2 - 2 TBSP

External use: It is effective at fighting itching and scratching from allergies or bites. When applied directly to a hot spot on your dog's skin, ACV will calm the redness and swelling while providing your dog with some much-needed relief. ACV can be poured directly on your dog's fur after a bath and then rinsed, which will cure dandruff, rejuvenate hair and **help balance the pH levels in the body. White vinegar is not recommended for use.**

Humic/Fulvic Acid (Minerals):
Many pet parents wonder if their dogs will be getting "too many minerals" if they are giving other products that also contain minerals such as a calcium supplement. The answer is no because Fulvic is extracted from plant material. Humic/Fulvic acid contains over 90 minerals, amino acids and several vitamins. When plant-derived Fulvic enters the system, it is immediately recognized as one of nature's essential substances. It triggers the proper metabolic responses that utilize the minerals where they're needed, discarding those that are not needed. It is impossible for plant-derived minerals to build up in the tissues. Fulvic/Humic Acid detoxifies the body of heavy metals, toxins, and pollutants, increases oxygen absorption in blood, enhances healing, repair, and rejuvenation of the cells - energizes cells, repairs and

detoxifies the thyroid. It can help decrease digestive issues such as SIBO symptoms (small intestine bacterial overgrowth), inflammatory bowel disorders, leaky gut, bacterial infections like respiratory and urinary tract infections or the flu and common colds. It's an all-natural plant form. It helps boost absorption of nutrients.

Do not give alongside medications. Wait 2 hours in-between. While overdosing is impossible, in higher amounts there can be nausea and diarrhea, similar to taking high amounts of vitamin C.

Dosage:
Small dogs: 1 teaspoon
Medium dogs: 2 teaspoons
Large dogs: 1 TBSP

B Vitamins (highly recommended):
The B-complex vitamins help ward off stress, alleviate neurological problems, and are essential for cell maintenance and growth, the production of antibodies and red blood cells, and the absorption of protein, fat, and carbohydrates.

The B-complex vitamins are grouped together because they work as a team. The team is made up of Thiamine (B1), Riboflavin (B2), Niacin (B3), Pantothenic Acid (B5), Pyridoxine (B6), **Methyl**cobalamin (B12), Biotin, **Folate (B9),** and Choline. The effectiveness of one B vitamin is to a large extent dependent upon adequate amounts of other B vitamins. For example, Pyridoxine (B6) is necessary for the absorption of **Methyl**cobalamin (B12). Natural food sources rich in B vitamins never contain only one B vitamin. It is best to supplement the B vitamins together. You can give your dog extra B-complex supplement when you know it is going to be stressed or the immune system is compromised. Vaccinations, surgery, traveling, separation anxiety and/or serious injury or shock to the body are the most extreme cases in which your dog's body needs a lot of extra support from the B vitamins. The B-complex vitamins will also reduce the toxic effects of antibodies and radiation from x-rays or radiation therapy. It has been found that dogs with seizures have shown to lack vitamin B-1(Thiamine) and B-6 (Pyridoxine) so B vitamins play a crucial role in maintaining the neurological system.

*Make sure the B-12 form is **Methyl**cobalamin and **not** **Cyano**cobalamin.
*Folic acid is a synthetic. Look for **Folate**. Folic Acid causes cancer.

Vitamins D, E, K, and A (DEKA) are fat-soluble.

Fat-soluble vitamins: Meaning they are stored in the liver. These should not be used in higher amounts unless recommended and supervised by your holistic vet or nutritionist.

Vitamin D or D3 Supplementation:

Dogs with illnesses like cancer, chronic inflammatory conditions, heart disease, renal disease, hyperparathyroidism, or inflammatory bowel disease are likely to have low vitamin D levels. If your dog has been on kibble, your dog most likely has low Vitamin D levels. In some cases kibble has been linked to high doses of vitamin D so this is why your dog needs to be tested before giving this supplement but cancer prevention and diagnosed dogs can benefit from this vitamin.

Good sources of vitamin D are wild caught salmon, calf liver, and organic eggs (yolks). Vitamin D levels are usually low in prostate cancer and the above mentioned. Make sure to add in some healthy fats such as coconut oil to help with vitamin D absorption. Many raw diets don't need added vitamin D but again, always best to get tested.

Use extreme caution when supplementing with synthetic OTC products. Very low dosing and not giving daily is safe. Give a couple times a week and at most, every other day for safe levels. You may also have your dog tested regularly using a test from Patterson Veterinary called the VDI Vitamin D Test Kit for Canine/Feline. If your vet doesn't carry this test (mine doesn't) you may order the kit yourself online for $75 (much cheaper than what a vet would charge) and take it with you to the vets office when you have blood drawn next time. All you need is a dab of blood. Then you may send the test off yourself for test results.
You will find it here: https://deservingpets.com/vitamin-d-test-kit/

Breeds such as Golden Retrievers, have low vitamin D levels so you may want to check your dog if this is your breed but all dogs should be tested. Dog breeds prone to cancer may have low vitamin D levels.

The actual dosage depends on how much food you feed. It's approximately 225 IU per pound (lb) of food you feed daily.

Approximate Dosing:
Small dogs (< 30lbs): 100 - 200 IU
Medium dogs (30-75lbs): 200 IU - 300 IU
Large dogs (75lbs +): 400 IU

Pumpkin Seeds/ Powder (raw organic):
Pumpkin seeds contain the amino acid Cucurbitin, which paralyzes and helps eliminate worms from the digestive tract. A safe and natural dewormer. Studies have shown that adding pumpkin seeds to the daily diet helps reduce inflammatory response due to conditions like arthritis, and helps prevent calcium **oxalate** stone formation. You can find them on numerous websites. Pumpkin seeds contain magnesium as well. *Pumpkin seeds should not be given to dogs with health conditions that require a restricted phosphorous intake.*

Diatomaceous Earth (Food Grade-only):
Good for many uses. You can even clean house, brush teeth, use for the lawn for killing insects, fleas, ticks etc. Great to add into your dog's food and helps with:

- Detoxing
- Fleas and ticks
- Worming (with exception of heartworms and tapeworms)
- Reducing tumors
- Brushing teeth
- Digestive Issues
- Better Organ functions (Heart Murmurs, Kidneys etc)
- Reduction in Seizures
- Allergies
- Hot Spots
- Healthy Shiny Coats

This is extremely safe for ingesting (add into wet foods) and using externally as well. It has many uses including cleaning.

Food Grade DE *is safe to distribute without wearing a mask. The* ***pool grade*** *is what's dangerous. For deworming, use for 7-30 days for best results.*

Dosage:
Under 25 lbs: 1/2 teaspoon
25-50 lbs: 1 - 2 teaspoons
50-100 lbs: 1 tablespoon
100+ lbs: 1 - 2 tablespoons

Collagen (amino acids):
Collagen makes up 30% of the entire body in dogs. Collagen works on nails, coat, joints, and digestive tract to name a few. Most collagen supplements contain amino acids, what most bodies are lacking, especially in older pets. Collagen comes in many types including Type I, II, III and so on. Type II is specific for joints and I and III are specific to skin, hair, nails. Overall Collagen promotes healthy systems in all areas. The amino acid Glycine targets cancer cells as well as the digestive system. Some types of collagen comes from fish. I tend to steer away from fish due to any chances of mercury contamination. Collagen peptide is another term for hydrolyzed collagen. If purchasing human products, start with a low dose and work up in dosing over a few weeks time as it can cause loose stools in the beginning if too much at once is added. Normally human dosing is based off of a 150-160 lb human. Adjust accordingly. Not all Collagens are created equal. Collagen is a tasteless and odorless powder, so it is easy to use and mix into wet foods. At this time, I found the brand ForestLeaf to be superior in its ingredients and contains 18 amino acids including Glycine. There are 9 essential amino acids: histidine, isoleucine, leucine, lysine, methionine, phenylalanine, threonine, tryptophan, and valine. And 20 amino acids in total. This particular brand contains 8 of those 9 essential amino acids. Tryptophan is not in it. I found this common in many of them. Amino acids play a key role in our health as well as our pets. The body cannot make amino acids so they must come from the diet. Buckwheat is a plant-based food that contains all nine essential amino acids as well. Protein sources are meat, poultry, eggs, dairy and seafood contain all 9 essential amino acids.

Approximate Dosage:
Small dogs: 1/8 scoop
Medium dogs: 1/4 scoop
Large dogs: 1/2 scoop (1 TBSP)

Start with lower amounts and work up to the recommended dose with time as this can cause some diarrhea or digestive upset.

These dosages can be adjusted according to the results you may or may not be getting. It takes a little time to begin to see results. "Undenatured" Collagen Type II should be taken in very small doses – usually 10-20mg per day for a dog, humans up to 40mg.

Hydrolyzed collagen should be taken in higher doses which is the one I mentioned above.

Note: It is up to you as to whether it is safe to give your dog any supplements. If your dog has an illness or is taking medications, please research further to make sure they are safe to be taken especially along with medications. Your conventional vet may not know. Consult with a holistic vet or research on the internet. When I say research internet, which means read on some of the best natural sites, not bogus ones condoning supplements such as petmd, dvm360 or alike.

Chapter 5
Canine Arthritis and Joint Pain

When it comes to joint issues, it can be difficult to find the right path to help our babies. All dogs respond to medications, supplements and diet differently. So this isn't set in stone for every dog. This is a basic guide to help you get started in helping your dog to feel better quickly. And not all of these are recommended for one dog. These are just some choices available to you. I believe a good diet, filtered water, correct and balanced supplements, good preservative-free joint supplements, exercise and therapy with minimal to no medications and vaccines is the best way to go.

> *"Before you can prevent the disease you have to understand it."*

A Few Precautions:

Drug-induced joint problems:
The drugs most associated with drug-induced lameness are antibiotics, especially **sulfa drugs, Erythromycin, Penicillin's, and Cephalosporin's.** Genetics also play a role in the development of this syndrome as well. Doberman Pinchers are predisposed to develop drug-induced lameness when administered sulfa drugs.

BEWARE OF THE DAMAGING EFFECTS OF INFLAMMATORY DRUGS (NSAIDs):

If your dog is being treated for arthritis, most vets will prescribe steroids or non-steroidal anti-inflammatory drugs (NSAIDs). *(Steroids and NSAIDs should not be taken together).* Physical side effects can be scary - including gastrointestinal bleeding and kidney and liver damage. If your dog's stomach and liver survive prolonged use of NSAIDs, the joints may not. Used long-term, these drugs can destroy the cartilage making the arthritis and pain much worse and debilitating.

Rimadyl (one of the more popular dispensed NSAIDs) lists as reported possible adverse drug events by the manufacturer:

Gastrointestinal, vomiting, anorexia and/or abnormal stools; pathology of the liver with or without general hepatic dysfunction; neurologic (nerves and brain pathologies), urinary pathologies with increased urination, thirst, increased Blood Urea Nitrogen (BUN), Creatinine and/or abnormal urinalysis; behavioral change; dermatologic (skin problems), immunologic/ allergic pathologies and death. Some reports contained multiple events.

The pharmaceutical companies are really pushing Rimadyl hard. Watch out, it comes in all forms such as generic names like Carprofen. But all NSAIDs are dangerous.

In one study in people in Norway, physicians examined the x-rays of 294 arthritic hips. They found that the hip joints of patients taking NSAIDs had significantly **greater damage** than those not taking the drug.

Steroids like Prednisone, Prednisilone, injectables like Kenalog and Vetalog etc. are devastating to the body over long-term use. They can actually bring on heart disease, diabetes, eye damage, osteoporosis, non-regenerative anemia, weaken the immune defense to disease, and upset the body's water and electrolyte balance that weakens the body.

Here is a list of NSAIDs:
RIMADYL (Carprofen) caplets, RIMADYL tablets, and RIMADYL injectable
NOVOCOX (Carprofen) caplets
VETPROFEN (Carprofen) caplets
CARPRIEVE (Carprofen) caplets, CARPRIEVE injection
LIBREVIA (Carprofen) soft chewable tablets; now called QUELLIN (Carprofen) tablets
METACAM (Meloxicam) oral suspension, METACAM injectable
OROCAM (Meloxicam) transmucosal oral spray, Meloxicam injection
LOXICOM (Meloxicam) injection
MELOXIDYL (Meloxicam) oral suspension
Meloxicam Solution - injection
DERAMAXX (Deracoxib) tablets
PREVICOX (Firocoxib) tablets
GALLIPRANT- tablets
PIROXICAM (generic name) or FELDENE

All vets recommend NSAIDs for pain. NSAIDs are a very high-risk and a dangerous drug. Many dogs have died from taking these medications. I am not saying that they are not needed in some cases but should only be given short-term, no longer than 2 weeks. (It has been documented that dogs have died after taking the first dose). There is a high possibility not to have to give these for more than a week **or at all** if you use other means of pain relief depending on the cause of the pain. CanineActiv (mild-moderate) is available without a prescription and completely all natural. Holistic vets may offer you RJ+. It's the prescription (RX) version of CanineActiv. It is 100mg stronger although CanineActiv can have the same effect with an extra capsule added.

Pain meds like Tramadol (moderate pain), Robaxin (muscle relaxer), and Gabapentin (nerve related pain) have many of the same side effects as well. Gabapentin is being removed from shelves more every day due to the high-risk long term side effects. The trick is to change everything you have learned and was told. Vets do not have a clue when it comes to natural remedies or even nutrition. Some will recommend therapies like Hydrotherapy. But ALL will send you home with the NSAIDs. And not many vets recommend Adequan which I find baffling to me since it IS an RX medication in which they can prescribe and have access to. I believe the high cost upfront of Adequan is why it isn't and they may feel you won't follow through with it. I say phooey on them for assuming and not asking. So you will have to ask for it. And do the injections at home. You will save a ton of money that way. The high cost is the first month, after that its dirt cheap.

This is why we must find alternatives to what we are told and have been doing. The body works as a whole. You cannot put a band-aid on a pain and expect things to get better. That's all these medications do. If you want your dog to heal and become pain-free or close to it, you must do so much more. There are many steps to heal the body and they must all come together for positive results.

Before prescribing NSAIDs for long-term use, a Heska ERD urine test to look for microalbuminuria, which can be an early sign of kidney disease. If the Heska ERD test is positive, a risk-benefit analysis is used to determine whether to use NSAIDs, or look for other options.

Warning: *Steroids should never be combined with NSAIDs, which should be discontinued for at least 72 hours before switching from either one to the other. They can be combined with all other types of pain medication. When used for more than 4 months, monitoring of blood work and urinalysis should be done.*

Tramadol (used for moderate-mod/severe pain) contains the inactive ingredients:
Carnauba wax, cornstarch, hypromellose, lactose, magnesium stearate, microcrystalline cellulose, polyethylene glycol, polysorbate 80, sodium starch glycolate, and titanium dioxide.

I also found these listed as well.
Silica colloidal anhydrous, Iron oxide yellow, Indigo carmine, Sodium lauryl sulphate, Methyl parahydroxybenzoate, Propyl parahydroxybenzoate, croscarmellose sodium, gelatin, and brilliant blue FCF.

***Note that Tramadol should **not** be given with MAOIs (such as Anipryl/-Deprenyl/Selegiline, and the Preventic tick collar, which contains Amitraz, another MAOI). It should be used with caution when combining with SSRIs (such as Prozac, Zoloft and Paxil) or TCAs (such as Elavil and Clomicalm) due to the risk of serotonin syndrome. It may also be dangerous if combined with St. John's Wort.*

Tramadol is metabolized 70% thru the liver and 30% thru the kidneys, so dosage must be reduced when using with a dog that has liver or kidney disease. Tramadol in high doses has been known to lead to seizures. It should be used with extreme caution in animals that are prone to seizures. Tramadol can cause constipation. Give pumpkin if needed.

Tramadol is a synthetic drug. This means that Tramadol is created in laboratories and is the result of chemical reactions. It is NOT a natural product, like codeine, and Tramadol has been labeled an opioid.

*Tramadol is **not** FDA-approved for children under 18 years of age, as children are at greater risk of experiencing drug-induced breathing problems and death compared to adults.* **So my question is, is it really safe for dogs?** *This is why we need to know what we are giving to our dogs. Know the risks before you give it.*

Vaccine induced
Immune Arthritis is seen in dogs in which the Distemper vaccine may be involved in cases of Immune Arthritis, as Distemper vaccine

particles have been found in some of the affected joints. Vaccines play a huge role in illnesses. Consider Titer testing instead.

Diet

I truly believe that diet plays a major role in our dog's health. Remember, in the holistic world of pet care, you focus on repairing and cleansing the whole body. Vets treat with modern treatments and focus on the illness only. It's a band-aid to the real problem within. Veterinarians have no clue about diet or choose not to learn so that they can keep you coming back. You MUST heal the gut. You have to get the digestive system healthy, which in turn builds a strong immune system. If your dog is ill or overcome with arthritis, pain and inflammation, this is where to start. Change the diet, reduce inflammation naturally, and build the immune system by repairing the gut and organs.

So let's say your dog has arthritis or some joint disease and now we have to spend that extra time and money in our busy lives to help our dogs be pain-free or comfortable. It becomes a lot of work. Do you see where I am going with this? Think about all the visits to the vet to help your dog when he/she is hurting. If we had known in the early years that diet played a role in joint issues, we may have made extra time to pay attention to the diet. If you are lucky enough to have a younger dog without issues yet, maybe it's time to concentrate on the diet now. Start now thinking about what you can do for your dog **before** it takes on the pains of arthritis. And if they are already ridden by the joint pain and inflammation, let's make some changes today starting right now.

If you are feeding kibble, I hope by reading the earlier chapters of this book that you have already decided to change your dog's diet. Start now by getting your dog (if they are not already) on a good preservative-free joint supplement. Add in some vitamins and minerals. Watch the diet for potatoes, sugars, preservatives, corn, soy, wheat, and all grains including feeding of kibble or commercial pet foods. Carbohydrates (corn, wheat, rice, soy, millet, and even potato) are pro-inflammatory foods; they promote inflammation. All herbs are an optional alternative and it may take awhile to see the best results in some cases. Start with a joint support supplement according to the severity. I find a good combination of ingredients works the very best.

The Power of Massage
What you can do for your dog at home is give him/her a massage. A daily massage will keep blood circulating in the areas where arthritis is a problem, as well as contribute to better blood flow throughout the entire body. Your dog will truly love the attention and enjoy the time you spend with him/her. Take 5-10 minutes (depending on your dog) of your day, sit down on the floor or bed, and rub your baby. When you keep the muscles relaxed, there is less pressure on the joints
trying to pull the bones out of place, especially the spine. Even rub the paws and, if your dog will let you, work in-between the toes. If you get in the habit of massages, they may eventually let you rub in-between, which also helps when it comes time for a nail trimming.

Moist Heat and Cold Therapy
Using cold applications will constrict the blood vessels and numb the nerve endings. Using heat will dilate the blood vessels first and cause the nerve endings to be soothed. This further causes the tissues to be relaxed.

During the first 72 hours after an injury, use cold therapy. This is the acute stage and the cold will help stop hemorrhaging in the tissues while reducing swelling. After 72 hours, use moist heat therapy. It does not have to be applied directly on top of it. Even close to the area works as well. Also, when you over exercise or do exercises to regain strength and mobility after an injury, apply cold immediately after exercise for up to 15 minutes at a time. A lot will depend on how you apply the cold. I myself use a towel. Towels can be different in thickness. A thin towel over an ice pack will feel much colder so less time applied is needed. So consider what you are using and decide on the length of time. You can do this 3 times a day. After the first 24 hours, you can consider using both cold and heat. Make sure it is MOIST heat and not dry heat such as a heating pad. I myself purchase the gel-filled packs. I have used the beaded ones and they do not last long. So I don't recommend those at all. Gel packs have worked really well. I usually buy a couple of the sizes I need and throw one in the freezer and keep the others out for heating up in microwave. I always wrap them in a towel or on top of the microfiber type throw you buy in stores. Periodically feel of the skin to make sure it isn't too hot or too cold. The colder, the less time applied. The hotter well, let cool before applying so not to burn the skin. You don't want to burn your baby. If it is too hot for you, it's too hot for them. Moist heat makes those achy joints feel good especially in arthritic dogs. If your dog has been out on a longer walk than normal, apply ice once inside. The typical time is 5-10 minutes and 3 times a day. Speak with your dog's physical therapist on what he/she recommends as this may be altered.

Vet Checks with Injuries and Arthritis
When you suspect a joint issue or lameness in your dog, you take your dog in to see the vet. What I find a lot of times when people come to me after they have taken their dog in and the vet didn't do x-rays but yet diagnosed the dog with arthritis or hip dysplasia or whatever joint may be hurting at the time without doing much needed x-rays. Wait, what? Let's say that again; the vet did NOT do x-rays but yet diagnosed the dog with arthritis. How can a vet do that? They can't! This is no guessing game. You **must** have x-rays and blood work or further testing to determine the cause of the pain and/or lameness. Tests are important and should never be overlooked. You need a diagnosis. Oh and another thing I find vets doing, saying they cannot x-ray a dog unless under anesthesia. This is so far from the truth, it's baffling. Find a vet that will do them without anesthesia. If they are so incompetent that they can't do it with going under, they are not a confident or worthy vet. My vet never puts my dogs under ever for x-rays. They can also use a sedative (valium) without putting them under if needed.

If you suspect a problem with a joint, it **should** be x-rayed immediately so that you know what you are dealing with. You cannot treat something if you don't have the correct diagnosis. A guessing vet isn't going to cut it. This happens so many times that it frustrates the vets that actually DO care about their patients and do get x-rays right away so they know how to treat the dog. This is beyond my comprehension that vets wouldn't do x-rays. Laziness perhaps or in a hurry and doesn't have time for you. Either way it is **unacceptable!**

For an example; your dog is limping and you are concerned so you take your dog to the vet and the vet says, "Oh your dog has a sprained wrist" or "Your dog has arthritis in his back" and sends you home with pain medication without doing any tests, blood work or x-rays. REALLY? Is this your kind of vet? If so, fire him/her and find a new one right away.

This vet not only put you off, but also didn't have a care in the world on how to help your dog. If you find your vet hesitating, request x-rays. Don't wait for your vet to suggest it. You need a proper diagnosis to be able to treat your dog correctly. I am finding this happening a lot more than it should and it really has me concerned for pet parents and of course the welfare of the dog. This is why I want you to know so that when/if you walk into a clinic one day with a lame dog, you will know what to do and what to expect. If for any reason your vet is not willing to work with you on ALL levels, by all means find a new one. They are a dime a dozen. It's your dog; your requests should be taken seriously. Be firm with your vet!

Just because you like them because they are polite to you or nice to your dog doesn't make them an ideal vet. You are the one paying the bill. It is YOUR dog. You have every say-so on what happens when you walk through those doors. Same goes for your children and so does it for your pets. You want the best care for your dog so find the best vet for you and your pets.

If your dog has had any type of trauma or injury, participates in any type of agility or repetitive exercises; your dog should be on a joint supplement. When playing with your dog, don't tug on any part of the body too hard. For example, playing tug of war with your dog will put some stress on the neck and possibly pull the spinal bones out of line causing injury. Same goes for pullers that wear collars. Purchase a harness instead. Don't forget to make sure you have studied the breed of dog you have and know the genetic history concerning hip dysplasia, degenerative joint disease and alike. If your breed is susceptible to diseases of the joints, take action now while they are young (6 months). There is so much to do to keep your dog moving way into his/her teen years. Remove kibble from the diet. Kibble is one of the main reasons for so much cancer and arthritis in pets. It's not real food. Feed a homemade unprocessed diet. To learn how, you can pick up a copy of my book called *"Natural Health and Nutrition For Dogs-Revised Edition 2"* for in depth details on how to do just that. Reduce all vaccines, medications, change to organic all-natural yard fertilizers, and use all-natural flea and tick repellants and shampoos. Do not apply topical flea and tick killers. They ARE killers (chemicals) to your dog. To learn more on this, again, check out my other book. Remove chemicals from your home such as cleaning products as well as laundry detergents. There are plenty of alternative safe chemical-free choices.

Also, make sure your vet does blood work to rule out other ailments or diseases such as Lyme disease. Have them listen to your dog's heart. Everything should be in tiptop shape; otherwise you may not get the correct diagnosis. And if they don't do blood work and they send you home with pain meds such as Rimadyl or alike, it could be a death sentence to your dog. Blood work should be performed before prescribing NSAIDS and I don't know of any vet that does this which is **against** AVMA guidelines.

Having What You Need
Make sure you have all the right supplements including a good joint supplement. In these supplements, make sure there aren't any preservatives or artificial fillers or additives and there are many out there that are full of this junk. Go for the smallest amount possible with preservatives. Sometimes they can't be avoided but knowing which ones are the worst, is also crucial. Find a good mix of substances. Giving just Glucosamine/Chondroitin isn't your best bet.
I find supplements that have a combination of good ingredients work the best or you can give several joint supplements with different ingredients. Add in high quality fish oil (sardine, green lipped mussel or squid), Ester C (Magnesium Ascorbate) along with a mix of anti-inflammatory herbs.

Better yet, go with the all-natural form and add in Rosehips, Amla or Camu Camu. These contain the highest concentration of natural vitamin C than any other food with Camu Camu having the highest. Vitamin C (Ascorbic Acid) is synthetic so it's harder for the body to absorb and you are risking the product being from China, as most all (95%) vitamin C in the USA is sourced from China. Ascorbic acid is very hard on the stomach so buffered vitamin C is safer for dogs.

Boswellia, Turmeric, Ginger, Yucca, and Devil's Claw are just a couple of some really good herbs that work well. Add Milk Thistle for 30 days to help filter the liver from all the toxins in his/her body. For extreme pain, give the pain meds you received from the vet or better yet, try a supplement called CanineActiv (found on *CanineArthritisAndJoint.com* website) to go along with your joint supplements and reduce or eliminate the pains meds. Increase the amount of the recommended dosage on your joint supplements as well. You need higher doses of the joint supplement.

If that isn't enough, there is a good combo I like. When a dog is hurting, I go straight for the anti-inflammatory herbs mix, Glucosamine with mixed ingredients, CanineActiv or DC-Y, Ostinol 350, and CBD oil. I also give Actiflex (equine) in higher doses as this is what I use for a daily joint supplement. Also, a liquid form of homeopathic herbs mix with Arnica, Rhus Tox, and Symphytum. I do everything I can to keep from giving any pain meds if the pain isn't so severe that they are showing clear signs like whining and/or struggling to even take a step.

Try not to give NSAIDs any longer than 2 weeks if you must give them. Actually NSAIDs break down cartilage and make the joints even worse so try to stay away from these as much as possible but please, if your dog is in horrible pain, by all means, give them something for pain if needed and know the risks involved. Even one dose can be deadly so use extreme caution and make sure you are ready for any consequences. Ask your vet how he would treat a severe reaction to NSAIDs and what you can watch for in an emergency. As far as I know, there isn't one. I also have found vets to deny these claims even though they know the risks involved with these medications.

Adequan works well also when you have a dog that has chronic joint issues. It takes up to 4 weeks (sometimes longer) to kick in but it is well worth it once you get the body primed with it. Giving injections at home is much cheaper. Adequan is not to be given to dogs with kidney disease or diabetes. Check with your vet about getting you a prescription for possibly ordering online, as it is cheaper that way most of the time. If my vet gave them, it would cost me $35-$40 per injection. If I give them at home, it's about $15 per injection for a large dog. Well worth learning how to give one. Have your vet show you how.

There are many questions on whether to give subcutaneous injection (under skin-Sub Q) or in the muscle (IM). Per manufactures recommendations it should be injected into the muscle. The reason for this is it takes effect a lot faster being injected into the muscle. So make a note of that if your vet recommends Sub Q. I give in muscle and that's how I will always do it.

Don't let your dog jump off of beds, couches, out of vehicles or jumping at any extent if your dog is in pain or has severe joint issues. I never let my special needs girl jump out of my vehicle or when playing. I lift all 60 lbs of her and sit her down on the ground. When she gets in the truck, I put her front feet on the seat and support her rear evenly and lift her slowly to get her even with the seat then let her move forward to get in the back seat. I don't have a backdoor for my truck's backseat, as it is an older model, so she has to go over the console. You may find a ramp or something to do this a lot easier but this is what I do. She doesn't move without me helping her either. She knows the routine.

Rest works well for an arthritic dog in pain. Once the pain has subsided, take daily short walks (5-6 houses down and back if possible). You can work up to further walks but do not push it. You can do several short walks daily. Again, you can use CanineActiv for that extra support during times that your dog may be pushed to walk for exercise or has over-extended themselves. Don't forget your ice packs.

If you have a doggie door, make sure it fits your dog properly. A dog constantly ducking its head, stepping up high to get over the bottom of door, or having to squeeze through a small door will make the problems much worse. The pet door should be low at the bottom of the door, wide enough for your dog and tall enough (shoulder height) for your dog to comfortably fit through it.

Keep slick floors covered with non-slip rugs so your dog doesn't slip or have to work hard to stay on all fours. They also make non-slip doggie boots.

Some of us pet parents have wood, laminate or tile flooring that may be slippery for our pets and possibly for ourselves as well. I have tile flooring and I myself cannot walk on it. I have slipped and fell recently with bare feet. And when it is wet, it's 10 times worse. I have injured my arms trying to catch myself. My dog with hip dysplasia refuses to try to walk across my tile floors. I have carpet pieces laid over the top of the floor for all of us to walk safely on. I think all vet clinics should have this applied to their floors as well. Talking about some slick flooring. I have to put booties on her when we go to vet clinic.

I would like to share what I discovered. I was totally unaware of these types of products and upon doing a project here at home, ran across this. If you have flooring and it is slick, you can put these products on your floors and it will stop the sliding. It's easy to apply and fairly cheap. This is my next project. I am excited to try this and will be doing this soon. They offer different size of bottles for different sq ft. You can also do concrete and wood as they make products for that as well. This is a golden find for those slick floors. Highly recommend you try this if you have slick tile floors. Can also be applied to shower floors and pool areas as well. How awesome is that? It's called InvisaTread! Found at local Home Depot stores or online. Do wear protective clothing when applying. Good ventilation is best. This should remain a safe-on-contact product. Most surfaces are ready within 5-25 minutes depending on what you are applying it on.

Allow InvisaTread to dwell (exact time shall be determined by your pre-application testing). Keep surface saturated with the product during the entire dwell time. DO NOT allow to dry out, puddle, or run off. Apply more InvisaTread as needed. Two coats may be needed but not usually. Test it yourself then reapply if needed. You will rinse off once ready for walking on. Read manufactures instructions for best results. Easy and safe to apply; simply pour or spray on, let stand and RINSE AWAY!!

After your grout with tile has completely dried out, you may notice some white residue form in a few spots over the next few days. This is a salt residue left over after application; it is not harmful and will be removed with regular cleaning. To remove right away, scrub with 1:4 dilution of vinegar to water, or 1:32 dilution of TractionWash to water.

NOTE: This does not occur on every application or every type of grout.

Works on porcelain, ceramic, granite, unpolished travertine, concrete, brick, honed stone, unpolished limestone, slate, quarry tile, stamped concrete and much more.

InvisaTread® is not for use on Wood, Polished Marble, Polished travertine or Polished Limestone.

They make other products that work on these other materials, including wood, laminate and alike.

It states that it should be reapplied after 3 years but this is only for high traffic areas such as commercial use. One application should be permanent. You can always reapply anytime to help it more.

Note from manufacture: *InvisaTread is not a coating so there is no dry time. But there is a DWELL TIME in the application process. CLEAN, APPLY, DWELL, RINSE. Dwell time is the biggest variable, the longer you leave it on the more traction it creates. Most surfaces are 5-25 minutes some are multiple dwell times. Best practice is to lay out 3-4 tiles (or a small hidden area) and test different dwell times for your particular surface. If after 25 minutes it's still not as strong as you'd like; rinse, dry, and do another application. Read all directions!*

Cork/Foam Flooring
Here is another option you may use. Cork doesn't hold up that well or nor does the foam flooring like you find in gymnasiums etc, but it's definitely a good move for temporary flooring. The more expensive cork flooring should hold up much better, as it is much higher in price. For an area of 280 sq ft, foam flooring tiles are under $400. For cork flooring, it's around $1300. I feel like the cheaper flooring will last a few years anyway as opposed to continuously buying rubber backed carpet that needs to be washed a lot. Even the cheaper foam is waterproof, but not toenail proof. Do a little research on this type of flooring. Some dog owners have purchased this and they love it for their senior dogs. Others complain of not holding up to your dog's nails. I suppose this will depend on your dog and how well you keep the toenails trimmed. It appears easy to lay as well, as it comes in large squares you snap together. Just lay on top of your old flooring and remove it when you are no longer wanting to use it. It's super simple.

Following My Suspicions
I had a few things that happened a couple years ago that I was unsure if I was onto something or just thinking crazy things. The first time that was the worst is when Diamond (my oldest girl) went down (in severe pain and couldn't walk). I had adopted her a year earlier. I took her into the vet and nothing was discovered from the vet. It was brushed off as a stomachache. Needless to say, not much was done either on that visit. We came back home and she was fine a day or two then back down again. A week later, I took her back in for x-rays thinking possibly she may have hip dysplasia. The x-rays confirmed she had Lumbosacral Spondylosis. At the time, I had no clue what that was and didn't take it that serious nor did vet seem concerned and didn't offer any help or suggestions at all. A few days before I took her in on the first visit, I had started giving her some Cephalexin for a UTI. When I discovered how bad she was in pain, I stopped everything. After she was back up and walking a day or two later, I started the antibiotics up again. That's when she went back down again and I took her for x-rays. This was in March. In November of that same year, I took her in for a teeth cleaning (different vet), a Rabies shot, and blood work. Little did I know at that time, you don't give Rabies on the same day you do surgery (things vets won't tell you). Three days after her teeth cleaning, she went down again and she went down hard. This was November 2012. Since that day, it had been nothing but a daily struggle to keep her pain-free. I took her back to the vet when she went down and I told them it had something to do with the surgery.
I told them I thought she had had a reaction to antibiotics previously. They looked at me as if I had two heads. Since then I have spoken with many vets about this. The only thing that was mentioned is the possibility of the bacteria could have caused it that was released from the teeth cleaning, or possibly the anesthesia but we just really didn't know.
In the back of my mind, I have wondered if the connection was the antibiotics. The vets looked at me crazy when I kept mentioning my thoughts on this. So when I met my new vet to discuss her Stem Cell surgery, I told him all of this and how it has put her down (in severe pain daily) since the teeth cleaning. So he was concerned about the anesthesia and would make sure he didn't give any antibiotics etc. So, she had the surgery and it didn't put her down at all. So now, I know it wasn't the anesthesia.

I was reading a book on Canine Arthritis (that was written by a DVM) and BINGO...there it was; my answer.

A N T I B I O T I C S !

It states: *While RARE, many doctors feel that drug-induced joint problems are becoming more common. Your dog's immune system can react to ANY drug, and drugs are usually considered foreign substances. A hypersensitivity or allergic reaction occurs when antibodies form chemical complexes with the administered drug, these drug-antibody complexes are then deposited into the joints of the body. The drugs most commonly associated with drug-induced lameness are antibiotics, especially sulfa drugs, Erythromycin, Penicillin, and Cephalosporin's.*

It further states genetics can play a role also especially with Doberman Pinchers when sulfa drugs are administered.

SO, when I read this, my jaw dropped and my thoughts were, I was right, I WASN'T CRAZY! So why didn't these vets **not** put this together or even possibly think it was drug-related? They have this knowledge right? Maybe they knew and chose not to tell me.
I can give my girl Diamond, Doxycycline and Clindamycin without any issues but Cephalexin puts her down. Looking back in her records on the day she had her teeth cleaning, she was given an injection of Penicillin and sent home with Amoxicaps. So obviously, she has a sensitivity to these as well. The bad part about this is, it put her down from November until the day of her stem cell therapy (Sept 12th the next year). Ten months of pain.

Why so many antibiotics? It's just a teeth cleaning. Skip the antibiotics and when you get home, do oral mouth rinses using Probiotics and Colloidal Silver. Mix probiotic in with filtered water and mix a liquid, then draw up into a syringe and squirt along the gums. Colloidal Silver -spray undiluted onto the gums several times a day. Add in Apple Cider Vinegar to the diet as well.

Note - Pets allergic to antibiotic class of Penicillin will naturally be allergic to Amoxicillin as well. Please make sure your pet's veterinarian is aware of this.

And not only am I speaking about medications, but vaccines can also do this. Even vaccines can make a dog go lame that's never had any issues before, although it seems more common in puppies. Like the distemper vaccine, particles have been found in joints. I am not ruling out adults as well. Vaccines are very harmful in adult stages and titer testing should be done instead. Titer (Vaccicheck or Kansas State University is the cheapest way. Dr John Robb at protectthepets.com can direct you as well for cheaper prices on titering).

If you have a dog that gets ill, goes lame or acquires a disease, which one then will be expensive? So weigh the costs. Have titer testing done instead. I am aware Rabies is a law but every 3 years this should be the most that gets done. Find a vet that offers a 3-year option vaccine. Some want you back in every year so they can make money. Where did this mindset come from? And if your dog has an illness, weakened immune system, or autoimmune disease, they can and should be exempted from Rabies. Speak with your vet about this to see what can be done otherwise your vet will most likely inject your ill or lame dog.

The bottom line here is, always be aware of what goes in the body and don't think your suspicions are crazy or a little over the top. Always trust your instincts, ask a lot of questions, research before you have any surgery done or vaccines and medications given. And always feed your dog a species-appropriate diet. Don't forget filtering the water. Anytime the body is fighting any disease or illness, inflammation can flow through the body causing inflamed joints.

Also note: During wintertime, this is a time for our dogs to start having achy joints. So get ready before. Prepare. Have your medicine cabinet stocked with meds (preferably all natural like CanineActiv and TRF or Ostinol), herbs (start the herbs before winter if you haven't), vitamins and minerals and don't forget the ADEQUAN. It's wonderful stuff and can make miracles when you have lost all hope. It did for me and has helped many animals stay upright and walking. Ask your vet for a vial to take home with you to give the injections. Also, have him/her show you how to give the injection. Have on hand some moist heat/cold packs, funds saved up for chiropractic, water therapy and acupuncture visits. Give daily massages and take short walks. Watch your dog's weight and if you're not already, consider feeding a raw diet. You will be totally amazed how much your dog will be so much healthier. A raw diet won't fix your dog with joint issues but it will certainly help make the body as a whole much healthier in which provides more oxygen to the blood. The same blood that flows through your dog's limbs and spine.

If your dog has had any type of trauma or injury, participates in any type of agility or repetitive exercises; your dog should be on a joint supplement. When playing with your dog, don't tug on any part of the body too hard. For example, playing tug of war with your dog will put some stress on the neck and possibly pull the spinal bones out of line causing injury. Don't forget to make sure you have studied the breed of dog you have and know the genetic history concerning hip dysplasia, degenerative joint disease and alike. If your breed is susceptible to diseases of the joints, take action now while they are young (6 months). There is so much to do to keep your dog moving way into his/her teen years. Remove kibble from the diet. Reduce all vaccines, medications, change to organic all-natural yard fertilizers (and read any warning labels on bag to make sure it is really organic), and use all-natural flea and tick repellants and shampoos. Do not apply topical flea and tick killers. They ARE killers to your dog.

Now what I would like to discuss is, what makes our dogs with joint issues go from bouncy and pain-free to all of a sudden in pain and can't move. Well if you haven't pinpointed what causes a flare up, take a look at everything you have done for your dog. If you haven't missed anything mentioned above then consider other things, for example the weather. The weather wreaks havoc on us humans and it affects our pets the same.

A lot of the time the barometric pressure can drop causing the body to react and the joints will start to ache. Damp days of humidity followed by cold fronts are a big aggravator. It can start a few days earlier, so if you know it's coming, give a little extra joint supplement, therapy, and/or massage a day or two before this arrives.

If your dog has some type of infection going on, say the ear or tooth, expect the joints to become inflamed as well and cause pain and swelling in the arthritic joints. Any time you have an infection, it causes bacteria to travel throughout the body and affect the weakest parts of the body. If your dog has itchy skin with lesions or is inflamed and red, expect the joints to be hurting as well. Everything that happens to one part of the body, affects the rest of the body.

Bacteria attacks weak points in the body's immune system. The best things you can do for your dog is keep his/her system strong. So have a list of what is specific to your dog as how to care for your dog daily and then prepare for the worst days when something goes wrong. If your dog has a heart problem, giving herbs for the heart can also work for the arthritis. Herbs are good for many different uses and you will find that when you're helping the heart, you're helping the joints too.

As I said, the body works in sync and you have to treat every issue so not to affect the other. Again, these supplements can and do benefit an older dog and one with joint issues. Every dog is different and everything out there that helps one dog may not help another, so it is a constant job of trying to find that right mixture that helps. And, as luck would have it, once you find that right mixture, it stops working and so here you are looking for a different solution. This is why it is important to learn everything you can so that you have options when that day comes.

What To Do When Your Dog Has Had Surgery Or Is Lame

1. First of all, put rubber-backed rugs down everywhere if you have tile/hardwood/vinyl floors. Your dog will have an extremely hard time walking on these types of floors. Don't take a chance on them re-injuring themselves. I have found the thin rubber-backed carpet that you can cut to fit for around $60 for 5x6 sizes. I cut it to the size I need. You can find this at TownhouseLinens.com called Royale wall-to-wall bathroom carpet and rugs by Mohawk. It takes at least two weeks to get the carpet once ordered. Cut to the size you want and wash in non-chemical laundry detergent. Dry on delicate cycle using Seventh Generation dryer sheets or better yet, organic wool dryer balls. Also, they make a product called InvisaTread. You can apply to tile flooring,

let it sit for a few minutes then rinse off. It makes slick floors non-slick. They also make products for wood and laminate flooring as well.

2. Keep any other pets from pushing or shoving your dog around. They can re-injure your lame dog. Teach your other dogs they cannot push. This is teaching respect for others.

3. When your dog needs to go to the potty, walk with him. If s/he is an active dog that likes to run, put a short leash on so s/he can't. No running while the body is healing.

4. Every day you will need to do leg exercises and massage. Per your vet or your therapists home instructions of course, but massage will not hurt your dog. Be gentle and rub the muscle and skin. As you are able to do leg exercises, do these in short intervals 2-3 times daily or recommended by your orthopedic vet or therapist.

5. Try to slowly taper off risky NSAIDs or other pain meds. After two weeks, hopefully your dog will no longer need any pain medications. Add in some herbs specific for joint and inflammation issues. Don't forget to give CanineActiv a try as well or the TRF/Ostinol. Yes, you may give these while giving NSAIDs as well but the goal is to wean off of the prescription pain meds as soon as possible. Increase the joint supplement dosage. Add in anti-inflammatory herbs. Fish oils help along with glucosamine's.

6. Do water therapy when sutures have been removed or healed. Water therapy (Hydrotherapy) is good at all times and for all issues. It has the power to help heal your dog along with re-building muscle and strength and helps your dog to lose weight for those that are a little pudgy.

7. Make sure you have your dog on a very good joint supplement that does not contain preservatives or a very small amount. If you are unsure, I keep an updated list on my Canine Arthritis and Joint website so you will know what to look for or the ones recommended here in this book. I even have a list of ingredients to avoid.

8. Start your dog on Adequan injections immediately. Make sure your dog does not have kidney disease. Speak with your vet. You can get it online cheaper than what the vets sell a vial for usually, but giving it at home is your cheapest route. Have your vet show you how to give a shot and buy the **equine** version. It's at least $15-$30 cheaper a vial. The loading dose will be the most costly so buying Equine version is most cost-effective. The only difference is, the Canine version has a preservative in it for longer shelf life, and the Equine version does not. I have two large dogs on it and I buy the equine version and still do to this day. And of course, the bigger the dog, the more you will use from the vial. I can get 2 1/2 injections per vial. That's for 60-70 lb dogs. The loading dose says twice a week for four weeks then you will gradually work into once a month. That is just not possible in my household. First, Diamond with severe Spondylosis took two months with twice a week injections before I started to see an improvement. To this day, both dogs get an injection every 3 weeks. To find out where your dog's point is, is to wait and watch closely. As you extend the time out, if you see limping, slowing down or just not right with them, give an injection. If the next day your dog is back to being peppy and feeling good, then that's where your limit is. Find that happy place and stay with it. In winter, you may need to watch this as well so you don't need to go completely by the book on the timing. Make your dog comfortable but be smart. It beats the alternative. In the beginning, an injection lasts 3 days only until it gets built up into the system. That's why you can start to back off on the injections given per week as it builds up in the system.

Sydney has Hip Dysplasia and Spondylosis and even though she gets an injection every 3 weeks as well, she still had a slight bunny hop. So I give her the CanineActiv and it gets completely rid of her bunny hop. She can walk longer distances too. I give at least 2 capsules a day but she does well with 4 caps on her bad days. I have seen in extremely painful days, you can increase the amount to 6 caps per day. It won't harm your dog. If your dog doesn't take capsules, you can open these up and sprinkle into food. Do not mix in water. I use these mostly for those "off" days and not as a daily supplement. They may be a bit bitter sprinkled into food but mask it with a dash of garlic or sardines or something your dog likes to mask the smell and taste. The caps, when opened, you can twist and turn them and tap on plate or bowl. It does kind of get stuck in the capsules at times so you must work it out. I have been putting the caps into the raw foods and they haven't found them. Also, try TRF or Ostinol for daily use. This has worked very well for Sydney as well since her torn ACL.

9. For traveling, make sure you do not allow your dog to jump into or out of your vehicle. Lift your dog into and help out of the vehicle. Or invest in a ramp if they can go up ramps easily. Allow plenty of room for them to lie down and be comfortable in your vehicle.

If they are in a crate at times when you are away, make sure the crate has adequate space for moving around in and not just laying in one small space and put orthopedic memory foam in the bottom (you can buy anywhere for humans also and cut it to fit) so the dog will be very comfortable in there. I buy 2-3 inch thick toppers. Put a thin blanket/throw over the foam. Take them out of the overly sized crate and walk them every couple of hours. DO NOT crate your dog all day. The amount of time for crating any dog is 4-5 hours. The dog needs to come out of the crate and walk around and have some interaction. This includes healthy dogs.

Have good orthopedic dog beds all over the house for your dogs favorite spots. If the dog is large and usually sleeps in the bed with you, you will need to lift the dog yourself up onto the bed (supporting the hips or backend if that's where your joint issues are. Keep everything in line so it doesn't shift the body and hurt them more) or the best place is on an orthopedic pet bed next to your bed so he/she doesn't decide they want to jump off of your bed. It is safer on the floor. You can try a ramp or stairs for getting on the bed but these don't always work well and are just as difficult to get up and down.

10. If you have stairs in your home, you will have to work something out so that your dog does not under any circumstances use the staircase. They do make full body support harnesses. Invest in one if you can. Sleep downstairs with the dog if you have to. Put up a child safety gate. Anything to keep them off those stairs.

11. No Jumping, No Running, No sudden or jerky moves!

This is a basic guide to help you through the healing process.

Remember; never let a vet tell you water therapy won't work. It works in ALL cases. Trust me on this one! And the sooner you can start the better. Speak with the therapist that will be doing the therapy and get a time frame set with him/her.

Once arthritis has become fully developed to the point where we have active joint degeneration and/or excess bone formation, we can't cure them but we can certainly make them comfortable throughout their lifetime and live a close to normal life. What I hope for is to reduce your dog's pain so that he/she can move around relatively pain-free, and create a healing environment around the joints so the animal's natural healing abilities can work their own miracles.

Sometimes holistic therapies take a while before results can be seen, so don't give up too soon. And also, understand that you will have to continue with the herbs and other treatments throughout the dog's lifetime. I am confident we can improve your dog's quality of life for the time they have remaining, and I am happy to know that with the holistic approach, I am helping you and your dog without causing harm.

Walking Your Dog and Exercise
All dogs need some form of exercise. It's good for their overall physical and mental health. When joints hurt, it's harder for them to do a lot of exercise. According to the severity of each dog, take short walks as often as possible without causing the dog any pain or overdoing it. Like Diamond, she started out walking about 6 houses down and back, some days a little further. On the way back though, she walked at a snail's pace. So pay close attention and don't overdo it or you could cause more pain and problems. Keep any excess weight off also. Weight can cause more problems as well. Diamond is now on Adequan and good joint supplements and a raw diet and she is able to walk a mile now. She is doing exceptionally well considering the severity of her disease and her age.

This is one thing that is important for your dog, whether he/she has joint issues or is healthy, young, and vibrant. Let me be honest and say, I hate exercise and walking included. I really haven't ever been an exercise person so I must say, my dogs have me walking and I know it is good for me and so my dogs are good for me in more ways than I could mention. Gotta love how dogs help us humans. And it is good for your dogs too. Dogs require exercise for so many reasons as do us humans. For spirit, longevity, and stress relief.

Like children, they can get cabin fever and need to burn off some energy. If your dog is digging, chewing, or destroying things, your dog needs exercise! Even a dog with fears and aggression need to get exercise. It helps on so many levels. Now with dogs that have joint issues, we must make some adjustments. Dogs with joint issues cannot walk or play like a normal dog. These are the dogs I am going to refer to in this discussion. If your dog has joint issues and is use to walking five miles a day when healthy, that same dog may not be able to walk near that far now. Every single dog is different but you must be aware and know the signs when you have pushed your dog too far. If your dog is in pain or limping before you ever start, that dog should only walk a short distance or not walk at all that day. A short distance is approximately 50 feet and back. If your dog is not limping and having no pain but has severe hip dysplasia, your dog may walk 100 yards and back up to about 1/2 a mile. If your dog is used to walking a mile without any pain during or after that walk, your dog can handle that walk. You have to pay very close attention to your dog's body language as to how your dog is feeling especially after the walk.
If your dog has really bad hips (hip dysplasia) and you walk your dog two miles, you may be putting more wear and tear on that joint than what needs to be happening. So, do not over-walk your dog no matter how your dog is feeling.

With Spondylosis, you may be able to walk further without issues because the hips are doing the work because the Spondylosis is in the spine. The spine is moving back and forth and sometimes those bone spurs can poke the spinal nerves and cause more pain so you have to pay attention to your dog. Same goes for ACL tears, luxating patella's etc. So every case is different and unique in its own self. Just please do not try to walk your dog five or ten miles EVER! Not a dog with joint issues. Those days are over for walking that distance. No marathons ok?

You can try and walk your dog two or three times a day with several short walks but I do not recommend pushing your dog if the dog is doing well with one mile or even 100 yards. Why push the dog and take a chance on causing more pain and inflammation? It's not worth it! Make sure he/she is getting their joint supplements and you can even give the CanineActiv an hour or two before your walk and give more later that evening. So I hope you are getting my point. When someone says to me that their dog is getting short walks, a short walk could be three miles. That's not short ok?

Here let me break down walks so we are on the same page:

Short walk: up to 50 feet (5 minutes)
Medium walk: up to 50-100 yards (10 minutes)
Long walk: up to 1 mile (20 minutes)
Extra long walks: over 1 mile (30 minutes)

So stick with this list and know what is too far and what isn't. Don't over walk your dog. I brought this up when I recently spoke with someone that has a dog in severe pain and walks her dog about **10** miles a day. Oh My God, NEVER EVER do that to a lame dog. It takes a special dog to walk that far even in the healthiest dogs without joint issues. That's like walking a marathon. Don't do this please! By the way, after speaking with her she has reduced her dog's walks to at least half. I am hoping she will reduce it more for the dog's sake.

If you are interested in Homeopathy..here are some products.
Homeopathy - Arnica 200 (Try not to touch the pellets. If you do, make sure your hands are clean). Arnica and Symphytum are available in the 200c, all others will be in the 30c strength. When using the 30c, administer one dose, then wait an hour and dose again. This seems to deep-seat the remedy. Arnica and Hypericum helps with pain can lessen bleeding and bruising under the skin and is great for sprains and muscle injuries.

Other remedies for arthritis, joint issues, tendons and ligaments - Homeopathic herbs:

- Rhus Tox

- Hypericum
- Bryonia
- Symphytum
- Ruta Graveolens
- Ledum

I must confess, I have a tiny issue with the pellets. Most all are non-organic. Organic being for the inactive ingredients such as sucrose (sugar) and corn starch (GMO). (Hylands brand has lactose and Acacia Gum.) If you use these short term, I am ok with it since the amount of sucrose/corn starch is relatively low. I know people swear by homeopathic and are 100% safe but many vets, holistic vets, holistic Drs and alike do not consider inactive ingredients nor are they looking for organic. This is why I am suggesting a different form of homeopathic in which I have not researched further but may also contain other unwanted ingredients such as alcohol, Potassium Sorbate or Citric Acid to name a few. Avoid these types of liquid forms. I am only bringing this to your attention so that you are aware.

However, I have found one that is made in Canada that claims to be organic and lactose free. The brand name is **Ollois**. Check them out at www.ollois.com. I also have banner ads on my website for these as well.

It isn't easy to find things that don't have JUNK ingredients but try to find the best ones. I like buying organic herbal powders because of this. Because most are all pure and organic from herbal companies and will always be my preferred choice although homeopathic has no interactions and are 100% safe in all situations. You can add these into foods or you can put pellets in the mouth or put into a glass bottle, add filtered water, shake, let dissolve then squirt into your dog's mouth using a syringe, spray, or dropper. Keep refrigerated up to 2 weeks.

Types of Glucosamine to Avoid:
Glucosamine alone is ok, but you should avoid Glucosamine Sulfate * NaCL (or KCl) (or if the ingredients list says Potassium or Salt after the Sulfate). Some companies are very tricky about this - **unless it just says Glucosamine Sulfate or HCL**, you likely are getting an inferior

product. It is easy for people to see the Glucosamine Sulfate and simply ignore the KCl on the end. We are not all molecular scientists after all. The NaCl and KCl ("the salts") refer to even more (unneeded but cheaper) carrier molecules that can be up to 30% of the product's weight. Some carrier molecule is needed (such as sulfate or HCL alone) because raw Glucosamine is unstable by itself - it needs to be bound to the Sulfate or HCL carrier in order to be stored for any period of time. So if you have one of the KCl or NaCl forms of the Sulfate when you think you are buying a quality product, you are actually getting 30% of your dose as ordinary table salt. Be advised to watch out for products with those markings. The less active amounts of glucosamine you get, the slower your relief will be. At some point, it will likely be so low that you will get no benefit at all. NAG (N-Acetylglucosamine or N-Acetyl-D-Glucosamine), is another rare form of Glucosamine but should generally be avoided due to its relative ineffectiveness and expense.

What Kind of Glucosamine Should I Buy?
There are so many different forms and types and brands of Glucosamine out there and the quality varies widely. It is advised that one seek out a reputable manufacturer (one that offers a full, no questions asked, money back guarantee) and follows the old rule of, you get what you pay for. It can also be helpful to look at the label before you buy or get recommendations from other people you know that use Glucosamine and don't contain junk ingredients. Glucosamine in **tablet** form is not recommended due to low absorption issues.

Functions:
Although Glucosamine HCl is normally found in shellfish, it can also be created from the fermentation of corn. Glucosamine is necessary in the body for the structure and function of the articular cartilage. It assists in maintaining the elasticity and integrity of the connective tissue and assists in building, maintaining and repairing cartilage, tendons, and ligaments. It is most commonly used as a topical ointment or oral supplement to treat Osteoarthritis. The same anti-inflammatory and elasticity properties that make it a great treatment for Osteoarthritis may also contribute to its use in skin products and cosmetics. It's also been known to help in the treatment of Psoriasis and cancer.

If your dog has a new injury like an ACL tear, rest is best for at least 3-4 weeks. Use PROM (passive range of motion) exercises and do daily massages once pain has subsided. Pay special attention to rubbing up and down the spine and on the sides of it as well as it is the lifeline to the limbs.
I do recommend giving it a couple of weeks of rest until you know your dog isn't in a lot of pain or is doing better mentally and physically as possible. Then start PROM. Go slow!

What is P.R.O.M.? I will answer that later in this chapter.

After four weeks, get your dog in a pool for swim therapy or find a facility that offers water therapy. It can be a pool or underwater treadmill. Laser therapy, acupuncture, chiropractic all work well too. Use several different means of therapy to get a faster recovery for your dog. Once walking without pain and has little to no limping, do short walks. If they do well and not limping hard that day or the next day, you can do that walk for a week then slightly increase the walks to a little further. Do NOT overdo these walks. Find a distance that works well for your dog. **There should not be hard limping or pain before the walks.** Give CanineActiv before or after the walks will help.
Invest in a pool; say an above ground pool just deep enough for your dog to paddle his legs. Even a pool when the water comes up to the top of the legs can work very well. Buy a life vest as well, if the water is deeper than what they can walk on. It helps a lot, it really does. If they get tired and stop swimming, they won't sink wearing a life vest. Never leave your dog alone in a pool that is deeper than they are.
Start the swimming out slow. Say 5-8 minutes of swimming the first time. You can increase that as you go as they progress. Always try to extend your therapy slowly and back off if you see a setback. Don't push it. You will get there. It just may take some time. Continue therapy year round for chronic issues but you can reduce the amount as your dog starts to get better. Walk your dog at least 3 times a week. Swim as much as you like. During wintertime, use a therapy facility for indoor swimming, laser etc. Keep your dog moving. That's the key. If you can find one in your area, hyperbaric oxygen chambers work well for faster healing too. It provides more oxygen in the body therefore supplying the limbs with more circulation and faster healing. It also

works well on cancer. It has wonderful healing properties beyond your imagination.

If your dog has Osteoarthritis or a tendon injury that doesn't seem to recover, look into Stem Cell therapy or PRP (Platelet Rich Plasma). Stem cell does cost but your dog shouldn't need any meds afterwards and can function as a normal dog and wouldn't need another injection for a year or two. You must bank the fat cells though and you pay for them to be stored as well. PRP is much cheaper and a great tool for older dogs that cannot go under anesthesia.

For stem cell, your dog will require surgery like being spayed to remove the fat cells. It is somewhat costly but it is completely natural and nothing foreign is going into the body. I tried it on Diamond even though results were unknown for her Spondylosis. It was a 50-50 chance. It worked for four months. A year later though we did another injection and it lasted six months. This was good results for her having Spondylosis and no research done on it. But it does work well on Osteoarthritis. Hip Dysplasia is a 50-50 shot as well. They haven't progressed far enough into helping all dogs at this time but they are striving to help in the future. There is also PRP (Platelet Rich Plasma) therapy to look into although I have no experience with it. Others that have tried it have seen good results and this also works for other illnesses as they are discovering. Such as pancreatitis in cats, severe wound healing in animal limbs etc. The costs are lower and no surgery required.

Just know that if you try one thing for a while and it doesn't seem to help, try something else, or change what you are doing. It may be the dosing of supplements. Every dog is different and every dog will need different things. What's important is to keep chemicals and toxins of all kinds out of the body. Keep the body moving. Find the correct combination of supplements and physical therapy that keeps your dog moving, and provide a good healthy balanced diet. This will take work on your part to find your dog's best regimen. All commercial pet foods are toxic.

If you will do all of these things, you will find your dog walking pain-free in about eight weeks depending on the injury or joint issue. Then you continue to build them up and get them really going and getting them back to normal. Yes, it is possible.

You must work at rehabilitating your dog. In the long run, the cost is less than surgery. I have heard vets say "Your dog needs surgery NOW or else" when in fact, that dog didn't. After 6-12 weeks of making dietary changes and adding in supplements along with rehab, the dog was walking much better and pain-free after following everything I have recommended above. Now so you know, any recovery takes at least 6 months to a full year depending on the injury.

I spoke with someone that had her dog on NSAIDs for 2 years and the dog was still barely moving and having a hard time rising from sitting. That dog's organs were starting to give way I am sure. I got her to get her dog off of NSAIDs after starting CanineActiv, Actiflex for horses in liquid form, and Adequan; the dog is now walking well and pain-free with only an occasional flare up. This same dog has severe hip dysplasia. There are almost no hip sockets left. The dog really needs a THR (Total Hip Replacement) surgery. But the dog is doing well even in these extremely severe cases. Its unreal he can walk but he is doing great and off pain medications completely.

Never give up hope until you have tried all alternatives before ever considering surgery or euthanasia. Many things can be done and each dog is different, so please if you are still having trouble and have done all the above, get in touch with me. Your case would be considered unique with other options to try. Of course, every case is unique in my opinion.

What is P.R.O.M.?
PROM stands for (passive range of motion). This is where your dog is laying down, bearing no weight on the leg and you work the leg by placing your hands on the leg and rotating in a bicycle motion slowly and carefully. Start with 10 repetitions and work up. Doing these repetitively 3 times a day in short intervals will increase muscle mass in your dog's leg. Go to YouTube. There are many videos on how to perform this on your dog. I suggest you watching several different videos to get an idea of what each orthopedic vet or therapist is

recommending. Or better yet, ask your dog's therapist to show you how.

Hydrotherapy
Hydrotherapy can be used in the treatment of Osteoarthritis, orthopedic conditions, neurological conditions, muscle, ligament, and other soft tissue injuries. Muscle waste begins in approximately 3 days of any injury so to reduce more wasting or re-injury, it is important to rebuild muscle using safe exercise and help rebuild any muscles that have deteriorated. It is better for dogs to swim in warm water since cold-water cause's constriction of the blood vessels near the skin and restricts the flow of blood therefore making the muscles less efficient.

Hydrotherapy can help with:

- Relief of pain, swelling & stiffness
- Muscle strengthening and maintenance
- Alleviating muscle spasms
- Increase range of motion in joints
- Improve circulation
- Cardiovascular fitness (heart & lungs)
- Increase tissue healing
- Increase speed of recovery

Being in water reduces the heavy load on the limbs and in the back in which helps to reduce pain and re-injury to other joints. Hydrotherapy can also help with nerve regeneration.

When the chest area is under water, the lungs must work harder so this increases respiratory breaths therefore increasing oxygen into the blood supply. Using water creates a harder workout therefore rebuilding and healing works much faster. Hydrotherapy can be used for many conditions:

- Obesity
- Joint and soft tissue injury
- Pain and inflammation
- Increasing muscle

- Spinal Injuries
- Muscle Spasms

Hydrotherapy is also considered to be a natural anti-inflammatory through its ability to reduce tissue swelling.

Water therapy works very well (2-3 times a week is ideal). It's one of the best things you can do for an arthritic or injured dog. Don't forget your chiropractor and acupuncturist. There are so many things you can do to help your dog and it doesn't have to cost a fortune. Find what works for you and your dog and work at helping him/her to be a happy pup again. You can also do an Epsom Salt bath. If your dog is really having a tough time and you can get them in the tub without causing further pain or injury, let them sit in a tub of warm water with Epsom salts. Help those achy joints. Or a small kiddie pool outside (during warmer weather of course) with lukewarm water and add in Epsom salts. Even baking soda in the bath along with Epsom salts is refreshing, helps relieve itching and absorbs toxins from the body.

As for Hydrotherapy, you will find vets and surgeons that will tell you to wait eight weeks at least of rest before walking, doing Hydrotherapy or anything. In speaking with my therapist, he says this is where therapists and vets/surgeons don't agree. He feels the sooner you can get them into therapy, the quicker the recovery. I agree on this and this is why. If you end up having knee surgery, the next day, they have you up walking around the hospital. Then they want you in therapy as soon as possible. So why is it that vets and surgeons are taught differently? Makes you wonder. I don't have a good reason but in my personal opinion and what I have gone through with my dog, I think getting the dog walking as soon as possible is better for a quicker recovery. I will give you examples.

When Sydney, my big girl, had an unknown issue with her right knee/leg bowing out, we laid around for a month before I started her on therapy. By then, she had no muscle left in that leg. She almost couldn't walk due to muscle wasting. So when she tore her ACL/CCL, the vet told me eight weeks of rest. I knew when he said it that was **not** going to happen. I let her rest for four weeks and we headed off to Hydrotherapy. BUT during this rest time, I massaged her daily. I loaded her up on all of her supplements. Nothing seemed to help but I knew in my mind it was helping in some way. I started her back on Adequan that I had stopped giving her 2 months earlier. Bad mistake on my part! The ACL/CCL was slowly healing but she was using her muscles during Hydrotherapy so she had strength to walk on her own and recover quicker. It brought us to the point of being able to take walks without causing much pain and less chance of re-injury.

In other words, Hydrotherapy gave us time for the knee to start healing and repairing itself. It creates scar tissue around it and forms some sort of support again. We did not choose surgery for several reasons. My therapist isn't in favor of surgery. He has even seen surgery patients not recover well at all and sometimes come out worse. Get to know your surgeon. I will say every single dog and case is different. It depends on the size of your dog, the activity of your dog, the extent of the ACL/CCL tear and age and health issues of your dog. Second, I didn't have $3,000. So alternative therapy was our only option.

I purchased a soft leg brace for her and it has really helped a lot. At first, I didn't see much of a difference but now I am seeing a big difference. She can really be struggling to walk and I put her brace on and she can walk a lot better and faster. (I keep having this thought in my head from the movie Forrest Gump, "Lt. Dan got new legs." Ha!) She just tires out quick in the beginning which is understandable and is common with any injury and after lying around for a month. We also started short walks with braces on. I purchased one for both legs so to try to help deter a second ACL tear and it is also her knee that bows out. So we walked ten houses down and back at first. We have gone up to 1/2 mile but I may need to drop back on that a little since this last walk caused her some pain. How do I know she was in pain when she never makes a sound and never shows pain? Because she is limping much harder (head bobbing). It's understandable to limp harder after the walk but the next day, the walking should be back to normal; whatever normal is at that time. We do some P.R.O.M. exercises and daily massages along with chiropractic adjustments, Class 3b laser therapy, and sound wave therapy at home. It's been a lot of work. All of this you will have to do if you choose surgery or if you don't. We just skipped the surgery part.

Sometimes ACL tears don't heal well even after 6 months even without surgery so that's when you may consider surgery if it's in your budget. It usually takes a year to actually get back to normal with or without surgery. Time and patience is critical on your part. It's not an easy recovery.

Laser Therapy (also called Low Level Laser or Cold Laser)
Laser therapy works well in combination with other treatments. These lasers used by professionals are usually a Class IV. This type of laser is deep penetrating and can burn if used incorrectly. This is why only a professionally trained therapist should use them. Class 3b is surface type lasers and do not burn and can be used in a home setting. They do go below the surface but not near as deep as the Class IV. You can buy these in health stores and online stores. The time on it will need to be longer than the Class IV. Usually 15-30 minutes with a Class 3b. You will need to shave the hair in that area to penetrate the skin layers. Laser therapy works well on speeding up the healing process on joints and soft tissue injuries. Works well along using other methods of therapies.

PRP
Platelet-rich plasma, or PRP, is derived from blood that is drawn from the patient and run through a special centrifuge, which separates the bloods less dense components from its heavier ones. This process distills a portion of the blood to a platelet concentration level that is much richer than regular blood. At the same time, it helps to remove both red and white blood cells from the platelet rich part of the plasma.

PRP works for cruciate ligament injuries, orthopedic fractures and delayed bone healing, as well as degenerative joint disease of the shoulder, elbow, hip, knee, and ankle. The number of injections performed depends upon the severity and type of condition being treated. The use of certain anti-inflammatory drugs is not recommended during PRP therapy as they may diminish the success of the procedure by interfering with the initial inflammatory reaction induced by the platelets. Other therapy is recommended in conjunction with PRP such as laser therapy, hydrotherapy, and acupuncture. This is a low cost procedure.

Adequan
Adequan is an injectable substance known as a "polysulfated glycosaminoglycan," and is very similar to the more familiar oral supplement known as glucosamine. Adequan soothes and lubricates the joints, reducing inflammation and pain by reducing friction. Instead of just masking pain that NSAIDs do, it actually helps to rebuild cartilage in the damaged joint. It's not just pain control, its therapy. Speak with your vet on side effects from these injections. There are some but most are rare or uncommon.

When beginning Adequan, the costs are high. I found a way to slightly decrease that by asking your vet to prescribe the equine version. Equine vials cost about $15-$20 less than the canine version and the only difference is, the canine version has a preservative in it for longer shelf life. You can always switch back to canine version after the first month loading dose period if you so desire. This will help cut costs purchasing the equine version. I buy from Valleyvet.com (don't forget syringes). Once you get past the loading dose, it becomes very cheap monthly. Depending on the size of your dog, anywhere from a few dollars to $15 a month. One injection every 3-4 weeks. Doing them at home will save you drastically. I give two of my dogs' injections although due to the severity of their cases, they get an injection every 3 weeks. Wintertime is sometimes 2 1/2 weeks. To determine the time in-between injections is to just watch your dog. If you see signs of more limping, pain, harder to rise, yelping in pain, give an injection. The injection takes effect usually within a couple of hours up to 24 hours or so.

When you start giving injections, the goal is to get it built up in your dog's system. Normally an injection takes effect within a couple of hours and starts to wear off within 3 days. This is why you give two injections a week for the first month. The second month is when you began to taper off. Give one injection once a week. You can do this for 2-4 weeks, and then cut back to an injection every two weeks. This is when you will really begin to watch for limping. If your dog can't make it past two weeks, then two weeks is your point. You will give an injection every two weeks. After using this over time, the time in-between may become a little longer. Every dog is different and it depends on you to pay attention to your dog and let your dog tell you when it's time. If you take your dog to the vet for the injections, the cost is usually around $35-$40 an injection depending on the area in which you live.

There are many questions on whether to give subcutaneous injection (Sub Q) or in the muscle (IM). Per manufactures recommendations it should be injected into the muscle. The reason for this is, it takes effect a lot faster being injected into the muscle. So make a note of that if your vet recommends Sub Q. I give in muscle and that's how I will always do it.

More vets should recommend this prescription and I am not sure why they don't. It has minimal side effects and works really well. In fact, it has saved one of my dog's life. I call it a miracle drug for her. She was in severe pain and I was giving 4 different pain meds to her daily. Definitely harming her internal organs. I am surprised I didn't kill her with all those high-risk pain meds. The vet gave me the list and dosing, but it was a lot. She was still in severe pain on all those pain meds as well. It took two months of twice a week injections of Adequan to get her pain-free, then we slowly and carefully tapered off from there. So let your dog tell you how this will work for your dog. Start with the recommended dosing and watch closely. I think this is the best thing I have found that has worked well and has been safest overall for my dogs. It surely beats giving those high risk deadly NSAIDs.

Adequan should not be given to dogs with kidney or liver disease. Avoid use with dogs with bleeding disorders. Twenty five percent of dogs have had reactions or side effects so keep watch for blood in stools, diarrhea, or stomach upset/vomiting.

Hyperbaric Oxygen Chamber Therapy
Hyperbaric oxygen chambers are pressurized tubes where oxygen therapy is delivered. This technique has been used in humans to treat many conditions including air bubbles in blood vessels, decompression sickness ("the bends"), carbon monoxide poisoning, wounds that won't heal, crushing injuries, a skin or bone infection that causes tissue death, snakebites, smoke inhalation, burns, severe anemia, soft tissue injuries as well as joint inflammation and even cancer. HBOT can do so much for many ailments and diseases. It's beyond our scope on the possibilities. Adding a high concentration of oxygen into the blood

supply accelerates healing and kills cancer cells. Look for a facility in your area that offers this to pets. The costs are around $135 per treatment depending on what area you live in. The total treatment time is usually 1-2 hours as the pet rests quietly while in the chamber.

There are several supplements for joints I really like to recommend especially for moderate to severe cases. Or any dogs having a problem walking, rising etc. That is DC-Y by MVP (equine for inflammation), Actiflex (equine), Ostinol 350 (human) and CanineActiv (for pain in dogs). I am sure there are some that are even much better (organic) but these are more budget friendly although Ostinol isn't so cheap but a very unique product.

Actiflex (equine)
Actiflex is for horses and is stronger. It contains glucosamine that I feel should be in every diet for every dog. They make this in a liquid form as well as a powder/meal form. The powder contains alfalfa and getting too much can cause an estrogenic effect. If you use this and DC-Y both, you are getting way too much alfalfa. The liquid has a fairly strong flavor to it. Pina Colada flavored so your dog may not like it if you don't mix it in with something they like.

Ingredients: Glucosamine Sulfate, Chondroitin Sulfate, Ester C (Ascorbic Acid), Superoxide Dismutase (SOD), Boswellia Serrata, Hyaluronic Acid, Methylsulfonylmethane (MSM), Perna Canaliculus, Bioperine, Yucca, Purified water, Pina colada flavoring.

1 tsp is approximately:

Glucosamine Sulfate	1,334mg.
Chondroitin Sulfate	667mg.
MSM	500mg.
Ester C (Ascorbic Acid)	167mg.
Perna Canaliculus	167mg.
Yucca	25mg.
Hyaluronic Acid (HA)	21mg.
Bioperine	17mg.

Dosage:
1-2 tsp (5-10 ml) per 50 lbs. You can give more in extreme severe cases for loading dose for several weeks or until you see clear signs of no limping or pain. Usually within 3-5 days, you will begin to see change. If not, increase the dosage.

If your dog happens to vomit or have diarrhea after giving this, then your dog is probably having a reaction to the MSM, vitamin C or too much given too fast. Try reducing dose back down lower than recommended dose then work back up slowly. Some dogs cannot tolerate MSM although uncommon and vitamin C will cause loose stools and diarrhea if given in high amounts with first dose. Just start small and work up.

Making Your Own Organic Anti-inflammatory Mix
If you would like an organic version of anti-inflammatories, you can gather these ingredients online and purchase organic powders then combine. Choose Grape Seed Extract wisely. No skin or meat. Only seeds from grapes. Make sure it says 100% grape seed. If in doubt, please ask manufacture if it contains skins or meat. Grape seed extract has terrific healing abilities for many diseases including cancer. You want to add flavor? You can find organic flavored powders as well like blueberry or apple. You can find these on different sites like Starwest-Botanicals.com, Znaturalfoods.com, and MontainRoseHerbs.com.

Anti-inflammatory herbs:
Devil's Claw
Yucca Root
Grape Seed Extract (no skins or meat-seeds only and organic)
Fever Few
Cat's Claw
Turmeric
Boswellia
Organic Alfalfa
Ginger
Meadowsweet

List to purchase for a good combo in **organic:**

Yucca (25%)
Devil's Claw (25%)
Grape Seed Extract (seeds only) (20%)
Boswellia (10%)
Turmeric (10%)
Rosehips (5%)
Blueberry powder (5%)

You will measure and mix then add to wet foods daily. You can split it into two meals if you like. Use some and put into capsules for yourself.

Keep the amounts of Yucca lower as a higher dose has been known to cause bloat in horses and could cause bloat in large dogs. It's best to discontinue yucca for a while after about 3 months of use. Not for long-term use without interruptions in dosing.

Approximate dosing for dogs:
Small dogs: 1/4 - 1/2 tsp
Medium dogs: 1/2 - 1 tsp
Large dogs: 1 tsp - 1 1/2 tsp
Giant dogs: 2 tsp

Do not give along with cortisone medications.

Devil's claw may also lower your blood sugar levels. Devil's claw might decrease how quickly the liver breaks down some medications. Taking devil's claw along with some medications that are broken down by the liver can increase the effects and side effects of some medications.

Do not use Cat's Claw if your dog has Leukemia, bleeding disorders, autoimmune disease or low blood pressure.

If you have kidney disease, don't use willow bark.

Discontinue use 2 weeks before surgery. Do not give this if your dog is on heart medications.

CanineActiv

CanineActiv relieves pain and inflammation while promoting healthy, natural healing and repair of damaged tissue for dogs of any breed. CanineActiv Safe Pain Relief contains the anti-inflammatory ingredient, Alpha-GEE®, a unique compound made of naturally occurring amino acids found in natural sources and endogenous to a dog's body. They are part of a dog's normal healing process and CanineActiv helps optimize restoration of healthy mobility.

Ingredients:
Alpha-GEE/Amino Acids, Boswellia Serrata/BOSWELLIA, Glycyrrhiza Glabra/Licorice Root, Harpagophytum/Devils Claw, Curmuma longa/Curcumin-Turmeric, Medicago sativa/Alfalfa, Tanacetum parthenium/Feverfew, Yucca schidigera/YUCCA
Use to relieve pain and inflammation and help increase mobility. Can be used as a preventative before activity.

Note: CanineActiv can produce a false-positive test in blood work causing liver enzymes to be higher. If your dog has liver issues already, please discontinue using this at least 48 hours before blood work. If your dog has heart disease, do not give as Licorice Root can cause more harm.
Do not take with or add water to this. Can add whole capsule into food or treat or open capsule and sprinkle onto moist/wet foods.

TRF 150/350

TRF 150™ provides nutritional support for healthy joint function, repair, and relief of occasional inflammation. These products feature Cyplexinol™ PRO, a bone derived protein/collagen complex containing **Bone Morphogenetic Proteins (BMPs)** and key growth factors naturally contained in bones. This ingredient helps to support pathways involved in normal bone remodeling, and the <u>proper repair and regeneration of cartilage, thereby supporting good bone health and joint integrity.</u>

Tissue Regeneration Factor (TRF) is an ideal first line of defense for any stage of osteoporosis, broken or fractured bones, and for any condition in need of joint or cartilage repair.

- Stimulates new bone and cartilage formation
- Anti-inflammatory
- Can be taken with or without meals

TRF is available in 150mg and 350mg doses. Use TRF 350 when higher dosages are desired for more serious bone and cartilage support or large dogs.

Note: I started Sydney on TRF 150 for her ACL tear and I have seen some nice results. I really like this supplement.

Ostinol 150/350/450
Another product called **Ostinol 150/350/450** is lower in cost and appears to be almost identical to the TRF brand. I have started using it over the last several months and it seems to work just as well. Avoid the *Ostinol Advanced* as it contains junk ingredients.

Found on Amazon and other websites:

- 150mg is for **mild** support
- 350mg is for **moderate** support
- 450mg is for **severe** support

I also recommend starting out in the beginning giving a double dose for 3-5 days in severe cases. This product takes 1-2 weeks to begin to see any changes and up to 6 weeks for full results. This is a long-term supplement and may be taken for the rest of their lives. Without this supplement, Sydney cannot walk literally.

Of course, a small dog may do well with the 150mg but a larger dog may need a higher amount. Adjust accordingly.

Collagen
Collagen makes up 30% of the entire body in dogs. Collagen works on nails, coat, joints, and digestive tract to name a few. Most collagen supplements contain amino acids, what most bodies are lacking, especially in older pets. Collagen comes in many types including Type I, II, III and so on. Type II is specific for joints and I and III are specific

to skin, hair, nails. Overall Collagen promotes healthy systems in all areas. The amino acid Glycine targets cancer cells as well as the digestive system. Some types of collagen comes from fish. I tend to steer away from fish due to any chances of mercury contamination. Collagen peptide is another term for hydrolyzed collagen. If purchasing human products, start with a low dose and work up in dosing over a few weeks time. Normally human dosing is based off of a 150-160 lb human. Adjust accordingly. Not all Collagens are created equal. Collagen is a tasteless and odorless powder, so it is easy to use and mix into wet foods.

At this time, I found the brand ForestLeaf to be superior in its ingredients and contains 18 amino acids including Glycine. There are 9 essential amino acids: histidine, isoleucine, leucine, lysine, methionine, phenylalanine, threonine, tryptophan, and valine. And 20 amino acids in total. This particular brand contains 8 of those 9 essential amino acids. Tryptophan is not in it. I found this common in many of them. Amino acids play a key role in our health as well as our pets. The body cannot make amino acids so they must come from the diet. Buckwheat is a plant-based food that contains all nine essential amino acids. Protein sources are meat, poultry, eggs, dairy and seafood contain all 9 essential amino acids as well. Type II collagen is usually found sold alone or within other types of Collagens. I found a brand on Amazon called Active Supreme Collagen Complex. It doesn't contain any junk ingredients as well.

Approximate Dosage:
Small dogs: 1/8 scoop
Medium dogs: 1/4 scoop
Large dogs: 1/2 scoop (1 TBSP)

Start with lower amounts and work up to the recommended dose with time as this can cause some diarrhea or digestive upset.
These dosages can be adjusted according to the results you may or may not be getting. It takes a little time to begin to see results.

"Undenatured" Collagen Type II should be taken in very small doses – usually 10-20mg per day for a dog, humans up to 40mg. Hydrolyzed collagen should be taken in higher doses which is the one I mentioned above.

Some other supplements good for joints:
Camu Camu/Rosehips/Amla
Fish oil (high quality)
Glucosamine
Chondroitin
Cetyl-Myristoleate
Bromelain
Green Lipped Mussel
MSM
Hyaluronic Acid (HA)
Mushroom Blends

Note: Check out my book called "Canine Arthritis & Joint Pain: Healing Naturally-Revised Edition". It covers this chapter and more.

Stay away from Inactive type ingredients such as:

Sodium benzoate	Propylene glycol	Lecithin (soy)	Polyethylene glycol (PEG)
Sucralose	Canola oil	Corn Starch	Sorbitol or Mannitol
Safflower Oil	Vegetable or corn oil	Xanthan Gum	Carrageenan
Citric Acid (corn based)	Artificial Flavorings	Soybean protein isolate	Benzoic Acid
Rosemary Extract	Potassium Sorbate	FD&C Red #40 (all food colors avoid)	Caramel Color
Stearic acid	Gelatin (corn carrier)	Dicalcium phosphate	Dextrose
Magnesium Stearate	Dicalcium phosphate	Soy and soybean oil	Maltodextrin (corn based)
Titanium Dioxide	Sorbic acid (a preservative)	Brown Rice Syrup	Hydrolyzed Vegetable Protein

These are a small portion to avoid but some of your main ones to watch out for. I find that Magnesium Stearate is in many things. Try to avoid if you can although not always possible under certain circumstances. Avoid tablets (full of junk ingredients) and softgels (will not dissolve in dogs short intestinal tracts). You will need to poke holes in softgels and squirt into foods. Use powders, capsules, or liquid extracts that contain no preservatives or alcohol. You will find vegetable glycerin in place of alcohol. As I said, it takes work to avoid junk ingredients but try the best you can. If you can reduce most of the bad ingredients, then you are cutting down on what the body must try to filter out and not absorb into the body causing more issues.

Inflammation is the root cause of nearly every disease!

Chapter 6
Lawn Care with Weeds, Fleas, And Ticks

Pet Parents purchase toxic chemicals intended to kill fleas and ticks. These include collars, sprays, dusts and more. Other Pet Parents take their pets to vets to be dipped in chemicals. Same for groomers that dip dogs. Many consumers probably assume that the products used by both parties have been tested and deemed safe. After all, how could the FDA let deadly poisons be sold on store shelves? Well that's a loaded question.

Spot-On Pesticides such as Frontline Plus, Sentinel, Comfortis, Trifexis, Assurity, Revolution, PetArmor, Bravecto, Hartz, Sergeants, NexGuard, K9 Advantix II, Biospot and Advantage just to name a few, can trigger adverse reactions in dogs and cats, shorten life spans, cause terminal illness, and premature death. The active ingredients in these solutions include chemicals such as imidacloprid, fipronil, permethrin, methoprene, and pyriproxyfen, all of which have caused serious health problems in animals. Even some of the inactive ingredients can be hazardous to your pet. Other forms of flea control powders (including carpet powders), collars, and sprays are no less dangerous to you or your pets. These products are considered pesticides. Avoid these pesticides for safer alternatives. Pesticides in your home? Sigh!

Immediate effects of pesticide overdose include vomiting, diarrhea, trembling, seizures, and respiratory problems. If your dog or cat shows any of these symptoms after the application of a pesticide, immediately wash the product off and seek immediate emergency veterinary care.

Products containing cyphenothrin and permethrin were especially problematic for small dogs. Veterinarians have seen a huge increase in the rate of liver disease, nervous system disorders, cancers, seizures, diabetes, renal failure, and other diseases. These popular anti-flea and anti-tick medications are extremely toxic to the liver.

Any dogs under 15 lbs should not use any flea and tick medications or topicals ever. And use caution with Essential oils as well.

The EPA issued an advisory a couple years ago about spot-on products after receiving over ***44,000 reports of adverse reactions, including 600 deaths. Don't be another statistic.***

NEVER give your dog Spinosad and Ivermectin at the same time.
Effects are DEADLY!!

Please err on the side of caution and don't use these (or any OTC) toxic flea treatments on your pets. Feel free to email, phone or write the FDA and tell the chemical and pharmaceutical companies that we REFUSE to POISON our pets in order to kill fleas.

You can try different non-toxic products on the market. They are out there and I have found a few for you. While some may work better than others so depending on your situation, as to which one may work best or in combination. Just keep searching for the one that works best for you. It may take going through a couple before you do find that safe product.

Some of the Safe Products to try are:
Food Grade Diatomaceous Earth (DE) (Yard and internal dosing)
Triple Sure
PetSafe Pure Red Cedar Insect Repellent Granules
Mercola Flea and Tick Defense
FLEA AND TICK SPRAY (sold at Hare Today)
Wondercide EVOLV: Natural Flea & Tick Control
Ticked Off!
Green Pet Fleaze-Off Wipes
Petzlife
TickZ - Controls Ticks and other biting insects
Alzoo Natural Flea & Tick Spot On Dog Repellent
Fleabusters Rx for Fleas Plus Powder
No More Ticks
Pet Protector Disc
Apple Cider Vinegar
Ambertick
Cedarcide (contains soy)

For lawns:
The Orcon Flea Destroyer (7 million) (FD-C7M)
CedarCide Pco Choice Organic Yard Pest Control
Food Grade Diatomaceous Earth (DE)
Wondercide

It may be best to use several different types of things like Diatomaceous Earth for yard, the safe products above and be vigilant about where your dog roams and trying to keep the yard contained with a heavily treated perimeter. Be careful with any that contain Tea Tree Oil or Wintergreen oil, as these can be highly toxic in many cases.

You can also try your hand at homemade remedies:

Colloidal Silver
Fleas: Use as a flea spray- saturate the fleas with colloidal silver daily until gone.

How many sprays or droppers = 1 teaspoon
50 vertical sprays = 1 teaspoon (5ml)
30 fine mist sprays = 1 teaspoon (5ml)
6 (2 oz/60ml) droppers = 1 teaspoon (5ml)
5 (4 oz/120ml) droppers = 1 teaspoon (5ml)
5 (8 oz/240ml) droppers = 1 teaspoon (5ml)

1 teaspoon= 5cc
2 teaspoons = 10cc

Apple Cider Vinegar (raw, "Mother")
Internal Dosage:
0-25 lbs: 1 teaspoon
25-50 lbs: 2 teaspoon
50-75 lbs: 1 TBSP
75+ lbs: 1 1/2 - 2 TBSP

External:
Sponge on ACV diluted with equal amounts of warm water. All fleas drown in soapy water and the ACV rinse makes the skin too acidic for a re-infestation. If you are worried about picking up fleas when you take your dog away from home, keep some ACV in a spray bottle, and spray your dog before you leave home, and when you get back. Take some with you and keep it in the car, just in case you need it any time. ACV normalizes the pH levels of the skin, makes your dog unpalatable to even the nastiest of bacteria.

Don't give up in getting away from these deadly medications of all kinds. Try the natural products, many use essential oils and are diluted so that they will not cause harm to your dog. But always watch your pets when applying something new. Also, wash your hands once you use anything. No need to share it everywhere else. You could touch a baby and it have a reaction or in your eyes. Always wash your hands after handling anything whether it is safe or not. And be very careful using on small dogs or puppies. Even the natural products can cause serious reactions as well.

Cedar Oil is a great product to use. You can dilute it yourself with coconut oil and apply to your pet's coat. It works well. The Health Ranger (Mike Adams) is working on a pet product as I write this that contains cedar oil.

TIP: *When washing hands, do NOT use any anti-bacterial soaps. These are extremely toxic as well. Use a mild, safe, chemical free soap. They come in hand soap liquids, dishwashing liquids, bars of soap, shampoos etc.*

I personally use Seventh Generation dishwashing soap and pour into my old soft soap container pump bottles to wash my hands in.

Lawn Care, Plants, and Essential Oils
In today's world, we all want the perfect beautiful yard that's lush and green and makes your neighbors jealous. If you have that type of yard, either you worked VERY hard at it or you hired a professional to come in and maintain it. Either way, your yard is probably doused in toxic chemicals. If you have dogs, you probably don't have this type of yard. Dogs make paths and create trails beating down grass etc. That's ok, grass is always a work in progress, and there are several things you can do such as artificial turf in those hard to grow or high traffic areas. You can use sand trails or walkways in those areas. Make sure you provide a cover over concrete and turf so on hot days it won't burn those paw pads.

Weeds! Let's talk about weeds. Weeds never go away. I was talking with my neighbor the other day and we were talking about weeds. I told her I never apply anything to my grass and they do and they have more weeds than I do. Think about that one for a moment.

Have you ever noticed certain seasons or times of the year, you get different weeds and different grasses growing? In Texas, during springtime, the yards look horrible. During winter, they are all brown but springtime, they are both brown and green with wild grasses and aggressive weed growth going on. But if you wait a little longer, the weeds and wild grasses calm down and a lot of them disappear or go dormant, then the original grass comes up. Yes you still have weeds but when you mow, those weeds blend in with the grasses (hoping you HAVE planted some grass right?). Now this may not be a perfect yard but it still looks great. A well-manicured lawn always looks great even with weeds.

I do hand pick weeds at times. Some that are really unruly or is an overabundance of that one weed. I don't want one kind taking over my yard and grass. You will NEVER get rid of weeds no matter what you do unless you are continuously applying chemicals all over your lawn. Don't walk on that grass ever! With that said, if you have pets and they use your yard to even walk on it, do not apply any type of chemicals. That includes weed killers, bug killers, and fertilizers.

To use all natural products, try this mix:

Here is a recipe for killing weeds from the Dirt Doctor himself:

Herbicide Formula:
1 gallon of 10% (100 grain) vinegar
Add 1-ounce orange oil or d-limonene
Add 1-tablespoon molasses (optional - some say it doesn't help)
1-teaspoon liquid soap
Do not add water

*You can use 10%-20% white vinegar for natural weed killing.

Weed killers can be done using safe products and mixes. Many may work for you and others may not. A lot of times it is trial and error on your particular yard and where you live and if you get the mix right. Do not purchase the store bought chemical laden weed killers. This also applies to lawn fertilizers. You can make your own weed killers and also purchase safe fertilizers for pet safe lawns.

FYI, just because it says pet safe, it still may not be. Learn to read ingredients on these products. The Dirt Doctor is a good website to follow. You can learn a lot about gardening as well. Some other good ingredients to use are gypsum, lime, bone meal, corn gluten meal, and molasses to name a few. Remember, learn to read ingredients.
Some weeds are actually good. Many times, you may see a dog munching on a weed. That may be just what your dog needs. Maybe he has an upset tummy or it just tastes good such as Dandelion weed. I am not fond of the Dandelion weed growing in my yard but I know they are safe and good and if my dog needs them, they are available. They don't stay year round. These are only a late winter/early springtime weed around here.

As for fleas and ticks, this is a little harder battle using safer products but it is possible and don't give up. First, you can use Diatomaceous Earth (Food Grade) often or after any rain event. The dust particles are small and sharp and inhaling large amounts can cause respiratory issues. DE can be used for so many things, it's endless. Deworming, brushing teeth, internal flea control, external flea control, good for the soil, potted plants, you name it. Buy in bulk and use it often. You can use many products being sold on the market that are natural and mostly safe. Some include essential oils. Take a look at these. There have been some reactions to them in certain pets especially cats but most are safe to use. Follow directions. Be careful with cats though. Much more toxic for them.

Here are some to avoid or to use with extreme caution and by an experienced holistic vet.

Essential oils to "avoid" with animals or under supervision of vet:

Anise	Mugwort
Birsch	Mustard
Bitter Almond	Oregano
Hyssop (use decumbens variety only)	Pennyroyal (high in ketones that's toxic to kidneys)
Calamus	Red or White Thyme
Camphor	Rue
Cassia	Santalina

Chenopodium	Sassafras
Clove Leaf and Bud	Savory
Crested Lavender	Tansy
Garlic	Terebinth
Goosefoot	Thuja
Horseradish	Wintergreen
Boldo	Wormwood
Juniper (use j. berry only)	Yarrow

You can also plant around your yard or in pots, plants such as lemongrass, peppermint, eucalyptus, citronella, and catnip to ward off insects. Be very careful about plants, bushes, and flowers as most are toxic to pets. For example: Nandina's, Hydrangea's and Begonias. If your pets like to get into things or are not supervised at all times in the yard, don't plant them. Plant them in the front yard or where the pets don't roam. Otherwise, this could become fatal.

Here are a few toxic plants:

Autumn crocus	Oleander
Azalea	Yew
Baby's breath	Dahlia
Begonia	Iris
Calla lily	Daisy
Chrysanthemum	Carnation
Daffodil	Chrysanthemum
Elephant's ear	Peony
Foxglove	Lily Of The Valley
Geranium	Hydrangea
Japanese pieris	Poinsettia
Larkspur	English Ivy
Lupine	Boston Ivy
Morning glory	Morning Glory

Oak trees - acorns and leaves are poisonous. They contain a combination of gallic acid and tannic acid.
Tomato plants - contains solanine, a highly toxic element.

Also, don't forget the indoor flowers and potted plants such as English Ivy. Did you know that by just drinking water from a vase containing poisonous cut flowers can result in vomiting, diarrhea, seizures, lethargy, and lack of appetite in pets?

Here are a few **non-toxic** plants:

African violet	Ponytail palm
Bamboo	Rose
Blue echeveria	Tiger orchid
Burro or lamb's tail	Wild hyacinth
Hens and chickens (evergreen succulents)	Lemon Balm
Jasmine	Bee Balm (technically an herb)
Marigold (select varieties)	Petunia

If you use chemicals on your yard, your pets paw pads will absorb these chemicals through their pads along with when they go to lick their feet and are ingesting these chemicals. Pets absorb these chemicals on higher levels and are therefore much more toxic than to humans. Don't forget the thought of if your pet decides that they want to munch on some grass. More ingesting of chemicals. Does your dog eat dirt? Mine does. I certainly don't want my dogs eating dirt with chemicals in it.

You know those mushrooms that pop up overnight in your yard? Remove those immediately. They are extremely toxic to your pets. Only medicinal mushrooms are safe for ingestion. Not the ones in your yard.

Keep your pets safe. Eliminate chemicals in and out of your home. Your pets and your children will be much healthier.

Chapter 7
Heartworm Treatment and Prevention

It is important to understand that heartworm infections are not detectable until about six months after a dog has been bitten by a heartworm-infected mosquito. (This is why it's not possible to have a heartworm test performed monthly and give the preventative only if an infection is found.) Blood tests generally will not detect heartworms in a dog until the larvae have matured into an adult worm, which takes atleast six months following initial infection. Symptoms, such as coughing, lethargy, and difficulty breathing, will not show up until the infection is advanced. Coughing will be your first symptom in the earlier stages.

Once heartworm infection has been confirmed, additional tests should be done to try to determine how extensive the infestation is. Radiographs can reveal inflammation and damage to the arteries and the heart, and blood tests will show whether the liver and kidneys have been affected.

Heartworm infection is divided into four or five stages (depending on the model used), based on the severity of the infestation and the age and health of the dog.

- Stage 1 (mild) consists of young, healthy dogs with no symptoms and minimal changes evident on x-rays.

- Stage 2 (moderate) infection will show heartworm disease that is evident on x-rays, but symptoms are minimal, mostly coughing.

- Stage 3 is a (severe) infection, with weight loss, coughing, difficulty breathing, more damage visible on x-rays, along with liver, and/or kidney damage.

- Stage 4 and 5 are considered (critical), with the dog often collapsing in shock. These dogs will not survive ordinary heartworm treatment, and must have the worms surgically removed if they are to have any hope of survival.

I recommend using all-natural products and no chemicals to treat a heartworm positive dog. You can also use the slow kill as this would be safer than a vet pushing Immiticide injections upon you. Natural treatments are safer and work just as well as medications. I have a list on my **Holistic and Organix Pet Shoppe** website. Just know, NO medication or natural supplement PREVENTS heartworm. These do not prevent. They kill <u>after</u> being infected. The best thing you can do is keep a strong immune system and test your dog every 6-12 months. If you elect to use the chemicals using the slow-kill method (no Immiticide), then I recommend giving normal doses of Heartgard Plus

(Ivermectin) monthly along with pulsed Doxycycline. Some studies show that you can give Heartgard every 15 days for 6 months to treat heartworm positive dogs.

(Note that a dog may test positive for up to six months after the worms are all gone).

Remember that anything that increases your dog's heart rate increases the risk as long as your dog is infected with heartworms.

Ivermectin is not recommended for dogs with the MDR1 gene mutation that causes sensitivity to Ivermectin.

Options for pulsing Doxycycline:

Give Doxycycline for one month (one month on, two months off, one month on.) Dosage may be repeated 6 months later - Doxycycline for one month.
Dosage of Doxycycline can be cut in half if the dog cannot tolerate a higher dose. Giving it with food can help prevent digestive upset.

Here are the supporting details on Wolbachia and Doxycycline: Research has led to the discovery of a parasite called Wolbachia that lives symbiotically inside heartworms. Studies indicate that this parasite contributes to the adverse effects of both heartworm infection and heartworm treatment, including inflammation, embolism, and allergic reaction. Treatment with Doxycycline to kill the Wolbachia parasite weakens the heartworms and makes them unable to reproduce, lessens their adverse effects on the body and greatly reduces the chance of adverse reaction during heartworm treatment.

Studies published in late 2008 clearly indicate that treatment with a combination of Ivermectin and daily Doxycycline given intermittently will sterilize the heartworms, prevent the dog from being infectious to other dogs (via mosquitoes), speed up the death of the worms prior to (or in place of) Immiticide injection treatment, limit inflammation and damage caused by the worms' presence, and reduce the chance of serious adverse reaction from Immiticide treatment. All of these work best when the two drugs are used together than when either is given alone.

TIP: Start the Doxycycline one month before starting the Heartgard to lessen any reactions to the Heartgard that may cause the dog to throw a worm.

"Treatment with Ivermectin combined with Doxycycline resulted in a significantly faster decrease of circulating microfilariae and higher adulticidal [killed more adult heartworms] activity compared with either Ivermectin or Doxycycline alone. . . . Results indicate that the combination of these two drugs causes adult worm death."

Any dog that is currently infected with heartworms should be treated with Doxycycline. All dogs except those with multi-drug sensitivity should also be given a regular monthly dose of Heartgard (Ivermectin) every month until heartworms are gone. Some dogs with this sensitivity may do ok on Heartgard. This is up to your vet and what he recommends for your dog that may have the MDR1 gene.

A laboratory study done on Wolbachia showed that intermittent (pulsing) treatment with antibiotics was more effective in depleting Wolbachia than continuous treatment.

Immiticide Injections are NOT recommended..ever!

Affected Breeds of the MDR1 Gene

The University Of Washington states:
While the dose of Ivermectin used to prevent heartworm infection is SAFE in dogs with the mutation (6 micrograms per kilogram), higher doses, such as those used for treating mange (300-600 micrograms per kilogram) will cause neurological toxicity in dogs that are homozygous for the MDR1 mutation (MDR1 mutant/mutant) and can cause toxicity in dogs that are heterozygous for the mutation (MDR1 mutant/normal).

Approximately three of every four Collies in the United States have the mutant MDR1 gene. The frequency is about the same in France and

Australia, so it is likely that most Collies worldwide have the mutation. The MDR1 mutation has also been found in Shetland Sheepdogs (Shelties). Australian Shepherds, Old English Sheepdogs, English Shepherds, German Shepherds, Longhaired Whippets, Silken Windhounds, and a variety of mixed breed dogs. The only way to know if an individual dog has the mutant MDR1 gene is to have the dog tested. As more dogs are tested, more breeds will probably be added to the list of affected breeds.

Breeds affected by the MDR1 mutation (frequency %)

Breed		Approximate Frequency	
Australian Shepherd	50%	Long-haired Whippet	50%
Australian Shepherd, Mini	50%	McNab	30%
Border Collie	< 5%	Mixed Breed	5%
Collie	70%	Old English Sheepdog	5%
English Shepherd	15%	Shetland Sheepdog	15%
German Shepherd	10%	Silken Windhound	30%
Herding Breed Cross	10%	Chinook	25%

They also offer the MDR1 Test for a small fee. Well worth the life of your dog.

If your dog is safe from not having the MDR1 gene, you can purchase straight Ivermectin from a feed store and give it monthly at the same dosage. (Check with your vet on dosage). Please watch the dog for the first 12 hours very closely up to 72 hours after the dosage is given. Your dog could have a reaction to it so be prepared if it does. This is uncommon but can happen so always be prepared for an emergency. My dog did and it was a severe reaction and was very close to dying. She doesn't have the MDR1 gene but had some sort of reaction to the drug itself. So then, I put her on the monthly Heartgard without any issues.

**Most feed stores/vet supply houses that carry this can help you with dosage as well.

Have your dog tested every 6 months until she/he is clear and tests are negative. It can take approximately 9-18 months to become negative according to how badly the dog was infected.

It's not unusual for the microfilaria to be seen in the blood for well up to a year after killing the adult heartworms. The microfilaria cannot turn into adult heartworms without being sucked up by a mosquito and going through the 4th stage and being re-injected into a dog. While stepping up the post-treatment with a higher dosage of Heartgard and given every 2 weeks along with using a Heartworm Nosode, in 3 months, the dog should be cleared and test is negative. Just use caution!

** I DO NOT recommend having the injections done (Immiticide treatment) EVER, since this can cause serious with sometimes-deadly reactions. Only under severe cases of heartworm would I recommend surgery AND it may be the only option for removal!

When using the Immiticide injection treatment, the dog needs to be crated for months. Absolutely no activity, no running, playing etc. With the slow kill, they can continue their normal activities just as long as you don't get the heart rate up too much. However they are able to go to the potty off leash and do not have to be crated, as they would have to be when giving the deadly injections unless you have a super hyper dog then the dog would need to be leashed when outdoors. Always keep an eye on the dog right after giving doses for at least 72 hours with the first 12 hours being the most crucial time since reactions are possible with every dog in every case.

There are quite a few natural remedies out there that are much better. All of these have a 75% or higher success rate. You can try them and if they still don't kill out the worms, slow kill (Heartgard and Doxy) is your best way to go. Once you have completed the treatment, your dog will highly benefit from supplements recommended for heart disease. Definitely add in probiotics if using Doxycycline as all the good bacteria has been destroyed as well and will need to be replenished. You may give these while your dog is on Doxycycline.

Natural Remedies to Prevent Heartworm
There is a homeopathic nosode that is made from heartworm larvae that is used commonly by holistic veterinarians as a preventive to avoid the drug side effects. However, many question its effectiveness, though some people who use the nosode (apparently successfully) with animals

in heartworm endemic areas. I use this for my 5 dogs and all have remained heartworm negative.

Dosing for the nosode is as follows: 30C potency given once a week. These can be given to dogs that are heartworm positive in a higher dose.

As I had mentioned about using homeopathic remedies earlier in this book, this is one time I overlook the "why I don't use them" and use them. Heartworms are nothing to play around with so give this once a week for preventative using this nosode. You may add (3-5) pellets into a 4-ounce glass bottle using filtered water, shake vigorously until dissolved, and then squirt into your dog's mouth one full syringe. Store in frig for 2 weeks. You can also put pellets directly into the mouth to dissolve or add into foods. Don't touch the pellets with your hands.

Warning: *Doxycycline is a very powerful antibiotic and must be given with food. Doxycycline can cause severe diarrhea (blood also) and vomiting even after first dose. If this happens, stop Doxycycline and call vet immediately. It has caused death under these circumstances. Do not give to ill dogs or weakened immune systems. Give probiotics and digestive enzymes when using Doxycycline.*

See *HolisticAndOrganixPetShoppe.com* for more information on all-natural treatment and remedies and links to the products.

For use of the homeopathic heartworm nosode for **prevention**:
- 3 pellets for small dogs a week
- 4 pellets for medium dogs a week
- 5 pellets for large dogs a week

For treatment:
- 3 pellets for small dogs 2 - 4 times a day
- 4 pellets for medium dogs 2 - 4 times a day
- 5 pellets for large dogs 2 - 4 times a day

Don't forget; have your dog tested every 6 months until all negative results.

There are many all natural treatments and preventions out there so go to my website for an up-to-date list of all your options. Just please avoid those injections pushed by vets that are truly very dangerous and toxic if your dog ever becomes heartworm positive. The odds of a raw fed healthy dog becoming heartworm positive are next to nonexistent. Mosquito's feed on weakened immune systems. Keep your dogs healthy and strong by following this book of recommendations.

Herbs for killing heartworms but use under the guidance of a Holistic Vet only:

- Parsley
- Wormwood
- Black Walnut Hull
- Hops
- Grapefruit Seed Extract
- Sorrel
- Cloves
- Neem
- Garlic

Petwellbeing.com has a formula that is made without the Black Walnut and Wormwood. Contact them on the precautions. May be safer to use but anytime a dog has heartworms, you should closely monitor your dog for the first 12-72 hours after dosing with anything. Stay on the side of caution but this is fairly simple to remedy your dog using natural products without using toxic chemicals or medications. You can even speak with the makers of these herbal mixes and they can guide you and will be happy to do so. They probably won't claim that it kills heartworms but used in prevention of. Same thing. Ha!

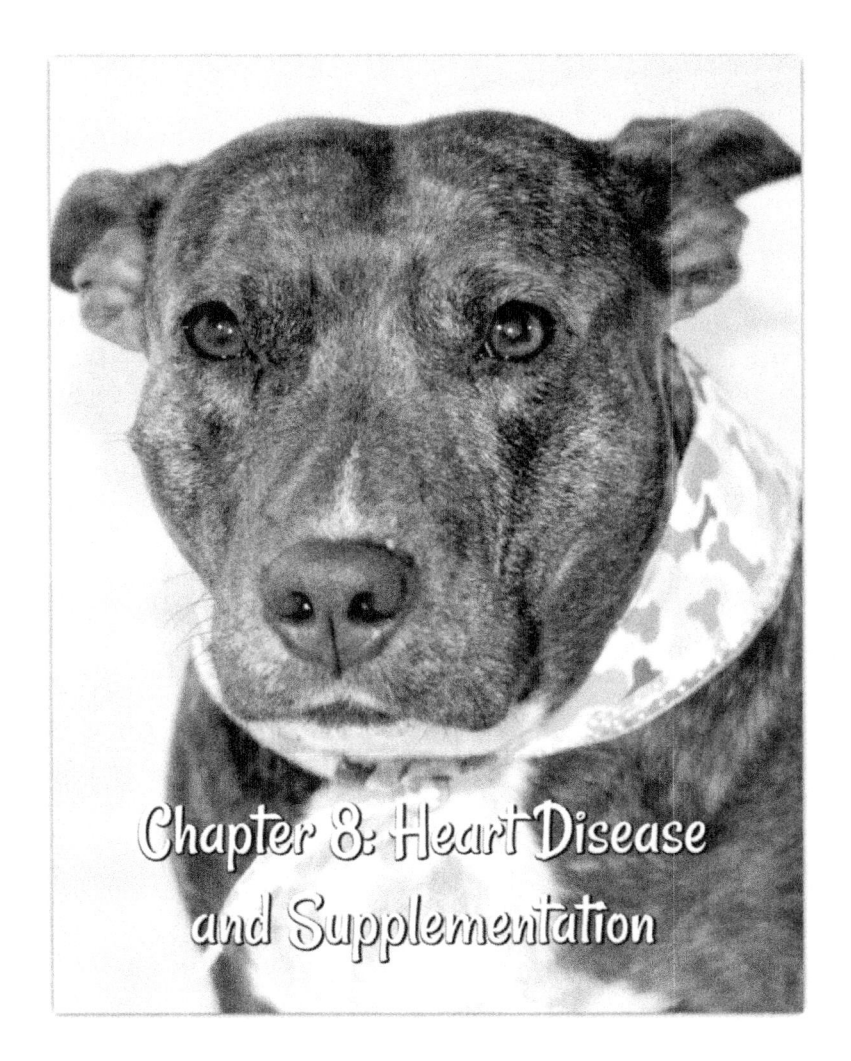

Chapter 8
Heart Disease and Supplementation

If your dog is getting into his/her senior years or has had heartworms now or in the past, you need to read this chapter so you will know how to help prevent heart disease in your dog.
If you wait too long and your dog shows signs of heart disease like lethargy, wheezing, coughing or has a hard time walking or running, it's often too late to save your beloved dog for living a longer life, but with supplements you can help extend his/her life and help them to be

comfortable throughout their lasting years and possibly extend their life further.

If your vet suspects heart disease, he/she will usually want x-rays, EKG or cardiac ultrasound. Many times he/she will find the heart enlarged, possibly fluid in the lungs. Your vet will also listen with a stethoscope for missed or skipped heartbeats causing a heart murmur.

Some breeds are predisposed to heart conditions, including New Foundlands, Cavalier King Charles Spaniel, Great Danes, and Dobermans. But no dog is excluded. Much depends on the breeding line, the diet, and overall care of the dog. Dogs with heart disease will be lacking sufficient nutrients. Many dogs on kibble will come down with heart disease as well.

Heart murmurs are ranked on a scale from 1 to 6, where 1 is considered mild and 6 is the worst case.

These symptoms are what to look for in heart disease:

- Abdominal distention
- Exercise intolerance
- Lethargy/weakness
- Coughing/Gagging
- Breathing difficulty
- Excessive panting
- Bluish skin/gums
- Sleeping more
- Loss of appetite
- Rapid weight loss

There is a blood test for early detection in heart disease. It's called the ProBNP test. (B-type Natriuretic Peptide) This test measures the peptide hormone that the heart releases. This only shows up when the heart is under pressure or working harder than it should be. This test can prepare you for the future to help your dog's heart function better and last longer without causing more stress. You can have this done at any age but in larger breeds, I would start around 4-5 years of age and check it either yearly or every other year depending on dog, but can be done as often as necessary.

Normal numbers range: <900pmol/l.
Moderate: 900 to 1800 pmol/l - Possible disease - Consider other tests such as x-rays or ECG.
Severe: >1800 pmol/l - heart failure is high, exercise intolerance, breathing difficulty.

Probiotics and Digestive enzymes are important. The goal here is to make the immune system strong and rebuild/repair muscles, liver etc. If you have a healthy gut, you will have a healthier body. Diet plays an extremely important roll. A homemade diet (raw preferably) is your best diet. **Do not feed commercial pet foods. Homemade only but make sure you have all the correct supplements for a homemade diet.** Do not feed anything with salt in dogs with heart disease. Provide fresh filtered multi-stage chlorine and fluoride-free water at all times.

If your dog is on medications, add milk thistle to the diet to help filter the liver. You can give milk thistle for five days and then off for two days weekly. After 1-3 months stop milk thistle for at least 30 days then you can give again. This is not an herb to be given daily and permanently. Normally 30 days is the recommended time to give.

If your pet is suffering from a heart condition, you may want to try these vitamins and herbs. It has been documented that these have shown improvement in heart conditions, and even eliminating medications or stopping them altogether.

For **prevention** of heart disease, you can give these supplements (several or all):

- Ubiquinol/COQ10
- L-Arginine
- Organic Hawthorn powder (or Ajuna)
- Taurine (try to find one not sourced from China because most are and/or feed raw heart meat)
- Propionyl-L-Carnitine /L-Carnitine
- Fulvic/Humic Acid (natural minerals, amino acids and some B vitamins)
- Organic Astragalus powder

- D-Ribose
- Astaxanthin
- Magnesium Orotate or Magnesium Taurate (contains Taurine)

I myself had a dog suffering from a heart murmur and with these supplements; I was able to stop all coughing and stopped all medications. Give it a few weeks to see if coughing subsides. Another dog with more severe symptoms was treated using all of these below and the coughing was cut in half but continued medications daily as well. Without the supplements, the coughing stayed the same even on medication.

This is a list of supplements that will work for heart disease if your dog has already been **diagnosed**:

- Ubiquinol/COQ10 (highly recommended)
- Pycnogenol or Pine Bark Extract
- L-Arginine
- Organic Hawthorn (or Arjuna) powder
- Taurine (try to find one not sourced from China because most are and/or feed raw heart meat)
- L-Carnitine
- D-Ribose (highly recommended)
- Magnesium Orotate or Magnesium Taurate
- Vitamin C (ester C-Magnesium Ascorbate) or better yet - Camu Camu or Rosehips)
- Vitamin E (soy free)
- Fish Oil (sardine/anchovy or squid)
- Organic Turmeric
- Organic Dandelion Leaf (diuretic)
- Fulvic/Humic Acid
- Astaxanthin
- Boswellia/Frankincense

Other Herbs for the heart:
Motherwort (Leonurus cardiaca)
Fo-ti root (Polygonum multiflorum)

Kudzu (Pueraria spp)
Bugleweed (expectorant and diuretic) not for use in hypothyroidism.

These are best when split into at least 2 doses per day. Do not throw all of these into one meal and not expect reactions. In other words, add two supplements into wet foods daily for 7-14 days, if no reaction (diarrhea, vomiting) then add 2-3 more into diet, give for 7-14 days then add a couple more and so on. Work up to getting all of these in the diet. It's a lot I know but, do this and see what happens. If your dog isn't better within 4-6 weeks, you can choose to cut back on them. But I would continue use as long as your dog is alive. You may cut back after 6 months to half a dose on some or even stop a few.

Ubiquinol/COQ10
Ubiquinol is better but COQ10 is acceptable as well.

Ubiquinol Dosage:
Small dogs: 50mg per day
Medium dogs: 100mg per day
Large dogs: 100mg twice per day
Giant dogs: 100 - 200mg twice per day

COQ10 Dosage:
Small dogs: 100 - 200mg daily
Medium dogs: 200 - 300mg daily
Large dogs: 300 - 400mg daily
Giant dogs: 400 - 500mg daily

Pycnogenol or Pine Bark Extract
Dosage: 1 - 2 mg per lb of body weight.

L-Arginine
Dosage:
Small dogs: 250mg
Medium dogs: 500mg
Large dogs: 750mg
Giant dogs: 1000mg

*Higher amounts of L-Arginine in some rare cases can cause diarrhea. Do **not** use with myocardial infarction.*

Selenium (Methylselenocysteine or Se-Methylselenocysteine):
Research notes show that breast cancer rates were low in areas where selenium levels in the soil and food were high. The same correlation was found between death rates and selenium levels. Similar correlations were subsequently found in animal studies.

Methylselenocysteine does not accumulate in the body and is considered to be non-toxic. The symptoms of selenium deficiency include hypothyroidism, a weakened immune system, and heart disease. Severe deficiency of the essential trace element selenium can cause myocardial dysfunction.

Dosage:
Small dogs: up to 10mcg
Medium dogs: up to 25mcg
Large dogs: up to 50mcg

Do not go over this dosage.

Astaxanthin
Astaxanthin is a very powerful antioxidant and it is 800 times stronger than COQ10. Astaxanthin can play a crucial role in helping your dog's heart function properly. Wild caught Salmon also contains Astaxanthin. Astaxanthin is also 65 times more powerful than vitamin C. Dogs and humans do not make Astaxanthin themselves so we must get it from other sources. When purchasing a supplement, make sure it is created from marine microalgae and not fungus. Look for oils and not powders. This may make your dogs poop a reddish orange color.

Dosage:
1- 2mg per 20 lbs or follow directions if in a pet supplement form.

I like to use human supplements a lot, as I don't trust many pet products plus they seem to be more expensive. That's my personal opinion. I am selective on what I like to purchase for my dogs. Astaxanthin is a very safe supplement to give so there is no known toxic effects.

Organic Hawthorn Berry powder
Dosage:
Small dogs: 1/4 tsp
Medium dogs: 3/4 tsp
Large dogs: 1 tsp
Giant dogs: 1 1/2 tsp

Taurine (Also good for Epilepsy. Helps heart muscle to contract.)
Taurine is best given on an empty stomach. Note that Taurine is abundant in raw meat, particularly heart, but much is lost when the meat is cooked. You may want to add some meat and canned fish with bones (low sodium sardines, jack mackerel, pink salmon-*wild caught*) to the diet if your dog suffers from heart disease. Cooking reduces Taurine, so feed raw or cook lightly. Canned fish is high in sodium, so rinse before feeding or look for low sodium fish. Vitamin B-6 is needed for the conversion of Taurine, so adding a B-complex vitamin supplement (better than supplementing B-6 alone) is also a good idea. B vitamins work together as a team the best.
Lamb and rice diets may contribute to Taurine deficiency, either due to the effect of rice or a lower availability of Taurine in lamb.

Dosage:
Small dogs: 250mg
Medium dogs: 500mg
Large dogs: 750mg

L-Carnitine (Angina, Heart Attack, Heart Failure)
Dosage:
Small dogs: 250mg
Medium dogs: 500mg
Large dogs: 750mg
Giant dogs: 1000mg

*Higher amounts of L-Carnitine in rare cases can cause vomiting, diarrhea, loss of appetite. It is always good to have a watchful eye when giving supplements to your pets.

D-Ribose
Supplementing with D-ribose can improve heart function following damage to the heart muscle. It helps the heart muscle manage energy, offering a solution to the slow-motion cardiac energy crisis that is heart failure. D-ribose improves blood flow and the exchange of oxygen and CO_2.

Dosage:
Small dogs: 500mg
Medium dogs: 1000mg
Large dogs: 1500mg
Giant dogs: 2000mg

Can cause some side effects including diarrhea, stomach discomfort, nausea, and low blood sugar. Stop taking ribose at least 2 weeks before surgery.

Magnesium Orotate/Magnesium Taurate
Dosage:
Small dogs: 10mg - 20mg
Medium dogs: 20mg - 50mg
Large dogs: 50mg - 100mg
Giant dogs: 75mg - 150mg
Or when using powder 1/8 teaspoon up to 1/2 teaspoon depending on size of dog.

Astragalus *(Astragalus membranaceous)*
Immunostimulant, antiviral, anti-inflammatory, hypothyroid (mildly depresses thyroid function), hypotensive, digestive tonic. Works on immune systems, lungs, liver, **heart**, kidneys, thyroid, and digestive tract. Astragalus is used for strengthening the body against viral infections of the respiratory and heart. Astragalus can be used for early treatment of a variety of respiratory infections, including kennel cough (Bordetella bronchiseptica). Astragalus helps to raise white blood cell counts and also boosts the body's immune system. Astragalus may be useful for helping the body protect itself and speed recovery from the damages of long-term steroid medications. Astragalus is also useful in early stages of kidney infection and/or renal failure. Astragalus is non-toxic in any dosages. Buy organic.

Powder
Dosage:
Small dogs: 1/4 tsp
Medium dogs: 3/4 tsp
Large dogs: 1 tsp
Giant dogs: 1 1/2 tsp

Vitamin C - (Buffered/Ester C-*Magnesium Ascorbate*) or Camu Camu or Rosehips)
Dosage:
Adjust accordingly but a good place to start or work towards.
Small dogs: 500mg - 1500mg
Medium/Large dogs: 1000mg - 3000mg
Giant dogs: 2000mg - 4000mg

Powder
Dosage:
Small dogs: 1/4 tsp
Medium dogs: 3/4 tsp
Large dogs: 1 tsp
Giant dogs: 1 1/2 tsp

Vitamin E (soy free):
Dosage (three times a week):
Small dogs: 200IU
Medium dogs: 300IU
Large dogs: 400IU
Giant dogs: 600IU

Fish Oil (Sardine/Anchovy or Squid)
Dosage:
Small dogs: 500 - 750mg
Medium dogs: 1000 - 1250mg
Large dogs: 1500 - 1750mg
Giant dogs: 2000 - 2250mg

Organic Turmeric
This herb is strong flavored and smells with a bright orange color. And it even will stain garments. May cause stomach upset for sensitive

tummies. Terrific for all ailments and diseases except kidney stones. It is important to note that turmeric is a binding agent and a good remedy for diarrhea as well. It can cause constipation as well as dehydration so be sure your dog drinks plenty of water when using it. Turmeric works for most all illness including, joints, heart, cancer etc. It's a great additive for most any ailment and for preventing future illness.

Dosage:
Small dogs: 250mg
Medium dogs: 350mg
Large dogs: 500mg
Giant dogs: 750mg
This can be adjusted up or down.

Powder
Dosage:
Small dogs: 1/4 tsp
Medium dogs: 3/4 tsp
Large dogs: 1 tsp
Giant dogs: 1 1/2 tsp

You can purchase capsules and slide into foods if possible or buy smaller (size 0) empty capsules and fill them yourself. Standard capsules are size 00. They go as small as size 4. You can buy them on Amazon, eBay etc.

*Turmeric should not be given to dogs prone to kidney stones. Turmeric isn't supposed to be given with blood thinners. Turmeric should not be combined with drugs that reduce stomach acid (Pepsid, Zantac etc), as the body will actually increase its production of stomach acid, and thus, lead to nausea, stomach pain, bloating, and esophagus damage.

Organic Dandelion Leaf Powder (Taraxacum officinale) (*Diuretic*):
Dandelion has been used for digestive and liver (root); Pancreatitis, edema (leaf), Anemia, Kidney/Bladder. The leaf and root are good for many conditions involving edema (water retention) and the flowers are

high in antioxidants. You can use root and leaf together and most of all for liver, kidney, and heart disease in dogs.

Dandelion should not be used in cases of bile duct obstruction or acute gallbladder inflammation. The high mineral content may affect the absorption of a certain class of antibiotics (quinolones). Dandelion leaf is particularly useful in animals that have a chronic problem with indigestion. If your dog has frequent gas and/or passes food that does not appear digested, apply a few drops of dandelion tincture on his/her tongue.

Dandelion Leaf is popular and is a safe but powerful diuretic and liver stimulant. Dandelion works with congestive heart failure, pulmonary edema, arthritis, gallbladder disease, and kidney stones. Drugs such as Lasix are often used to drain off excess fluid from the body and help the elimination of waste. Pharmaceutical diuretics are fast acting and very effective, but while they do a good job at reducing fluid buildup, they tend not to discriminate between what the body needs to keep and what it needs to lose. The body often loses too much potassium, a crucial heart and brain chemical, through urination. In this case, potassium must be supplemented throughout the therapy. Dandelion leaf on the other hand, contains its own rich source of potassium that the body can absorb.

While dandelion leaves are used as a diuretic, the root holds its own usefulness as a safe liver tonic. The liver is the primary filtering organ and responsible for removing toxins from the blood for elimination in the kidneys. And while dandelion leaf tea or tincture may do much toward relieving the symptoms through a nutritive/diuretic action, the root will work closer to the underlying causes.

Dandelion does not further irritate an already inflamed condition. Dandelion root was shown to be effective in treating inflammatory diseases of the liver and the gall bladder including gallstones.

Dandelion helps reduce fluid in the lungs and around heart. It's a natural diuretic and helps to restore potassium levels lost while taking medications.

Dosage:
Capsules-up to 250mg a day

Powder
Dosage:
Small dogs: 1/4 tsp
Medium dogs: 3/4 tsp
Large dogs: 1 tsp
Giant dogs: 1 1/2 tsp

Note on the differences between the root and leaf
Dandelion <u>Root</u> is used mostly for liver, gallbladder, and better digestion. Aids in destroying cancer cells. A research study done in Ireland showed that dandelion root was especially effective against certain strains of bacteria that are responsible for staph infections and food-borne illnesses. High in vitamin K.

NOTE*: *May* affect the absorption of a class of antibiotics (quinolones).*

Fulvic/Humic Acid
Many pet parents wonder if their pets will be getting "too many minerals" if they are giving other products that also contain minerals such as a Calcium supplement. The answer is no because Fulvic is extracted from plant material – not rocks or clay. It is impossible for plant-derived minerals to build up in the tissues. Depending on the severity of health issues, you can give higher amounts. Fulvic/Humic Acid detoxifies the body of heavy metals, toxins, and pollutants, increases oxygen absorption in blood, enhances healing, repair, and rejuvenation of the cells - energizes cells, repairs and detoxifies the thyroid.

Approximate Dosing:
Small dogs: 1 teaspoon
Medium dogs: 2 teaspoons
Large dogs: 1 TBSP

Collagen:
Collagen makes up 30% of the entire body in dogs. Collagen works on nails, coat, joints, and digestive tract to name a few. Most collagen supplements contain amino acids, what most bodies are lacking, especially in older pets. Collagen comes in many types including Type I, II, III and so on. Type II is specific for joints and I and III are specific to skin, hair, nails. Overall Collagen promotes healthy systems in all areas. The amino acid Glycine targets cancer cells as well as the digestive system. Some types of collagen comes from fish. I tend to steer away from fish due to any chances of mercury contamination. Collagen peptide is another term for hydrolyzed collagen. If purchasing human products, start with a low dose and work up in dosing over a few weeks time. Normally human dosing is based off of a 150-160 lb human. Adjust accordingly. Not all Collagens are created equal. Collagen is a tasteless and odorless powder, so it is easy to use and mix into wet foods. At this time, I found the brand Forest Leaf to be superior in its ingredients and contains 18 amino acids including Glycine. There are 9 essential amino acids: histidine, isoleucine, leucine, lysine, methionine, phenylalanine, threonine, tryptophan, and valine. And 20 amino acids in total. This particular brand contains 8 of those 9 essential amino acids. Tryptophan is not in it. I found this common in many of them. Amino acids play a key role in our health as well as our pets. The body cannot make amino acids so they must come from the diet. Buckwheat is a plant-based food that contains all nine essential amino acids. Protein sources are meat, poultry, eggs, dairy and seafood contain all 9 essential amino acids as well.

Approximate Dosage:
Small dogs: 1/8 scoop
Medium dogs: 1/4 scoop
Large dogs: 1/2 scoop (1 TBSP)

Start with lower amounts and work up to the recommended dose with time as this can cause some loose stools, diarrhea, or digestive upset.

These dosages can be adjusted according to the results you may or may not be getting. It takes a little time to begin to see results.

The brand mentioned contains 18 amino acids including Glycine (for cancer) at 2330 mg. per scoop. This product is low in sodium. Some of the other brand of collagens contain higher amounts.

Boswellia (also called Frankincense):
Boswellia has also been shown in preliminary research to be effective at reducing swelling around brain tumors. A study performed in 2004 shows that Boswellia is an herb that lives up to its reputation. Twenty-four dogs with chronic joint pain were administered a dose of Boswellia once a week for 6 weeks. After just a couple weeks, 71% of the dogs showed improvement. The research showed that improvement was gradual but Boswellia did seem to help reduce local pain and stiff gaits. Boswellia is considered an anti-inflammatory herb. Boswellia is one herb that seems to work well. Helps coughing and asthma along with inflammation.

Dosage-Powder:
Small dogs: 1/4 tsp
Medium dogs: 3/4 tsp
Large dogs: 1 tsp
Giant dogs: 1 1/2 tsp

Potassium may be needed:
Potassium needs may be increased, if you are giving digoxin or diuretics, or decreased if you are treating with ACE inhibitors such as Enalapril, or with spironolactone. Monitor blood potassium levels and make adjustments as needed. Check with your vet before adding any potassium supplements. If you feed a raw diet or are giving Dandelion Leaf, it is probably not needed.

Note that many prescription cardiac diets are high in potassium, which may be inappropriate depending on the medications being used. Some prescription diets are also low in protein, which is always inappropriate for dogs with heart disease. If you are feeding a prescription diet for heart disease, you can improve the quality of the diet by switching to high-protein animal-source foods such as meat, eggs and some dairy (raw goats milk, Kefir), but be careful not to add foods that are high in sodium. For example: Look for low sodium sardines in water. Avoid salmon, as it is high in sodium. Note that prescription diets are **<u>not</u>**

recommended. This can be maintained by a homemade diet (raw or cooked) best. (See Chapter 3)

While this seems like a TON of supplements, **it is**. But these are all known to help the heart. It is **not** recommended to use only one or two. Pick at least 5-8 of these and use them daily for moderate - severe cases. Combinations work much better than single ingredients. You can skip a day or two weekly for the system to have a break. Usually for the first 2-4 weeks, don't skip unless an issue arises. Like I mentioned, I have used them all at one time and had really good results. Start out with a couple for about 5-7 days and in lower amounts, if no loose stools or diarrhea, vomiting or loss of appetite, work up to full dose then add two more into the daily diet. Sometimes you may not see diarrhea until the second week so be aware. If all goes well, in 5-7 days, add in two more. Work your way up to all of the ones you plan on adding. Never throw all of them in at one time on the first day with a full dose and not expect something to happen. You may obtain cannon butt (diarrhea) if you do. Poop always plays a crucial role in knowing where your dog is at in his diet, or anything going into the body.

Vitamin C (all ascorbates) will cause diarrhea or loose stools in higher doses. Just back off of the amount you gave until no more diarrhea or give Camu Camu for all natural. Give 100% organic pumpkin to help with the symptoms of diarrhea or loose stools along with Slippery Elm. Organic diets for a diseased heart will help improve your dog's health overall as well.

Chapter 9
Storm Anxiety

Dogs suffer from anxiety caused by different things - loud noise, fireworks, strangers, children, being alone, car rides, and storms to name a few.

It is important to remember that behavior is transferable from one dog to another. If I had encouraged unbalanced behavior of who behaved in an unbalanced way, the behavior of the other dogs would have become unstable also. **It is also transferable from human to dog.** Dogs read our body language and sense tension in your voice. They know how you are feeling and sense your stress.

Some dogs can sense an earthquake minutes before we feel any sign ourselves. A dog's sensitivity to environmental changes (barometric pressure changes, noise, vibrations, visual, electrical energy etc.) varies from one dog to another. Some dogs can find environmental changes bothersome or even painful.

If your dog normally paces or runs around feeling anxious, stop your dog right away! One of the worst things to do is to allow a dog to run around or pace. At this point, the dog is driven by fear and does not know where to go or what to do to feel safe. It is really important (once again) that the dog's pet parent takes the leadership role and shows the dog what it should do. If your dog is crate trained, put him/her in their crate. They want guidance at that time - crating them tells them were to be and provides them with a safe haven. Don't baby talk, pat them or worry. Just treat them as normal. Cover the crate for adding a layer of security for them.

Some phobic dogs will seek out dark, quiet corners on their own where they can calm themselves, so consider providing a dark room, a closet, or space under a table or desk for a frightened pet. The goal is to provide your dog a secure spot that helps calm him/herself. Most dogs will find this spot every time fear strikes. Let them stay there and provide them with one of your pieces of clothing for security.

Don't feel stressed or tension within yourself. Your dog will sense this and it will increase his/her emotions. This is all about changing your dog's connection with thunderstorms and your bad habits of supporting and enabling psychological trauma with emotion. Keep the pitch of your voice low and calm as well.

Most dogs that are suffering from social anxiety have this behavioral problem because they have not been properly trained to socialize with other pups and humans.

To desensitize your dog from having "panic attacks" around other dogs or people, for example, slowly introduce a dog (preferably a calm one) or human to your dog, one at a time. Do not attempt to introduce a lot of dogs and/or people including kids to your dog all at once. You will only scare and stress your dog out! This could cause fear biting. You certainly don't want that to happen. Do this once or twice a week at least to help them adjust to people and other pets. This may take time but continue to reinforce this positive and secure behavior.

You may try soft music for your dog or drown out outside noises with white noise. You may turn on the television for background noise as well. If they are use to falling asleep to the TV and low light setting, then create that environment for them so they can feel normal. Put on something that doesn't have a lot of guns firing or screaming on the TV. A calm documentary or something to keep things monotone. Try playing with your dog to get his/her mind off of what is really going on. This will take his/her mind off what's going on outside and can help calm his/her anxiety as well. It is also helpful if you try to talk to your dog softly and reassuringly when s/he is having an "anxiety attack". Wrapping him up with a towel or blanket (or Thundershirt) helps as well as dogs feel more secure when there is a constant firm feel around their bodies. These techniques require time and patience for it to become effective.

Also, there are Calming Collars. These are made with herbs inside fabric to repel the aroma of calming herbs. Try diffusing Peace and Calming essential oils that contain like Lavender or other calming oils that reduce stress and anxiety. Ylang Ylang is another one. Sometimes they work, sometimes they don't. Same goes for the Thundershirt. But it's certainly worth a try.

There are also herbs you can try. They are to be given orally. A great website is *AldaronEssences.com*. You can even create your own mix of Bach Flowers. 'Rescue Remedy For Pets' is another mix. Bach Flowers are very safe.

Veterinarians are big on handing out medications such as 'Ace' for short, also known as Acepromazine and Chlorpromazine for fearful dogs. These should **not** be given to fearful dogs. EVER! These are used during surgery as well so know what your vet uses and request an alternative. Acepromazine or Ace (Promace ®) and Chlorpromazine are two commonly used phenothiazine tranquilizers in veterinary clinics.

While under the effects of Ace, the animal still has a very strong fear, anxiety, avoidance or arousal response, but it does not physically display these reactions and is less able to react. The dog or cat appears calm and relaxed but mentally is lucid and still having an intense emotional reaction to its surroundings. Ace is a dissociative agent and prevents the patient from understanding his environment in a logical manner. So, the actual fear level of the animal is increased. Compounding the situation, the animal is being restrained and it makes a negative association with the entire experience.

According to veterinary behaviorist Dr. Vint Virga, DVM, ACVB, this is one of the reasons, why clinics are seeing so many animals, which have been previously given Ace, continuing to be fearful during veterinary exams. It becomes a never-ending cycle of chemical restraint and continued fear for the pet.

Ace is appropriate as a tranquilizer for the happy, jubilant, bouncy dog that has **no** anxiety, stress, or fear.

Note: Ace should never be used as a tranquilizer for animals traveling due to the erratic thermoregulation effects (inability to control body temperature in cold or hot conditions).

Ace, used to sedate fearful animals, is no longer appropriate. Its use should be discontinued.

FDA has recently approved a new drug called **Pexion** for anxiety in dogs. AVOID this medication. It is dangerous and has high-risk side effects such as ataxia (difficulty standing and walking), increased appetite, lethargy, and vomiting. Also 3 out of 90 of dogs became aggressive, including growling towards a young child and lack of restraint or self-control towards other dogs after being given this medication.

I don't know about you but I am not willing to take that chance in my home. Not worth it. This is why avoiding these types of medications is much safer and use natural products instead. Always research medications before giving. Remember this, with most all medications, ONLY short term studies have been done as well with no long-term side effects known.

One more "don't": Whatever you do, don't lock your dog in a room or area they can escape from. Dogs have been known to get out of homes and garages, destroy crates, and break leashes and collars to escape when terrified by storms and fireworks.

CBD oil or Cannabis oil:
Cannabis oil or CBD oil is legal in all states. This CBD/hemp oil contains less than .03 percent THC and it is considered legal under this amount in ALL STATES. I have personally been using this on my fearful dog and it has actually helped her to relax more. It doesn't take away her fears but it helps reduce the anxiety that comes with it and she rests better at night also. She isn't so restless. When purchasing CBD oil, human supplements work just as well. In fact, there have been some reports that the pet CBD oils may or may not contain any CBD oil so therefore will probably not work so well. It is hard to know without being tested. So thoroughly check out your sources and don't go by just hearsay. Pet products are also much higher in price I have noticed. Look for Full Spectrum (uses all parts of the plant) products for best results.

I like to buy organic CBD oil for humans for my dog. I found when searching for one, that the milligrams in them are very confusing. You have sizes that show milligrams and you have amounts that show milligrams. To keep it simple, I purchased a one ounce bottle...at 300mg. Now where it gets even trickier is how much on dosing amounts. No one can really say how much. They may or may not give you dosing amounts. Most of it is guesswork. Read the label as it may tell you something like CBD extract 31 mg per recommended dose. So I started with 5-6 drops. Then I decided to increase the amount since I wasn't seeing any changes. So I increased it to 10 drops. Now this is for a 60-70lb dog. I still didn't feel like I was seeing any changes so I decided what the heck, I will try a dropper full. That's when I noticed that she was not so restless and was sleeping much better. This was also given over a period of 30 days. Sometimes it takes awhile to start working. It has also helped her when she gets out of the home for trips or walks. She's very fearful of strangers and/or strange places so this helps her to handle it slightly better. I also think once you get it built up in their system, less is needed per day. This is all about playing around with the amounts. Start low and work your way up until you see some sort of results. Give it 1-2 months to start working. Sometimes you may get instant results but don't expect it.

Other things you can try:

- Soundproofing a crate or room
- Play calming (classical or high frequency) music or white noise
- Ashwagandha daily supplement. (used for depression, anxiety etc)
- Skullcap
- Chamomile (nervine herb-used for calming)
- L-Theanine (supplement that may help calm your dog)
- Essential oils such as Lavender, Peace & Calming or Ylang Ylang can be used for aromatherapy.
- Relora (Magnolia (Magnolia officinalis) and Phellodendron (Phellodendron amurense) barks.

I have tried all the above and I had the best results with Relora and CBD oil. Relora will make them sleepy but they are still alert if need be. Whatever you do, don't give up on trying to calm your dog. Each dog is different so it will take you finding the right solution. I hope these things will work for you. You can even combine some of these. Good Luck!

Tip: *For female dogs who exhibit signs of agitation (sometimes to the point of panic), generalized anxiety, fear of new people, other dogs or new situations, they may be deficient in estrogen as well as progesterone. Have your vet check for these things.*

Chapter 10
Cancer - Prevention, Treatment, and Diet

Being told that your dog has cancer is of course heart breaking. But don't take this as a death sentence and give up! Be proactive. Make it your mission to find out as much as you can about your dog's condition, the treatments available, and what you can do yourself to help rid this horrifying disease from your dog. Some call it a fungus.

I like to think of it as inflammation or infection. You may realize that there are more options than you think. Have faith and believe you can beat this. There is so much information on cancer; it will be impossible for me to even get close to the tip of the iceberg to cover all the great things you can do to fight this. But these are some of the most common things you can try at home along with or without conventional treatments.

I truly don't recommend chemo or radiation of any kind. Why? Because radiation and chemo are what comes from 2-4-D (Agent Orange) and mustard gas. Yeah, read that again. It's true. Scary thought there. I have also discovered that these treatments are the number one money making treatment in all of health care. Even though we have natural cures out there, the FDA and many other government agencies are not allowing these. Why? Because there is too much money to be made off of people and they don't care if we die anyway. Their goal is to reduce the population. Yes, they are doing that too, I am not kidding and I wished I was. I learned this straight from scientists, whistle blowers, and doctors. You would be shocked at what I have learned about our food, water, vaccines, and medications. You can learn this too by just watching videos, seminars of Drs and many that do care about human life. So you really honestly do not want to use these chemicals to try to destroy the cancer. Even cutting into a cancer cell may also allow it to spread throughout the body. So, always consider this before ever considering surgery. Weigh your options if it is critical and hindering the dogs life traumatically at the time to cut it out. Have your dr/vet guarantee you in writing that your dog will be cured from cancer using this type of treatment. I get worked up when I think about what's being done. It's truly horrific.

Cancer is one of the top killers in people and pets. Look at the latest numbers. The latest annual report provides the estimated numbers of new cancer cases and deaths in 2016, as well as current cancer incidence, mortality, and survival statistics and information on cancer symptoms, risk factors, early detection, and treatment. In 2016, there were approximately 1,685,210 diagnosed with cancer and 595,690 cancer deaths in the US. One out of two dogs will get cancer. That's extremely high numbers and a sad reality, unless we make changes today. Reduce the odds. Don't let your dog or you, be another statistic.

Conventional cancer treatments using chemotherapy and radiation may be effective in getting rid of or reducing cancerous tumors, but these treatments destroy the immune system as well and many times these treatments end up killing the dog or person instead of the cancer itself. Chemo and radiation can create secondary tumors that occur within 3-5 years. It causes cancer! So make sure you decide on the correct treatment. And if you are really struggling with this decision, you can try the alternative treatments for a while, also build the immune system and see it is working. Trust me; they will help in some form or fashion. If you choose conventional treatments, just know this will destroy the immune system leaving it vulnerable to fight disease and will make your dog much sicker. Even biopsies and surgeries can end up spreading the cancer further by releasing the cancer cells throughout when these cells are cut into or disturbed in any way. They need to stay contained. So only do these if you must. Many pets and people have lived many years with a tumor that has not grown or spread by using holistic modalities. When using herbs and supplements and making changes in your environment and diet, you can extend the life of your dog even if cancer is not cured and even if you choose to do conventional chemo or radiation. Supplements will always help. It will extend your dog's life without using harsh chemicals that will end up killing your dog sooner than you would with using natural treatments. And your dog will feel better and look and act more normal up until the very end.

In the meantime, you need to build the immune system the entire treatment time and keep the body's immune system strong throughout the rest of your dog's life. Do not get in a big hurry to make a decision on doing chemo or radiation treatments. Most all drs/vets will try to rush you into treatment immediately. This is a scare tactic used to hurry and get your money before you change your mind and find other alternative options. Cancer didn't get there overnight. It took a long time to grow, so there is no hurry to run out tomorrow and fix it, so to speak. Make a plan. Any plan is never set in stone and there are many options that can be done in conjunction with. So no ONE decision is the correct one. There are only a select few of aggressive growing cancers (ex: Chondrosarcoma, Hemangiocarcinoma etc.) where immediate intervention is needed. Speak with the Oncologist on which cancer your dog has. But take a few days no matter what the diagnosis is just to get your mind right after the initial diagnosis before making a decision. Consider all your options. And remember, there is a very high probability that conventional treatments will cause secondary cancers within 3-5 years of treatment.

If you find a lump under your dog's skin, it is important to ask a vet to check the lump to see if it is a benign fatty tumor, or something malignant. Never assume that any growth under the skin is just a fatty tumor. There are cancerous tumors such as mast cell tumors that mimic fatty tumors and only tests such as a fine needle aspirate or biopsy can give a correct diagnosis.

It is known that certain purebred dogs also have a common inherited tendency for cancer. Cancer prone breeds include Golden Retrievers, Labradors, Bernese Mountain Dogs, Boxers, Cocker Spaniels, Rottweiler's, and Beagles.

Spaying or neutering at an early age (before 18 months) has been known to cause cancer (conventional vets with argue this but holistic vets are speaking out on this) along with commercial pet foods. All pet foods break down into at least 50% of pure sugar. Also, these pet foods have been sprayed with grease or fats that become rancid and in which cause cancer as well.

Now first, let's revert back to the diet. You MUST change this if you have been feeding anything other than organic or grass-fed diets. Kibble and canned pet foods do not count. You cannot feed these if your dog has cancer. You MUST clean the entire body of toxins inside and out.

Homemade Diet for Cancer
If your dog has been diagnosed with cancer, an intermittent or pulsed fasting can/should be done. You will feed meals within 6-8 hours *(pulsed)*, and then fast until the next day at the same time each day. This helps the body to go into ketosis. You can also fast your dog several times a week. Calorie restriction is important.

As for cooking the food, dogs **cannot digest, cooked animal fats** like humans can. This can also increase the risk of pancreatitis. Keeping fats and proteins raw is feeding a species appreciate diet as they would in the wild. Some people worry about feeding raw diets with dogs with cancer. This would be when you should seek the advice of a holistic vet or Oncologist that knows about raw diets or the Ketopet Sanctuary for more information. But overall, raw diets are usually always acceptable. If your dog is getting chemo or radiation treatments, you may want to try cooking the meat for awhile. Just remove any fat and don't feed cooked bones.

Once you have a diagnosis of cancer or you want to prevent cancer, follow this protocol. Now I want you to know that it is very important to add supplements in at this time. You must do this and not just one supplement will cure your dog. Not the perfect diet will cure him/her either. It is a combination of things. They all need to come together to cure your dog. This will take hard work, time, patience and a few extra dollars in your pocket. Supplements are not cheap (neither is chemo) and you will be using many different ones. But it's cheaper than conventional treatments. So get prepared to do everything different if you haven't had your dog on a homemade diet already. This will be a fast learning course and this book will tell you how.

Despite articles on the internet saying cancer is down, this is simply not true. How many family or friends that you know have passed away or been diagnosed with this horrible disease? One in three people die or get cancer. The numbers are up on our family pets as well. One out of two dogs will get cancer. Every day you hear about a pet being put down or dying from cancer. It's time to be proactive.

Why are we getting cancer at alarming rates? Many reasons and it all revolves around our own government. In the USA, we have the FDA. The very people that are supposed to be protecting us are the ones harming us. They are in cahoots with Big Pharma and Monsanto/Bayer. We have Monsanto and DuPont and others that are adding chemicals to everything, genetically modifying our foods and using pest resistant pesticides that are getting into our soils and our foods and slowly poisoning us. It's been mentioned time and time again about the FDA and what they seem to **not** be doing. Don't trust our government to protect us. It is those very people that are destroying us. Bill Gates (creator of Windows for computers) is pushing vaccines to reduce the population. Hitler used Fluoride to dumb down the human population and make them docile and obey orders (and it's still happening to us today). Watch out for those flu vaccines and alike. You think it stops there? Not even close. So learn, be aware, and always research before giving anything to your pet. You have options so find the one best for you.

Water *(filtered fluoride and chlorine free including pesticides, chemicals etc)*
Many chemicals are in our tap waters. Over 60,000 to be exact. Chemicals and preservatives are also in our medications, vaccines, foods, and the air we breathe. We put it on our lawns and wash our clothes in chemicals. It's overwhelming. Our bodies just cannot protect us from getting sick or diseased from so many chemicals overloading our immune systems. We just don't have a chance to fight so many. So we must reduce these toxins as much as possible. Start with the food and water. You can test your water for chemicals and pesticides by doing a simple water test. But ALWAYS buy one that also filters out fluoride and chlorine. I find so many people with water filters that have not even considered the fluoride. Fluoride is a drug. This stuff is toxic. Both chlorine and fluoride are now considered neurotoxins. Don't take this lightly. Remove all of these chemicals from your home. Make huge changes here. It's critical for everyone. Water is just as important as the food.

Buy organic pasture-fed eggs. You will see egg cartons saying cage free. What does that mean? NOTHING! It means nothing! A chicken is out of a cage but packed into a barn and the chickens still can't flap their wings. They are eating grains like GMO corn. When you eat that chicken or egg, you are getting what they eat going into your body as well. So buy organic pasture-fed eggs. Even if it isn't organic, pasture-fed is better than cage free. Also, when it says in stores that the chicken says "hormone and antibiotic free"; not true! Ask any holistic integrative doctor or holistic vet. You can even find that info on the internet. For example, Sanderson Farms chicken has all over their packaging 100% natural. But yet, go to their website and it says the opposite. They are proud to be using hormones and antibiotics and even say that buyers support this. This couldn't be further from the truth.

What are the people running that company thinking? There is nothing logical in that. Lies, lies, and more lies.

I know this book is for dogs but everything in it also applies to humans. We must be the change. We must protect our bodies and heal them using what God gave us; the plants from our earth. In 2022 they are coming out with a stronger and more deadly pesticide than Round Up. The main ingredient of Round up is Glyphosate. It's on our wheat and most every food out there unless organic. Then you question how much is getting sprayed in the air and falling onto our organic foods. But organic is your best bet no matter what.

When you throw all of these things into one pot (your body and your pet's), you have a recipe for disaster. Cancer is inevitable unless you have a strong healthy immune system. You can choose to stick your head in the sand or better yet, make some changes to help prevent and protect your loved ones and you. I had someone ask for help recently. Their dog has cancer. I explained in a very respectful simple way that she really needed her dog off kibble and on a homemade diet and was going to have to add in supplements and makes some big changes to save her dog. I never heard from her again. This is what makes me sad. It's hard for me to understand that type of person. I would give my left arm for my dogs and do whatever I could to save them if I thought there was even a remote chance.

So for starters, you must change the diet, provide filtered (multi-stage filter) fluoride/chlorine free water along with an Ionizer /Alkalizer, stop all vaccines (titer test instead) and medications (if possible), and remove chemicals and toxins from your home. You should see the inactive ingredients in medications. They are horrible. Food colorings, propylene glycol, maltodextrin, soy, caramel color, and so many other horrible ingredients. For water filters, a reverse osmosis works well but also add on a fluoride filter and mineralizer/alkalizer. RO removes the much needed minerals so you must add these back in as well.

You cannot avoid all chemicals but you can make a huge dent in avoiding many by doing a few things differently especially within the confines of your home and yard. And in by doing this, you can help reduce you and your dog's chances of getting cancer or feeding the cancer.

There are 85,000+ chemicals being used today in this world. There are new ones being invented every day. So start with cleaning out your home, your lawn, your foods, and your water. Throw away the foods that are GMO or processed foods. Things such as boxed foods as well as canned. BPA/BPS is in the lining of cans and in plastic. You want clean foods in your house. Rid your home of chemicals. Store bought bleach, dryer sheets, laundry detergents, sprays such as air fresheners, furniture polish, Windex etc. Don't worry, there are alternatives.

Stock up on vinegar, baking soda and rubbing alcohol and a few nice smelling safe essential oils that's safe to use around all pets. Buy organic and non-chemical laundry detergents. I like the organic brand called FIT laundry detergent but they do make other organic detergents or at least some without chemicals that aren't organic. Try Soap Nuts; Some people swear by these. Use organic dryer balls in dryer. (It's better for your dryer anyway) but if you insist on using dryer sheets, Seventh Generation makes some that I know are safe and work well. Clean your carpets using vinegar and water. Mop using the same or water only or dilute using vinegar. You can make your own homemade window cleaner. I make my own using 1 part rubbing alcohol, 1 part water, and 1 part vinegar. You can even make stain removers for clothes. I use 1 part dishwashing liquid (still contains some chemicals unless you buy chemical free such as Seventh Generation), 2 parts water, and 1 part Hydrogen Peroxide. The internet is full of natural ways of doing things. Again, learn ingredients. If you aren't sure, go to sites like EWG.org and do a search. It will give you an idea. The best thing you can do for your dog and family is learning to read labels. Pay special attention to supplements and medications with the INACTIVE ingredients. That's where you find a lot of the toxic chemicals and/or fillers. I call these JUNK ingredients.

Get your dog off of commercial pet foods of all kinds period. Yes, this is a must! It is at the top of the list of what is causing cancer as well as many other diseases in our pets today. With so many mycotoxins and preservatives, it's inevitable. This applies to human foods as well. (Buy organic, organic, organic).

The best diet you can feed your pets is a homemade raw diet. Veggies can be given in raw juiced/pureed/finely chopped or in a steamed form. Raw form is always better. Steamed is second best. You will need to add in some supplements. Many supplements are sourced from China much of the time, so it's best to try to find vitamins in a natural form. Whole foods like an organic greens powder and/or organic veggies and fruits. If you provide fresh organic raw veggies and fruits to your dog, make sure you puree/juice or finely chop them up. Dogs cannot digest chunks of veggies and some fruits so they need help to get the nutrients needed from them. Fruits are softer and do digest easier so eating small chunks is fine but you can puree these as well. Keep fruits at a minimum. Yes, fruits contain natural sugars but are fine in small amounts. Fruits with lower sugar content are best. As for cooking your dog's food, it removes a lot of nutrients that may be needed and it is harder to digest than raw. You will need to add in supplements no matter how the food is prepared.

I have created a list in this book and on my website for supplements needed to be added to any and all diets. I am always updating them when I find even better things. Remove dairy (with exception of raw or fermented), sugar, carbs (potatoes) of all kinds (no grains of any kind).

Remember, cancer cannot survive in an oxygen enriched blood supply so therefore adding oxygenated supplements and/or foods to the diet are important. Also, look into Hyperbaric Oxygen Chambers. Hyperbaric Oxygen Chambers are really a great tool. They can be expensive ($135 per session) but it will get oxygen into the blood fast and start killing cancer. You may get grief from your vet or therapist that you work with using natural sources but stick to your guns, provide them with only information that they REALLY need unless they are open to natural therapies. But do the hyperbaric chamber if you can add it in. I feel this is a critical therapy in beating cancer. Also, invest in a good HEPA air purifier for your home. Buy several and place in main rooms and where your dog and you sleep or stay in most of the time.

Get rid of the plastic food and water bowls. Make sure you use glass, high quality ceramic or stainless. I use stoneware dinner plates for my dog's raw diet every day.

Dogs are extremely sensitive to EMF (Electro Magnetic Frequency) and Radio frequency waves. That would include cell phones, Wi-Fi, and Smart TV's. Anything you can plug in. That includes your electric toothbrush, computer and more. Unplug these things when not in use and turn off your Wi-Fi as well when not in use. These make people sick and even our pets as they are much more sensitive than us humans. Start turning these things off when not in use and see if you notice any difference. Give it some time to see any changes. It may take awhile but you will reduce exposure to all of these radiation waves.

Do not use fertilizers or weed killers on your lawn. They do however make all organic natural ingredients completely safe for pets and kids. Some may work, some may not. Use Diatomaceous earth (food grade only) for pest control. For insect control, you can try using Borax (laundry) but don't let the dogs eat it. It isn't to be ingested. They also make products that are all-natural for this or mix your own. You can find many recipes on the internet. Remember, learn to read all ingredients. If you don't know them, Google it. Research before you buy or use. I have a huge list of these junk ingredients that are in medications and foods on my websites as well.

After walking dogs in public places, wash off the paws by sticking them in a bowl of water with some raw unfiltered apple cider vinegar or Povidone iodine and water (dark tea colored) added in for a few minutes, then wipe/pat dry.

Do **not** use any topical flea and tick medications. These are deadly and full of toxic chemicals. Use all natural products. Find one that works best for you. A lot of these contain essential oils. Stay away from some of the oils no matter who sells it.

Listed below in the graph are some essential oils to **avoid** using on your pet's skin or ingesting. I would avoid diffusing these as well unless specifically directed by a holistic vet.

If you have cats or small children, you may want to avoid most essential oils or do extensive research on each.

Anise	Boldo
Birsch	Calamus
Bitter Almond	Camphor
Cassia	Chenopodium
Clove Leaf and Bud	Crested Lavender
Garlic	Tea Tree Oil
Goosefoot	Horseradish
Hyssop (use decumbens variety only)	Juniper (use j. berry only)
Mugwort	Mustard
Oregano	Pennyroyal (toxic to kidneys)
Red or White Thyme	Rue
Santalina	Sassafras
Savory	Tansy
Terebinth	Thuja
Wintergreen	Wormwood
Yarrow	Tarragon

Work with a holistic vet before using these essential oils that I have listed but avoid them in OTC products for pets unless your vet gives you the ok. Essential oils should be diluted with a carrier oil or alike such as coconut oil, olive oil etc.

You may need to experiment with different natural flea and tick products but they do exist and work well when used correctly. Add some scented herbs and plants around your yard that repels. Like peppermint, lavender, lemongrass, eucalyptus etc.

And for goodness sake's, DO NOT SMOKE around your pets! Stay at least 50 feet from your pets when smoking. Go outside to smoke but do not allow them out with you.

Vaccines!
DO NOT vaccinate your pet **at all** if he/she has been diagnosed with cancer. That includes the Rabies vaccine. Get a waiver and titer. Every time you turn around, a new vaccine has been invented/created for some sort of new disease. It's totally nuts. Vaccines contain mercury and aluminum and other toxins including preservatives and bacteria. These are the very things that cause cancer. Do not buy into what your vet may tell you. The flu vaccines for people and for pets are nothing more than a moneymaker for the people that created them. I even read where they are adding something into the human flu vaccines to reduce sperm counts in men so to reduce population. I know, it's crazy. We just don't know do we?

If you do everything listed here, you will not have to be concerned about the flu. Give your dog the 3-year rabies vaccine every 3 years if they do **not** have cancer. Your vet must be on the same page as this. Yes, they make a 3-year vaccine. Request it before ever going in to see your vet and ask for the Thimerosal-Free Rabies vaccine. If they do not offer it, find a new vet. Their mission isn't about helping your dog.

Puppies should have their vaccines to help protect them getting through their younger years. Some vaccines may be better off avoided. If you have a concern about the protection they may have against certain diseases, try titers. Have your vet sign up with Vaccicheck or check out Dr Robb at ProtectThePets.com. Titer test for antibodies. Over all, a vaccine is a cancer causing injection and to repeat these year after year, can become fatal. Dr Robb can do this cheaper than your regular vet. Just follow instructions on his website.

For small dogs less than 12-15 lbs, ask for half the vaccine. You can request this with all vaccines except for Rabies. Yep, a 12 lb dog gets the same dose as a 100 lb dog. The law requires the FULL dose of the Rabies vaccine. Ugh! The risks involved with that are extremely high. Vaccines also can cause diseases and joint issues and even aggression in some dogs.

Before, during, and after a Rabies vaccine, you can use nosode pellets to help curb any reactions or side effects to it. Using Lyssin (preferably 200c) for Rabies vaccines. Thuja is used for the other vaccines. But it doesn't reduce the toxins taken in. The vaccine is still doing its damage to the system. Ask for the Thimerosal-Free Rabies vaccine (Merial IMRAB TF). Again, if your dog has cancer, get a waiver. Do not vaccinate! Vaccines are NOT to be given to sick pets at all. The manufacture prints that on the labels and/or warning labels and have your vet read this so he can get your message that you know what you are saying. So you have every right and a good argument for not giving a Rabies vaccine to a dog with cancer. Any vet that forces this upon you, walk out that door and find a holistic vet or one that's not pushy.

Also, know that spaying/neutering your dog too early can cause problems with the endocrine system and also create cancers as well. It is recommended to wait till at least 18 - 24 months to spay/neuter.

Any time you put medications and vaccines into the body, you are adding toxins that can grow cancer cells. Avoid all as much as possible. If your dog has cancer, limit the use of all medications if at all humanly possible. There are herbs to help with certain issues. Much safer than medications of any kind.

I have to tell you a story. I spoke with someone one day helping them with their dog that had joint issues. In our conversation, she bragged about how wonderful her vet was. She went on and on and on about her wonderful vet. Well, then we got into this discussion about vaccines. She said to me, "My vet says it is **"by law"** that dogs get the Bordetella vaccine every time they stay at their clinic". WHAT? I was in shock. This woman was also a nurse. She had no idea. Her dog gets a Bordetella vaccine like every month. I told her that was incorrect and that the Bordetella vaccine does not work and it should NEVER be required. This is the type of vet you want to **<u>avoid at all costs.</u>** You are paying the bill. It is YOUR RIGHT and your decision on vaccines. If they cannot agree to your way, find a vet that will. Remember your vet works for you. I can't stress this enough!

Kennel cough (Bordetella) is equivalent to the human cold. A vaccine isn't going to fix or avoid this. Again, this is for moneymaking purposes. Kennel cough is however contagious so make sure you keep pets separated until it passes. Give your dog Echinacea, Astragalus and Mullein until the illness has passed.

The FDA is well aware of cures and all natural treatments for cancer but it is not allowed to be marketed or advertised. In fact, Big Pharma (and others) has a say so in that. Doctors that have used and are treating patients with cancer using all-natural treatments and that have actually cured cancer are being criticized and harassed by our own government. Some have been thought to have been murdered. Some have been shot, homes and businesses raided, multiple Supreme Court hearings trying to put these life saving Drs in prison, and for what, saving a life. Wrap your brain around that one for a minute. Mind blowing! In Mexico, it is legal for these natural treatments and there are several cancer centers in Tijuana. So we must take this into our own hands to cure ourselves and our pets here in the U.S.A. since we are not given any choices.

There is also a doctor in Texas that uses anti-neoplastons to cure cancers and he has succeeded many times. It's a long story but he has been in front of the Supreme Court like 6-7 times. Even the mainstream media has ridiculed him and called him a quack. It is the FDA and the Texas State Medical Board that's harassing him. He even has an FDA approval to use this patented concoction but yet, they still want him behind bars so they can steal his work. He invented this cure and patented it. He was fined $60,000 during the last court hearing but kept his license that they were trying to revoke. This man is brilliant. The point is, the government is trying to stop cancer cures. There is too much money to be made on sick people. This is our government. Welcome to the U.S.A. So we MUST learn what we can ourselves and do what we have to do to cure ourselves and our pets. Don't be afraid. What do you have to lose?

I keep talking about this because I want people to know, this is really happening and how critical it is to know what you are dealing with and up against. We have been brainwashed to think chemotherapy is the cure and it's just not. I am trying to reiterate that into your brain that this is wrong. Think about how they could care less for our pets?

Supplements
Make sure you add in supplements listed below into the diet to help prevent and treat cancer and other diseases. These have been known to prevent and/or destroy cancer cells. Use organic any chance you can. I added some recommended supplements to help build the immune

system since cancer feeds off of weakened immune systems. You do not need to run out and buy them all; find the ones that you feel will work best for you to start. Don't be overwhelmed. It will all fall into place as you go. I do however recommend several important ones. The Apricot kernels/B-17 capsules, Humic/Fulvic acid, Probiotics and Digestive Enzymes and a good mix of anti-inflammatory herbs. Also, Cell Stop appears to build the immune system and offers herbs for taking out those cancer cells. Read on all the other supplements to see what you may want to add. A good combination of these will help battle cancer as well as help prevent it. Preventative doses will be lower than doses for diagnosed cancers.

These supplements will help to detox the body, help kill cancer cells and build the immune system. If you do happen to cure your dog's cancer, your dog will still have to remain on the same regimen but with lower doses. You may be able to eliminate some of these supplements but you will have to remain on the ones that helped cure your dog for the life of the dog. Also, the same type of diet as well. This is life changing. If your dog doesn't have cancer, change the diet right away, homemade organic or grass-fed. Start now! Prevention has always been the best medicine. But before you can prevent the disease, you have to understand it.

Let's get down to the details on supplements now shall we.

CBD for Dogs (cannabinoids):
Numerous studies have found cannabinoids and particularly CBD to have anti-tumor effects and anti-inflammatory properties. Additionally, CBD has been shown to regulate and stimulate appetite, modulate pain and improve the overall vitality and health of animals.
There is a lot of hype about Cannabis oils (CBD) going on and let's talk about them. This is my opinion but I am still doing my research on it. It

is a good addition to the dog's diet. All 50 states allow the purchase of CBD oils that do not contain THC or less than .03 percent. While this may or may not fight certain cancers, it can help relieve pain, reduce stress and help reduce tumors in certain cases. It can help many ailments and I will always recommend this as 'an addition' to using other supplements. I wouldn't use it alone for treating cancer unless you have a medical card allowed by states where it is legal and used under the supervision of a holistic vet. Only the CBD oil that is over the legal limit with THC that will have the profound effects on killing cancer. Work with a holistic vet when using THC products over the legal limit.

Remember, you can't treat cancer using ONE ingredient. It takes an army to knock down this enemy. The medicinal CBD oils that contain over .03 percent are illegal in most states although this is changing every day. THC actually kills the cancer more so. Do not give products over .03% without close holistic veterinarian supervision. Suppositories do not cause any high effects. CBD oils do not cause a toxic effect. It is used for medicinal purposes only. Make sure your CBD is from the leaves, buds, and **flowers.** Not from seeds. And also, it is processed through what is called solvent extraction. Not pressing which is usually done with seeds. Many sold now are Full Spectrum, meaning they use **all** parts of the plant.

Organic Greens Powder Blend:
Organic Greens Powder or juicing (pureed or finely chopped raw veggies). Organic greens and veggies are full of natural vitamins and minerals and is the key to healing the digestive system. When your digestive system isn't functioning properly, you are open to disease and illness. Absorbing raw nutrients from the greens (powdered or juiced) provides your much-needed body and your dogs, a path to building a strong immune system. This is important for recovery and prevention. These can also help heal a leaky gut. Leaky gut can cause cancer as well. Leaky gut is determined by small holes in the lining of the intestines therefore leaking out foods, toxins etc into the bloodstream causing cancer and many other illnesses and disease.

What causes Leaky Gut? Well it's from a poor diet and vitamin deficiencies to keep it simple. (See chapter 2) Using greens high in chlorophyll helps to rebuild the lining. Also using probiotics, digestive enzymes and Slippery Elm will help. Feeding organic is best. You need to keep all those chemicals and pesticides out of the body. Many of our foods are layered with Glyphosate. Regular foods are GMO foods. Both will cause severe intestinal issues including Irritable Bowel Disease (IBD), allergies, bad behaviors and much more.

Dosing for greens powder:
Small dogs: 1/4 - 1/2 teaspoon
Medium/Large dogs: 1/2 - 1 teaspoon
Giant dogs: 1 - 1 1/2 teaspoons

Also, it is known that iodine in the body helps to conquer cancer cells, so provide a small amount of Kelp or Dulse or some type of sea-iodine if not giving the greens powder blend.

Digestive Enzymes and Probiotics (Recommended):
Builds a strong digestive tract, weeds out the bad bacteria and adds in the good. Great for building a strong well-functioning digestive tract. This is important in every cancer patients diet. Double dosing recommended.

Humic/Fulvic Acid (Recommended):
It can be very beneficial to take a double dose, depending on body size and severity of your health issues. This contains over 90 natural occurring plant derived minerals, trace elements, vitamins, and amino acids in an unaltered ionic solution. It increases oxygen absorption into the blood. Remember, oxygen enriched blood kills cancer cells.
In a perfect world, we would all consume nutrient rich fruits and vegetables and there would be no need to supplement our diets with Fulvic; it would be available in our food supply. Unfortunately, our current farming practices use chemicals and pesticides that kill the microorganisms that create Fulvic, and because of this, Fulvic minerals are severely lacking in today's fruits and vegetables. Even our farm animals, which are now consuming Fulvic deficient greens, are mineral deficient themselves.

Do not give Humic/Fulvic acid with medications or juice. Allow 2 hours in-between for best absorption.

Dosage:
Small dogs: 1 teaspoon
Medium dogs: 2 teaspoons
Large dogs: 1 TBSP
Or follow label on human dosing.

Apricot Seed/Kernels (B-17 / Amygdalin) (Raw and Bitter) *(works well on Breast, Lung, Colon and Prostate and many other cancers):*

This is an important food to take for killing and preventing cancer.

You want ORGANIC RAW BITTER SEEDS. The more bitter the better. Seeds that are not bitter do not work for cancer. Each kernel contains 20mg of B-17/Amygdalin. **B-17 is the killing agent.** It is what contains the Cyanide. Do not go overboard using this. Use lower amounts for longer periods of time.

For actual seeds/kernels dosage for treating cancer:

Approximate Dosage:
Preventive doses:
2-4 seeds up to 50 lb dogs or (100mg in capsules)
5-8 seeds for 50-100 lb dogs (100mg - 200mg in capsules)
10-12 seeds for over 100 lbs (200mg - 300mg capsules)

For cancer treatment, see dosage below.
If nausea or loss of appetite occurs, just reduce the amount you are using daily. You can grind these up or buy the already ground up organic ones.

Cancer Treatment Dosing:
For actual seeds/kernels to treat aggressive or late stage cancer in dogs:
5-10 seeds/kernels (100mg - 200mg Amygdalin/B-17) up to 50 lbs
10-15 seeds/kernels (200mg - 300mg Amygdalin/B-17) for 50-100 lbs
15-20 seeds/kernels (300mg - 400mg Amygdalin/B-17) over 100 lbs

You will **not give this for first dose. You need to work up to this amount over a period of a few weeks.*

You can give up to 600mg (30 kernels) of Amygdalin/B-17 safely in med/large dogs for short-term use (2 weeks). Give less (100mg-300mg) for smaller dogs. To cut down on that many kernels, you can use both the kernels and capsules. The kernels contain B-15 also which is needed to help absorb the B-17.

Remember, B-17 is the killing agent. Apricot Power now makes a capsule called Apricot Seed Capsules. It contains 50mg per capsule of B17. This is the whole seed.

Vitamin C helps to absorb B-17. So does zinc (be careful with using zinc-very low doses only) and B-15. B-15 is also in the whole kernel. No need to add this in if you use the kernels. Capsules come in 100mg and 500mg sizes of B-17. There is 50 mg in the whole Apricot Seed capsules. I would recommend the 50mg or 100mg to start. If there is cancer and it's at a critical timed treatment stage, I would use both capsules and kernels. Doing the math is critical. Remember you can use up to 600mg safely for short-term use. What I mean by "safely" is the side effects. Like nausea or loss of appetite. If this happens, stop using this supplement immediately. If your dog doesn't bounce back quickly, seek a vet. Yes, these kernels in very high doses possibly can cause organ failure or damage as can anything in high amounts. This is also true with certain vitamins and other supplements. You must use caution with using high doses of anything and never use high amounts for long-term use. When you get to a point that you don't think this is working or your dog is declining fast, you may want to try the higher amount for a week or so. If there are any signs of vomiting, loss of appetite or diarrhea, just back off on the dose or discontinue and switch to something else. You use your own judgment and don't be afraid to take an extra step if your dog is at a critical stage but keep it safe so not to cause more harm.

As with any food, supplement, medication etc, don't overdue or go over recommended dosing without consulting a holistic vet or you may see some more serious side effects. In other words, doing higher doses for a long period of time or bombarding your dog with everything may just cause more issues. Use common sense please and take it slow and easy. Sometimes it isn't about higher dosing; it's about lower amounts for longer extended periods.

*Note on the fear of eating foods that contain cyanide: Amygdalin contains four substances. Two are glucose; one is, benzaldehyde and one is cyanide. Yes, cyanide and benzaldehyde are poisons **if** they are released or freed as pure molecules and not bound within other molecular formations. There are 1200 foods we eat every day that contain Laetrile (Cyanide). In fact, many healthy foods such as bitter almonds, millet, sprouts, lima beans, spinach, bamboo shoots, and even apple seeds have quantities of cyanide in them, yet they are still safe to eat.*

Laetrile/Amygdalin/B-17 is in our foods but the amounts are much lower and because of nutrient deficient soils, the amounts are even lower. Apricot kernels have the highest amount therefore the best option for fighting cancer.

If your dog has been diagnosed with cancer in its early stages, I would work somewhere in-between the preventative dosage and the late stage dosage. Also, if the tumor is in a life threatening area such as brain, near the brain or an organ, I would use the higher doses for a week or so, but start low and work your way up. Don't overwhelm the body too fast. Let it adjust to what's going in. This is important.

Curcumin (found in turmeric):
The herbal compound Curcumin has a mechanism of action as a natural COX-2 inhibitor (COX-2 is an inflammatory enzyme). Inhibitors of this type have shown to have the capability to help relieve common everyday inflammations triggered by a host of lifestyle factors.

- It helps to reduce the risk of ulcers due to stress and drugs by increasing the mucous protective lining of the stomach.
- It can also help to reduce elevated blood cholesterol levels and has a protective effect on the liver.
- Is a natural antiseptic and antibacterial agent, useful in disinfecting cuts and burns.
- May prevent metastases from occurring in many different forms of cancer.
- Works as an anti-inflammatory agent for arthritis and rheumatoid arthritis by lowering histamine levels.

- Is a natural painkiller and cox-2 inhibitor. In many instances, works as well as anti-inflammatory drugs but without the side effects and potential risks associated with NSAIDs.
- Used in treating depression. (Yes, dogs can suffer with depression)
- Has been shown to stop the growth of new blood vessels in tumors.
- Speeds up wound healing and assists in remodeling of damaged skin and other inflammatory skin conditions.
- By enhancing liver function, helps to cleanse the blood of toxins and impurities.
- Helps to regulate intestinal flora if taken during and after a course of antibiotics by dogs suffering with Candida (yeast infection).

Buy organic and do not buy any types (including organic) that comes from China or India. This includes Ginger, Turmeric, and Garlic spices.

Ginger:
Ginger, a cousin to turmeric, is known for its ability to shrink tumors. It is even more effective than many cancer drugs, which have been shown to be completely ineffective and actually accelerate the death of cancer patients. The medicinal properties of ginger far surpass even advanced pharmaceutical medicines. Ginger is also a good treatment for chemo side effects like nausea.

Salvestrol Platinum:
Salvestrols may not be effective for cats because they do not produce the CYP1B1 enzyme the same way as humans, but the results for dogs may actually be greater. Use one Salvestrol Platinum capsule (1,000 points) for up to two meals per day for every 40 lbs of dog's weight. For smaller dogs, empty the contents of the capsule proportionally by the pet's weight into your dog's food. If the dog doesn't respond after two weeks, gradually increase the dosage up to two capsules per meal for every 40 lbs. Salvestrol capsules should be taken with meals.

Avoid using Resveratrol while using Salvestrol. Give Salvestrol separate from other remedies, herbs, and/or medications. Avoid using Apricot kernels when using this product.

*NOTE: Why Resveratrol is not listed here in this Chapter for cancer. The reason is, I have found that **higher** amounts of Resveratrol may actually increase the growth of cancer. I wouldn't want to chance where that fine line is, so I switched to recommending Salvestrols which appears to be better and stronger and can be used safely in higher amounts without causing cancer growth. But you will find Resveratrol mentioned often for cancer treatment.*

Not many people know about Salvestrols. I found thousands and thousands of comments from people (over 2600 pages to be exact) using this for cancer on how well Salvestrol Platinum worked and even for their dogs.

Salvestrols in North America **do not** contain grape extracts in which grape SKINS/MEAT are toxic to dogs. (Grape **seeds** are **not** toxic.) Salvestrols in North America do not contain grape extracts nor are the compounds extracted from grape products.

Note: Many of your Resveratrol products contain grapes. Use caution. Specific enhancers to Salvestrols are Niacin (Vitamin B-3), **methyl**cobalamin (vitamin B-12), magnesium, and selenium so you can add these into the diet.

Cat's Claw-(particularly urinary tract cancer):
Works on Allergies (environmental), Alzheimer's (canine), Asthma, Arthritis, Osteoarthritis, as well as Rheumatoid Arthritis. Can also have effect on the blood, eyes, lungs, heart, and nerves.

Also works against:
- Chronic fatigue
- Digestive disorders
- Colitis
- Gastritis
- Stomach ulcers

- Leaky Gut Syndrome
- Cancer (particularly urinary tract cancer)
- Cleansing of the kidneys
- Parasites
- Viral infections
- Wound Healing

If your dog has low blood pressure, Cat's Claw may lower blood pressure even more. If your dog has leukemia, do not give Cat's Claw.

Cat's Claw may help create support for the intestinal and immune systems of the body, and may also create intestinal support with its ability to cleanse the entire intestinal tract. This cleansing helps create support for people and pets experiencing different stomach and bowel disorders, including Colitis, Crohn's disease, Irritable Bowel Syndrome and Leaky Gut Syndrome.

Organic Sulfur:
Organic sulphur has been known to turn malignant tumors into benign tumors. Remember, the difference between true "organic sulfur" and inferior MSM (especially with added chemicals) is so important it could mean the difference between life and death when using this protocol!

Air is 21% oxygen. Water is 89% oxygen. The oxygen from air gets to the lungs, heart, and muscles. However, it is the oxygen from water that needs to get inside the cells to make the cells healthy, to give them energy, and to kill microbes inside the cells. True organic sulfur is what grabs the oxygen from the water and transports the oxygen inside the cells. This produces a surge of oxygen into the cancer cells. True organic sulfur is important in the treatment of cancer, brain disorders and many other health conditions! Every part of the body (including the brain) is made of cells. Getting sulfur and oxygen inside these cells is critical for all aspects of health! So remember to use FILTERED water with organic sulfur. For dogs, I would recommend adding to wet foods that contain a lot of moisture like raw diets do.

Wait at least 30 minutes after using Organic Sulfur before adding other supplements into the daily regimen for best results. Organic sulfur only stays in the body for 12 hours so this will need to be given twice a day at least. This may need to be given in fairly larger amounts than what any label tells you or any normal dose. There is nothing normal about having cancer so dosages in most products will need to be much higher.

Always watch for the poop change. If diarrhea or loose stools, simply reduce amount a little until you get to a point of no diarrhea or loose stools. If for some reason your dog vomits, you may have to reduce or eliminate this from the diet. Some dogs have sensitive tummies with using this supplement.

Flaxseed oil (keep amounts low):
Flaxseed oil mixed with small curd organic cottage cheese is used in the Budwig Diet for humans, has also been reported to be effective against dog cancers. I do NOT recommend this diet alone. For one, flaxseed oil or powders usually aren't organic. If you do find some that are organic, the ALA is hard for a dog to break down into Omega-3 fatty acids. Fish oils don't need to be broken down and are easily absorbed by the dog's body. I am not saying this won't work, I am saying add fish oils long with vitamin E three times a week also into the diet.

Black Cumin Seed:
Black cumin is a part of the buttercup family and the seeds are dark, thin, and crescent-shaped when whole. The seeds have been used for many centuries in the Middle East, the Mediterranean, and India. Black cumin seeds are used as a seasoning spice in different cuisines across the world due to their nutty flavor. Besides their culinary uses, black cumin seeds also have a wealth of important health benefits and are one of the most cherished medicinal seeds in history. The seeds of the black cumin plant contain over 100 chemical compounds, including some yet to be identified. In addition to what is believed to be the primary active ingredient, crystalline nigellone, black cumin seeds contain: thymoquinone, beta sitosterol, myristic acid, palmitic acid, palmitoleic acid, stearic acid, oleic acid, linoleic acid, arachidonic acid, protein, vitamin B-1, B-2, B-3, folic acid, calcium, iron, copper, zinc, and phosphorous.

One recent study on black cumin seed oil demonstrated that it was effective against pancreatic cancer, one of the deadliest and most difficult to treat cancers.

NOTE: Those who decide to use black cumin seed oil should check labels and product information carefully. Black cumin is commonly referred to as black seed oil, black onion seed, black caraway, black sesame seed, and other names, but **only Nigella sativa is true black cumin**. Black cumin seeds lower blood sugar levels and therefore should be consumed only after consulting with a vet/holistic vet. This has a strong taste. Mix with something tasty your dog likes.

Dosage:
Small dogs: 1/2 - 1 teaspoon 2-3 times a day
Med/Large dogs: 1 teaspoon up to 1 TBSP 2-3 times a day
Give preferably on an empty stomach.

Noni Fruit:
Taking a daily dose of Noni Fruit is as beneficial to pets as it is to humans. Adding Noni Fruit to the food of dogs, cats and other animals has been shown to strengthen an animal's immune system. The average pet diet is usually comprised of low quality ingredients. A low quality diet compromises a pet's immune system and lessens the ability to fight illness and disease. Noni Fruit contains 17 of the 20 known amino acids, including all 9 essential acids.

Veterinarians who practice both traditional and holistic animal medicine recommend Noni Fruit daily in the diet to assist in the treatment of viral infections, worms, digestive disorders, food allergies, recovery from surgery, and arthritis to name a few. There has been much success using Noni Fruit in treating pain, inflammation and ridding animals of worms. Using Noni Fruit eliminates the need for muscle relaxants, NSAIDs, and steroids. Noni Fruit enhances an animal's immune system, joint health, circulation, digestion, and numerous skin conditions. Noni Fruit can be added to the diet of dogs, cats, birds, hamsters, pet mice and larger animals such as horses and cows to strengthen and support the immune system, assist in cell regeneration, boost nutrient uptake, offer digestive support and increase energy.

Dosage:
Up to 10 lbs: 5ml - 20ml per day
11-25 lbs: 20ml - 50ml per day
26-50 lbs: 50ml - 70ml per day
51 lbs and above: 70ml - 90ml per day

Powder:
Small dogs: 1/4 - 1/2 teaspoon
Medium dogs: 1/2 - 1 teaspoon
Large dogs: 1 - 2 teaspoon

ESSIAC TEA:
(Ingredients in Essiac tea - Organic burdock root, organic sheep sorrel, organic (Turkey) rhubarb root and organic slippery elm bark.)

- Building immune system strength.
- Helping the body to destroy benign growths and tumors.
- Strengthening muscles, organs, and tissues.
- Removing toxic accumulation in the body, including heavy metals and other environmental toxins.
- Aiding in bowel detoxification and elimination.
- Adding strength and flexibility to bones, joints, and lungs.
- Blood purification.

As a general guide for treating animals, it is best to assess the dosage according to your pet's weight.

15-40 lbs: 1/2 ounce of tea, twice per day
40-80 lbs: 1 ounce of tea, twice per day
Over 80 lbs: 2 - 3 ounces of tea, twice per day

WHO SHOULD **NOT** TAKE THE ESSIAC TEA:
If your dog has kidney disease, are prone to kidney stones, or kidney infections. The varying amounts of oxalic acids in this tea are irritating to the kidneys. If your dog has ulcers or colitis do not give.

The Essiac has an action of being a laxative (depending on how much you take). Some properties in this root can be highly irritating to ulcers and colitis, exacerbating (or worsening) these conditions.

If your dog has tumors that are close to a major blood supply or an area of an organ that expansion of the tumor could have dire consequences. In Rene's work, she reportedly noticed that in the beginning phase of a person taking this tea, the tumor could appear to enlarge before it began to break down. (One of the reasons she was adamant that they take very small doses.) If you notice any sudden pain or unusual symptoms after beginning this tea, stop taking it. **Do not give to patients with a brain tumor.** This can be extremely detrimental in the brain tissue. Rapid or excess growth can put pressure on areas of the brain that affect body/mental function. If the tumor would break down, it can release pieces of the malignant tissue, which could cause a stroke. Circulation in the brain is unlike the rest of the body.

Astragalus (Astragalus membranaceous):
Immunostimulant, antiviral, anti-inflammatory, hypothyroid (mildly depresses thyroid function), hypotensive, digestive tonic. Works on immune systems, lungs, liver, heart, kidneys, thyroid, and digestive tract. Astragalus is used for strengthening the body against viral infections of the respiratory and heart. Astragalus can be used for early treatment of a variety of respiratory infections, including kennel cough (Bordetella bronchiseptica). Astragalus helps to raise white blood cell counts and also boosts the body's immune system. Astragalus may be useful for helping the body protect itself and speed recovery from the damages of long-term steroid medications. Astragalus is also useful in early stages of kidney infection and/or renal failure. Astragalus is non-toxic in any dosages. Astragalus may help prevent the immunosuppression caused by chemotherapy. It has been found that Astragalus contains an alkaloid that inhibits the spread of melanoma, a skin cancer.

There is a mixture that I really love and use on my dogs for prevention and immune building. I buy organic powders of Astragalus, Dandelion, Ashwagandha and Ginger. This is my favorite mix of herbs for daily use. I mix them all in together equally. And there is one more I would love to add in; Grape Seed Extract. Make sure this is SEEDS only.

Check and double check before buying. The skin and meat is toxic to dogs.

Panagamic Acid (B-15):
An ester derived from gluconic acid and dimethylglycine. Based on research in humans, 125mg - 2500mg per day in divided doses is most commonly used. Although it can be taken with or without meals, it is most often advised to take between meals. It is best to divide the doses throughout the day. Panagamic Acid (B-15) is also found in apricot kernels. For dogs, you will need to half that dose and in smaller dogs even reduce it more. Human dosages are determined on a 150 lb person. So adjust the dose for your dog by his/her weight.

Artemisinin (Wormwood):
It is recommended that kidney and liver enzyme levels be monitored though out your dog's treatment with Artemisinin. Artemisinin is an extract isolated from the plant Artemisia annua, or sweet wormwood. Artemisinin can kill iron-enriched breast cancer cells similar to the way it kills malaria, making it a natural cancer treatment option for breast cancer. Wormwood is used in natural heartworm treatments and should be used with caution and under care of holistic vet. If your dog is undergoing radiation, you must **not** use this herbal. Works against bone cancers and may work on brain cancers. Although amounts are listed here, I recommend you giving this under the guidance of a holistic vet.

Dosage:
Small dogs (up to 30 lbs): 50mg twice a day
Medium dogs (over 30 lbs): 100mg twice a day
Large dogs (over 60 lbs): 150mg twice a day
Giant dogs (over 100 lbs): 200mg twice a day
Use this for two weeks on, then 4 - 5 days off, and then back to two weeks. Repeat!

Bindweed Extract (toxic to horses):
Bindweed extract has been shown to be helpful for numerous cancers, including prostate cancer, lung cancer, liver cancers, and more. It is so helpful, in fact, that it completely destroyed lethal cancer tumors in laboratory mice. Also called convolvulus arvensis, or Field Bindweed.

Bindweed has also been used medicinally for centuries for many ailments.

I had to dig hard for Bindweed to find the right information. Field Bindweed (convolvulus arvensis) is considered an antioxidant by the NCBI website and sold under the name of VascuStatin and upon reviewing the ingredients of VascuStatin (Allergy Research Group); it contains maltodextrin which falls under the avoided ingredients. With that said, two other brands sell this and it contains the exact same ingredients. So this is when you have no choices, do you want to give this. It is also VERY expensive. They are proud of their product and I assume because of the limited variety out there. The other brand names are made by Nutricology called Angioblock and Aidan brand called C-Statin. (sounds like a high cholesterol medication don't it). On Amazon I found the VascuStatin being the lower priced. You will also find reviews on these of people using on their dogs.

These are approximate doses only. This appears to be safe to give in higher doses. If cancer is aggressive or in late stage cancer, you may give the higher end doses. Start with lower dose and work up to higher dose over a couple weeks time. Don't rush it unless the dog is at end stage cancer.

Approximate dose:
Small dogs (up to 30 lbs): 2 - 4 caps per day
Medium dogs (over 30 lbs): 3 - 6 caps per day
Large dogs (over 60 lbs): 4 - 8 caps per day
Giant (over 100 lbs): 6 - 12 caps per day

Do not give for 14 days before surgery. High amounts may cause digestive upset. Heart patients should not use Bindweed.

Medicinal Mushroom(s):
Yun Zhi is also known as *Coriolus versicolor (Turkey Tail)*, *Trametes versicolor*, and *Polyporus versicolor*. Most current cancer research in the United States refers to it as *Trametes versicolor*. *Coriolus versicolor* is the most well studied medicinal mushroom in the world. While there is not enough evidence to support using Turkey Tail alone for cancer treatment, there is plenty of evidence showing its efficacy as

an adjuvant therapy. Especially in cases of breast cancer, colorectal cancer, and gastric cancer, this mushroom therapy should be a component of the treatment plan, both during and after conventional treatments.

Mushrooms alleviate the side effects of chemotherapy. Promote vitality and stamina, inhibit pain, and stimulate appetite. Mushrooms also stabilize the white blood cell count. White blood cells are the cells responsible for fighting infections and attacking tumor cells.

Many integrative oncologists prescribe 3000 - 4500mg (human dosage). Human dosing is based on a 150 lb person. Adjust accordingly to your dog's body weight.

Approximate dosage for dogs: 300mg per 50 lbs.

More on mushrooms:
I believe taking Turkey Tail along with a mushroom combo would be great for the immune system and to help fight off the effects of chemo treatments if given. Great for building a strong immune system and fighting off radicals.

Note: The Reishi mushroom has a strong flavor.

Vitamin E (Soy Free):
Each cell of the human body has a tiny furnace in it, known as the mitochondria, in which fuel (food) is burned to give energy to that cell. What vitamin E does is block that process in cancer cells. Without fuel, a cancerous cell soon dies of starvation no matter what stage it is in. Many vitamin E supplements contain SOY! Avoid soy if at all possible. All soy contains GMOs. Look for this in a non-soy formula. Vitamin E should always be used with fish oils and alike as higher amounts of fish oils can cause vitamin E deficiency.

Bromelain:
Taken from Washington State University...(pertains to people, not dog dosage. Dogs dosing is below) Bromelain has been shown to inhibit growth of lung tumors in mice inoculated with tumor cells as well as breast cancer. Oral doses of Bromelain given in breast cancer

Bromelain in doses of 3000mg have been found useful in preventing post surgical adhesions and is used, often in combination with other plant enzymes in the treatment of lymph edema. Reduce this amount for dogs (see below).

Because Bromelain has been shown to be generally safe in oral doses, integrative oncologists often use it for a variety of cancer-related conditions including post-radiotherapy fibrosis, post-surgical edema ileus, lymph edema, immunomodulation, and inflammatory bowel disorders.

Dosage:
Small dogs: 100mg - three times a day
Medium dogs: 200 - 300mg - three times a day
Large dogs: Up to 350mg - three times a day

Fucoidan
In studies, fucoidan had a success rate of 75% or higher in the elimination of cancer or reduction in tumor size by a minimum of 50%. This includes tough cancers like lymphoma, ovarian and pancreatic cancers. Fucoidan's success rate with stomach, lung and esophageal cancer, as well as leukemia, was almost 85%.

Approximate Dosing:
Small dogs: 1/2 cap daily
Med dogs: 1 cap daily
Large dogs: 1 - 2 caps daily

As with any supplement, this may take several weeks to a couple months to really show its working. Be patient, it's working undercover.

L-Arginine (amino acid):
The basic reasons Arginine would be helpful for cancer patients is its ability to safely deliver more oxygen to oxygen-deprived tissues in the body. The entire world of alternative medicine agrees that getting more oxygen to the tissues is going to be bad news for any and all cancer cells because they have given up normal respiration for fermentation. When acid levels are high and oxygen levels are low, we find cancer flourishing, a situation that orthodox oncology

ignores. Arginine opens up the veins and arteries to increase blood flow and volume, thus increasing oxygen to the cells. *L-Arginine in higher amounts in some cases may cause diarrhea.*

Quercetin:
Human Dose is up to 1000mg/day for up to 12 weeks have been shown well tolerated for human consumption. Quercetin is used in naturopathic medical practice in doses of 500-3000mg/day as post-chemotherapy adjuvant therapy to stabilize the P53 gene. Since it inhibits the release of histamine it is also prescribed for cancer patients with Ig E-mediated allergies. Courses of Quercetin treatment may range from weeks to months.

Quercetin is an:

- Anti-allergenic
- Anti-carcinogenic
- Anti-fungal
- Anti-Inflammatory
- Anti-microbial
- Anti-viral

Used for allergies in place of Benadryl as well. Quercetin works for cancer but specifically these cancers for prevention and treatment.

- Breast cancer
- Colon cancer
- Endometrial cancer
- Ovarian cancer
- Prostate cancer

Use caution:
Very high doses can cause kidney damage. Do not give Quercetin to dog and cats with kidney disease. Quercetin can be administered for **up to** 12 consecutive weeks at a time. Only use Quercetin for as long as absolutely required. You should not keep your dog/cat permanently on Quercetin.

Dosage:
Small dogs: (Up to 20 lbs) 50 - 160mg
Medium dogs: (20-50 lbs) 160 - 350mg
Large dogs: (50-100 lbs) 400 - 600mg

Rosehips/Camu Camu:
Dogs can greatly benefit from Rosehips as well. Rosehips is a great additional supplement for treating and preventing arthritis and many other diseases. It contains a high amount of vitamin C. It has a tart flavor but dogs don't seem to mind it. It's less expensive than Camu Camu. Camu Camu has one of the highest concentrations of vitamin C of any food source.

Daily Dosage:
Small dogs: 1/4 - 1/2 teaspoon
Medium dogs: 1/2 - 1 teaspoon
Large dogs: 1 - 2 teaspoon

Unfiltered Raw Organic Apple Cider Vinegar ("Mother"):
The body can be acidic and cancer grows in an acidic environment. Add to daily meal if feeding wet foods. Add to cottage cheese or yogurt. Taken internally, ACV is credited with maintaining the acid/alkaline balance of the digestive tract. To check your dog's pH balance, pick up some pH strips at the drug store and first thing in the morning test the dog's urine. If it reads anywhere from 6.2 - 6.5, your dog's system is exactly where it should be. If your dog has cancer, you need the pH level slightly higher than normal. If it is 7.5 or higher, the diet you are feeding is too alkaline, and ACV will re-establish the correct balance as well.

Dosage:
Small dogs (0-25 lbs): 1 teaspoon
Medium dogs (25-50 lbs): 1 - 2 teaspoons
Large dogs (50-80 lbs): 1 TBSP
Giant dogs (80+ lbs): 1 1/2 - 2 TBSP

Echinacea:
Echinacea stimulates the white blood cells that help fight infections in the body. Research has shown that Echinacea enhances the activity of a particular type of white blood cells-macrophages. A particular glycoprotein in Echinacea was found to significantly increase the killing effect of macrophages on tumor cells. Echinacea benefits dogs by boosting their immune system and helping their bodies fight bacteria, viruses and other germs. Echinacea also has anti-inflammatory and antimicrobial properties. Echinacea is used in treating the common cold and yeast infections. Can cause laxative effects and works on constipation. Works on skin infections, bee stings, UTI's and helps heal wounds. Do not take more than recommended as it reverses the healing effects. Not for use in seasonal allergies. This is to be used short term of two weeks only. Echinacea should be given at the onset of symptoms. Echinacea should NOT be used on dogs with immune systems that are already overly active and functioning abnormally, such as those suffering from autoimmune diseases, leukemia, or diabetes.

Colloidal Silver:
This has many medicinal uses. It is a true antibiotic as well. It works on cancers and helps build the immune system. Make sure you get colloidal silver that is pure and of high quality. I recommend Sovereign Silver brand. For fighting cancer, you can mix colloidal silver up to 50/50 with drinking water and then after a couple of weeks or so gradually back off from 2 tablespoons per day for small dogs up to 2 ounces per day for large dogs until the cancer is gone. Adding IP-6 along with colloidal silver makes this a powerful cancer fighter.

IP-6:
IP-6 (inositol hexaphosphate) is a component of certain dietary fibers, particularly most cereal grains, legumes, and seeds high in oil. Many researchers believe that some of fiber's health benefits may be due to the antioxidant, immune enhancing, and cardiovascular supporting activities of IP-6. IP-6 has shown to have significant protective and growth regulating effects on various cells and tissues, including those of the colon, breast, and prostate. IP-6 has consistently demonstrated positive research results in animal and cell studies and has reported that IP-6 is effective in cancer prevention and control of tumor growth, progression, and metastasis. Its anticancer activity likely involves

IP-6's immune stimulatory, potent antioxidant and anti-angiogenic effects. IP-6 has been shown to help treat kidney stones as well as high cholesterol and lipid levels.

Directions:
Powder: Mix 1 1/2 teaspoons (or up to 9 grams per day) with water. For systemic support, take on an empty stomach. For direct colon support, take just prior to or with meals.

Dosage for dogs:
Small dogs: 400mg twice a day
Medium dogs: 800mg twice a day
Large dogs: 1200mg twice a day
Giant dogs: 1600mg twice a day

Recent human studies of inositol for lung cancer showed that in a daily dose of 18 grams for 3 months, inositol was safe and well tolerated. IP-6 has anti-platelet activity, so it may increase the risk of bleeding when used with other anticoagulants or anti-platelet drugs. IP-6 can also bind with calcium, iron, magnesium, and zinc in the stomach and reduce their absorption. Doses listed in this paragraph is based on research in humans. Dosage for dogs listed above.

Cell Stop:
Nature has given us an army of cancer therapeutic substances from herbs, mushrooms, fruit, and vegetable extracts that can help fight the very mechanisms cancers use to grow. Cell Stop is great for immune building as well as cancer killers. This contains Curcumin, Astragalus, Green Tea, a three mushroom blend, Quercetin, Broccoli Extract, Bitter Melon, Mangosteen fruit, Milk Thistle, Beta Glucan, Chamomile, Flaxseed, Pterostilbene and Se-Methylselenocysteine (Selenium). It contains these 17 powerful plant compounds that work together to target and disrupt abnormal cell growth on a cellular level. This is a great combination of ingredients all in one product. Whatever the dose is on the bottle, base it off of 150-160 lb person, then adjust for your dogs weight.

Note: I would give Cell Stop for 3 months then take a break from it for 30-60 days.

Selenium (Methylselenocysteine or Se-Methylselenocysteine):
Research notes show that breast cancer rates were low in areas where selenium levels in the soil and food were high. The same correlation was found between death rates and selenium levels. Similar correlations were subsequently found in animal studies.

Methylselenocysteine does not accumulate in the body and is considered to be non-toxic. In humans, it has been observed that a 200 mcg daily supplement given for four years led to a big reduction in cancer deaths and reduction in the incidence of prostate, lung, colorectal and some types of skin cancer. The symptoms of selenium deficiency include hypothyroidism, a weakened immune system, and heart disease. Do not go over this dosage.

Dosage:
Small dogs: up to 10mcg
Medium dogs: up to 25mcg
Large dogs: up to 50mcg

Colostrum:
Colostrum from pasture-fed cows is much higher in immune factors than a human mother's colostrum! It's the immune boosting properties that make Colostrum an important cancer-fighting weapon.
Research has shown that Colostrum is one of the most important nutritional supplements available for enhancing the immune system and helping in tissue repair. Colostrum works well for dogs and cats with diarrhea and for weakened immune systems. Colostrum can be used in all animals and humans. Colostrum contains IgF (Epithelial growth Factors), IgF (Insulin-like Growth Factor), Transfer Factor, IgG (20 times that in human milk), PRP, etc. IGFs act as endocrine, autocrine and paracrine hormones enhancing cellular glucose uptake, and enhance synthesis of proteins, DNA, RNA and lipids. Without adequate EGFs, the body cannot repair damaged cells, no matter how good the patient is being fed.

Lactoferrin is another component of colostrum, which inhibits the growth of pathogenic organisms. Colostrum shows that it can be used to treat allergies, cancer, ulcerative colitis, diarrhea, poor wound healing, hepatitis C, bacterial and viral infections, multiple sclerosis, obesity and peptic ulcers. Colostrum is useful in the treatment of chemotherapy-induced mucositis. It's best to give at least 30 minutes before feeding time.

Dosage:
1/3 tsp per 25 lbs of body weight once per day.
You may notice changes as soon as one day up to two months.

Collagen:
Collagen works on nails, coat, joints, and digestive tract to name a few. Collagen peptide is another term for hydrolyzed collagen. If purchasing human products, start with a low dose and work up in dosing over a few weeks time. Adjust accordingly. Not all Collagens are created equal. Some do not contain amino acids. Collagen is a tasteless and odorless powder so easy to use and mix into wet foods. There are 9 essential amino acids: histidine, isoleucine, leucine, lysine, methionine, phenylalanine, threonine, tryptophan, and valine. And 20 amino acids in total. These amino acids play a key role in our health as well as our pets. The body cannot make amino acids so they must come from the diet.

Approximate Dosage:
Small dogs: 1/4 scoop
Medium dogs: 1/2 scoop
Large dogs: 1 scoop

Making Your Own Organic Anti-inflammatory Mix
If you would like an organic version of anti-inflammatories, you can gather these ingredients online and purchase organic powders then combine. Choose Grape Seed Extract wisely. No skin or meat. Only seeds from grapes. Make sure it says 100% grape seed. If in doubt, please ask manufacture if it contains skins or meat. Grape seed extract has terrific healing abilities for many diseases including cancer. You want to add flavor? You can find organic flavored powders as well like blueberry or apple. You can find these on different sites like Starwest-Botanicals.com, Znaturalfoods.com, and MontainRoseHerbs.com.

Anti-inflammatory herbs:
Devil's Claw

Yucca Root
Grape Seed Extract (no skins or meat-seeds only and organic)
Fever Few
Cat's Claw
Turmeric
Boswellia
Organic Alfalfa
Ginger
Meadowsweet

List to purchase for a good combo in **organic:**

Yucca (25%)
Devil's Claw (25%)
Grape Seed Extract (seeds only) (20%)
Boswellia (10%)
Turmeric (10%)
Rosehips (5%)
Blueberry powder (5%)

You will measure and mix then add to wet foods daily. You can split it into two meals if you like. Use some and put into capsules for yourself.

Keep the amounts of Yucca lower as a higher dose has been known to cause bloat in horses and could cause bloat in large dogs. It's best to discontinue yucca for a while after about 3 months of use. Not for long-term use without interruptions in dosing.

Approximate dosing for dogs:
Small dogs: 1/4 - 1/2 tsp
Medium dogs: 1/2 - 1 tsp
Large dogs: 1 tsp - 1 1/2 tsp
Giant dogs: 2 tsp

Do not give along with cortisone medications.

Devil's claw may also lower your blood sugar levels. Devil's claw might decrease how quickly the liver breaks down some medications. Taking devil's claw along with some medications that are broken down by the liver can increase the effects and side effects of some medications.

Do not use Cat's Claw if your dog has Leukemia, bleeding disorders, autoimmune disease or low blood pressure.

If you have kidney disease, don't use willow bark.

Discontinue use 2 weeks before surgery. Do not give this if your dog is on heart medications.

Shark Cartilage:
I wouldn't normally recommend this because of the over killing of sharks but in the case of cancer, I will make an exception. There are some species of sharks not on the endangered list. So depends on manufacture on what sharks they are using as to whether I felt ok with it. Shark cartilage is expensive but consider the costs of modern treatments as opposed to safe alternatives. Initial studies showed in rats that when shark cartilage extract was injected into one eye along with a cancerous tumor and the other eye received only a cancerous tumor. After 19 days the eye that had injected both the tumor and the shark cartilage there was no tumor growth. In the eye with only the tumor, the tumor had grown much larger. So shark cartridge works at combating tumors by cutting off the blood supply. In these studies, it shows that it doesn't have a direct effect on the tumor but yet cuts off the blood supply to the tumor therefore causing it to shrink. There is one made for dogs and is called Wholistic Shark Cartilage. This brand claims to use non- endangered species.

Dosage:
Up to 30 lbs: 1/4 teaspoon
31-60 lbs: 1/2 teaspoon
61-90 lbs: 3/4 teaspoon
91 lbs and over: 1 teaspoon
I would double this amount for treating cancer. It's also great for joints. For preventative/maintenance dosing, go with recommended dose on label.

Graviola (Soursop):
Soursop contains folate, niacin, thiamine, vitamin C, calcium, magnesium, potassium, and fiber. This fruit is used to treat an upset stomach, coughs, asthma, skin conditions, gout, fever and as a mild, natural sedative. Graviola is considered an antioxidant and anti-inflammatory. Graviola has the ability to kill cancer cells specifically pancreatic cancer. A study that was conducted by the University of Nebraska Medical Center found that the extract can greatly reduce pancreatic cancer. Also used for treating bacterial infections. A really good brand is called **Amazon Thunder** at amazonthunder.com. It is organic and freeze-dried.

Dosage:
Under 5 lbs: 1/4 capsule (or 4 or 5 drops for liquid types)
5 to 10 lbs: 1/2 capsule or 15 drops
30 to 50 lbs: 1 capsules or 25 - 30 drops
75 to 100 lbs: 1-2 capsules, 1/2 tsp or 2 droppers
Over 100 lbs: 2 capsules, 1/2 tsp or 2 droppers for every 100 lbs.

Start with low dose and work up to recommended dose. Give probiotics and digestive enzymes along with Graviola as well.

Paw Paw:
PawPaw is said to be superior over Graviola, so you may use this if not using Graviola.

- Supports the immune system
- Selectively affects specific cells
- Modulates ATP production in specific cells
- Modulates blood supply to specific cells

Nature's Sunshine uses an extract of the twigs of the North American paw paw tree, which contain the most concentrated amount of acetogenins. These twigs are harvested when they are most biologically active. This is a renewable resource since the tree is not harmed during the harvest. Yes it is safe to use with antioxidants. Their website says otherwise but I asked them and they said their website was wrong and has not been updated.

Brand: Nature's Sunshine Paw Paw Cell-Reg. Use caution on buying fake replicas on Amazon.

Small dogs: 1-2 capsules
Medium dogs: 2-3 capsules
Large dogs: 3-4 capsules
Giant dogs: 4-6 capsules

Do not exceed this dose as nausea can occur. You may adjust accordingly.

NOTE: CoQ10, Thyroid Support and 7-Keto may decrease the effectiveness of this product. Only those with cellular abnormalities should take this product on a regular/daily basis.

Other Options:
Other options I would highly consider include intravenous vitamin C in high doses. This should be done by a holistic vet or Oncologist.

Mistletoe -Two to three injections of Mistletoe per week are required to treat most cancers, and it is recommended that the injections be given in the morning. Can only be given by a veterinarian. It is widely used in Europe for cancer (more than 50% of all cancer patients in Germany are treated with it).

K9-ACV Immunotherapy:
There is a clinic called **Medivet Biologics** also found at medivetbiologics.com that offers a cancer vaccine. Not sure why it is called a vaccine. It's more like 3 injections given 4 weeks apart. They create the vaccine/injections using your own dog's cancer cells. Pricing for this is around $1,300. You can check it out as well. I found this slightly fascinating to say the least. (Medivet also offers Stem cell therapy).

Medivet states it can treat these certain types of cancers:

- Lymphoma
- Mast cell tumor

- Sarcoma
- Osteosarcoma
- Melanoma
- Hemangiosarcoma (spleen or liver hemangiosarcoma cancer in dogs)
- Skin tumors
- mammary tumors
- Oral melanoma
- ***Ideal Canine Cancer Patients***
- Greater than 1 year of age
- Dogs with a solid cancerous tumor that is accessible for surgical removal
- Dogs must have a predicted survival greater than 1 month without therapy

The following list describes patients that are not suitable for the canine cancer treatment/vaccine.

- Leukemia or a cancerous tumor that cannot be removed
- Any previous forms of immunotherapy
- Pregnant dogs
- Histologic diagnosis of benign tumor in the resected tumor or low grade malignancy

This vaccine can be done by your own vet and it takes three injections given 4 weeks apart. Immunotherapy is a new groundbreaking treatment option for dogs with cancer. Many pet insurance companies offer coverage for the K9-ACV cancer treatment. In one case I followed, the dog was cancer free for one year after receiving these injections. The cancer has returned and injections have begun again. I do not know the update on this at this time, but it gave that dog another year of a normal healthy life.

Vet-Stem.com is now offering cancer treatment injections such as these.

Hyperbaric Oxygen Chambers (Recommended):
Find a place that can do oxygen therapy for your pets. It would help to oxygenate the blood. This does not allow cancer cells to grow and travel throughout the system. Cancer cells cannot survive in an oxygenated body. So by increasing the oxygen in the blood, the cancer cells die. Same for starving it from having any sugar. I highly recommend looking into this. Hyperbaric is used daily in cancer patients and has been extremely successful. Each session is about $135. Check your area for facilities for pets. Some animal emergency clinics may have them or Neurologists.

Magnetic Resonance:
The **Magnesphere** is an FDA approved class 1 medical device that has been proven to lower stress and cortisol (the stress hormone) and restores the body to rest, repair, and regenerate. This is relatively a new treatment and may be hard to access at this time. Go to YouTube to see this in action. Magnesphere has been shown to go from a dog dragging its hind legs to walking, a dog that had tumors and reducing, and killing the tumor. This machine can do so much. Stress causes cancer. Yes, even in our pets. Reducing stress heals the body as well.

Other things for your "To Do" list:

Get some sunshine: Soak up the rays. Just don't get burned and white dogs of course shouldn't stay out for more than 30 minutes or so in high heat since they burn much easier and faster. We all need sunshine. Soak up some vitamin D. Just know dogs do not absorb vitamin D much from sunshine. See more on vitamin D later.

Exercise
This is also **crucial** in cancer patients. Exercise helps reduce stress and providing oxygen to flow throughout the body. It's a healthy benefit for you and your dog. This will also help your dog go into Ketosis much faster with the Ketogenic diet. You want to keep your dog lean when fighting cancer. A dog with joint issues, use Hydrotherapy or short walks if possible.

Reduce stress: Make a calm quiet space for you and your dog. Stress can make cells grow. Play soft music, Meditate, Reiki, Acupuncture, and Yoga. Anything relaxing for you and your dog. If your dog seems stressed, you can add Ashwagandha to the diet daily. It helps for depression and anxiety. Also helps in fighting cancers.

Do **not** use air fresheners in your home or anything with a fragrance. No chemicals at all for cleaning either. Buy top of the line (Merv 11 or 13 and above) air conditioning filters. Stay away from smog and exhaust from vehicles and busy highways. HEPA filters with carbon block or high Merv ratings for your air filters. Check into HEPA air purifiers as well. Keep the air in your home clean and pure. Outside air is not clean and pure anymore.

Add an Essential oil diffuser to your home. They come in different sizes. Add 3 - 5 drops of Frankincense and/or Myrrh for fighting cancer. Run this at night especially when you are sleeping in a closed bedroom. No cats allowed. Cats are very sensitive to essential oils. Use extreme caution. Diffusers will cover only a certain amount of space just like your air purifiers. That's why it's good to have a couple of these in your house. I recommend a good organic essential oil.

Also, know that certain pet products - including the inflatable alternative to the so-called "cone of shame" are made of PVC, a known carcinogen. If my dog was battling cancer, PVC is the last substance I would put around her neck! Find a safe alternative.

And overall, give love love love. Hug/kiss your pets. Give them massages. Show them lots of love and attention. Make them feel warm and fuzzy inside. It is the heart that can heal. Keep a positive attitude always and be happy, even during the most worrisome times. Make the moments count!

If your pet experiences unusual side effects, substitute with something else. Adverse reactions to the herbs recommended are unusual. But just like people, allergic reactions are possible. Do not give your dog softgels. They will not dissolve. Poke hole and squeeze into foods.

If you DO decide on doing chemo, I highly recommend you adding D-ribose into the diet to help restore energy.

Chapter 11
Healing Herbs

Astragalus *(Astragalus membranaceous)*
Immunostimulant, antiviral, anti-inflammatory, hypothyroid (mildly depresses thyroid function), hypotensive, digestive tonic. Works on immune systems, lungs, liver, heart, kidneys, thyroid, and digestive tract.

Astragalus is used for strengthening the body against viral infections of the respiratory and heart. Astragalus can be used for early treatment of a variety of respiratory infections, including kennel cough (Bordetella bronchiseptica). Astragalus helps to raise white blood cell counts and also boosts the body's immune system. Astragalus may be useful for helping the body protect itself and speed recovery from the damages of long-term steroid medications. Astragalus is also useful in early stages of kidney infection and/or renal failure. Astragalus is non-toxic in any dosages.
A great immune booster and even kills cancer cells. Astragalus is a option for early treatment of various forms of respiratory infection such as kennel cough. Helps with anemia as well. It is an immuno-stimulant, antiviral, anti-inflammatory, hypothyroid (mildly depresses thyroid function), hypotensive, digestive tonic. Works on immune systems, lungs, liver, heart, kidneys, thyroid, and digestive tract.

Astragalus is used for strengthening the body against viral infections of the respiratory and heart. Astragalus can be used for early treatment of a variety of respiratory infections, including kennel cough (Bordetella bronchiseptica). Astragalus helps to raise white blood cell counts and also boosts the body's immune system. Astragalus may be useful for helping the body protect itself and speed recovery from the damages of long-term steroid medications. Astragalus is also useful in early stages of kidney infection and/or renal failure. Astragalus is non-toxic in any dosages. Astragalus may help prevent the immunosuppression caused by chemotherapy agents. In addition, it has been found that Astragalus contains an alkaloid that inhibits the spread of melanoma, a skin cancer. *Astragalus should not be given if active fever is present.*

Moringa
Moringa contains 46 antioxidants, 90 nutrients including calcium, trace minerals, iron, and all 9 essential amino acids. Moringa also contains powerful antioxidants, and has anti-fungal, antibacterial, and anti-inflammatory properties. A very powerful green food.

Dosage:
Small dogs/cats (up to 20 lbs): 1/4 - 1/2 teaspoon
Medium dogs (20-50 lbs): 1 teaspoon
Large dogs (50-100 lbs): 1 1/2 - 2 teaspoons

Giant dogs (100+ lbs): 1 tablespoon
This is just a general guideline and can be adjusted as needed.

Mullein
Mullein soothes and protects mucous membranes. It is an expectorant and can suppress cough (kennel cough) and treating asthma. Works with flu, coughs etc. The flowers, in the form of an oil infusion, also have antimicrobial properties and are effective in treating ear infections, including those caused by ear mites. The flower oil infusion can also be used to fight against fleas and mange.

Milk Thistle
Milk thistle is well known as an **herb for the liver** both for humans and pets. Milk thistle contains a flavonoid called silymarin. Extensive research has found that silymarin is safe and effective in treating a variety of liver diseases and other conditions, from kidney disease to mushroom or lead poisoning. It works by removing toxins trying to bind to the liver and by causing the liver to regenerate more quickly.

Works on:

- Chronic inflammatory liver disorders
- Liver tumors
- Leptospirosis
- Pancreatitis
- Fatty liver

Milk thistle is not effective in treating advanced liver cirrhosis. Milk thistle is safe for dogs. If milk thistle causes upset stomach, gas, or mild diarrhea in your dogs, simply reduce the dosage. Milk thistle should **not** be given to healthy dogs as a daily supplement. Some studies show that long-term use of very high doses of milk thistle will eventually suppress liver function. Give 5 days on and 2 days off weekly for up to three months, then remove from diet for six months.

Rosehips
Rosehips have been known for its ability to reduce the symptoms of rheumatoid arthritis, some respiratory conditions, prevent cancer, lower

cholesterol, manage diabetes, and boost the immune system. The vitamins and minerals included in rosehips is vitamin C, A, E, and B-complex, as well as calcium, iron, selenium, manganese, magnesium, phosphorus, potassium, sulfur, silicon, and zinc. The amount of antioxidants in rose hips is particularly useful in keeping the body healthy.

Rosehips have an impressive amount of vitamin C, which is one of the best methods to boost the immune system. Vitamin C stimulates white blood cells and is also essential in the prevention of asthma and the general health of the respiratory system. This also can be seen in the reduction of respiratory conditions such as colds and flu's through the intake of Rosehips and its high levels of vitamin C.

Rosehips can regulate the blood sugar levels of the body for anyone suffering from diabetes. By keeping the balance of insulin and glucose in the body and prevent fluctuations in blood sugar. Rosehips are also used as a diuretic which can help eliminate toxins from the body. Rosehips contain a good amount of iron which can help prevent anemia and also keep your organs well oxygenated. Collagen, along with the other minerals in Rosehips, can help prevent Osteoporosis. Safe for cats as well.

Dosage:
Small dogs: 1/4 - 1/2 teaspoon daily
Medium dogs: 1/2 - 1 teaspoon
Large dogs: 1 - 2 teaspoon

Slippery Elm (Ulmus fulva)
Slippery Elm is very safe and non-toxic. It can be used both internally and externally. Slippery Elm is one of the herbs used in Essiac Tea.

In the gastrointestinal tract, Slippery Elm acts directly. It resembles a natural "Pepto-Bismol." (Pepto-Bismol itself should not be used because it contains salicylate, a.k.a. aspirin). Slippery Elm coats, soothes, and lubricates the mucus membranes lining of the digestive tract. Slippery Elm is an excellent treatment for ulcers, gastritis, colitis, and other inflammatory bowel problems. It is high in fiber, and so helps normalize intestinal action. It can also be used to relieve diarrhea and constipation. It also may help with nausea and vomiting. Slippery Elm contains many nutrients beneficial for recuperating pets, and it may stay down when other foods are not tolerated. Slippery Elm may interfere with the absorption of certain minerals and pharmaceuticals, so is best given separately from any medications.

Give a dose before or with meals for digestive tract problems, such as inflammatory bowel disease, until symptoms resolve. Give for up to 90 days then take a break from it.

Powder Dosage:
Small dogs: 1/4 scoop
Med dogs: 1/2 scoop
Large dogs: 1/2 scoop - 3/4 scoop

Slippery Elm also has a calming effect creating a more relaxed sleep.

Turmeric
Turmeric is becoming very popular as a cure for cancers. Turmeric (Curcumin) has extreme anti-cancer properties. It has proven to cure some cancers because it inhibits growth of tumors, shrinks existing ones, and prevents new tumors from developing. Turmeric has been found to be a good pain reliever to dogs. No turmeric side effects to worry about, even if a large dose is given. It's a great herb to add to the dog's food if it suffers from arthritis.
An animal that's had a skin injury can be helped by turmeric's antibiotic and anti-inflammatory properties.

To treat a skin issue, simply mix honey with turmeric to form a paste and apply it to the abrasion.

Has been known to work on:

- Blocking inflammation
- Killing bacteria
- Improves health of the heart
- Antioxidant, carcinogenic, antibiotic, anti-inflammatory
- Stomach ailments

- Kills parasites
- Heals damage done from long-term diabetes

The dose for pain in dogs is 1/8 to 1/4 tsp. for every 10 lbs of dog's weight.

Turmeric should not to be given to dogs prone to kidney stones. Turmeric isn't supposed to be given with blood thinners. Turmeric should not be combined with drugs that reduce stomach acid (Pepsid, Zantac etc), as the body will actually increase its production of stomach acid, and thus, lead to nausea, stomach pain, bloating, and esophagus damage. Avoid Turmeric while giving any type of steroid medications.

Burdock Root

Burdock Root is a blood-purifying, hair-regrowing and cancer-fighting herb.

Its uses:
- Antioxidant
- Blood cleansing
- Liver and gallbladder stimulant
- Diuretic

Burdock is an effective herb for the detoxification of the body. It can remove toxic substances that are threatening the health of our dogs. Use it regularly as a preventative, especially if you have a breed of dog that's prone to cancer (such as a Boxer, Golden Retrievers, Labrador Retrievers, etc). Burdock can be used as a long-term liver tonic to clean and build the blood.

It is also useful in the treatment of arthritis, cancer, rheumatoid disorders, and kidney and bladder diseases. It also has been used as a diuretic that helps to eliminate waste materials from the body.

Chamomile

Used for anxiety, nervous disorders, skin inflammation, flatulence, and indigestion. One of the best known and most widely used plants in the world. Chamomile is gentle and can be used internally and externally in teas, tinctures, salves, compresses, and rinses. Helps to calm and relax the dog. Chamomile should not be given to cats. Helps with seizure disorders as well.

Dandelion
Dandelion has been used for digestive and liver (root); Pancreatitis, edema (leaf), Anemia, Kidney/Bladder. The leaf and root are good for many conditions involving edema (water retention) and the flowers are high in antioxidants. You can use root and leaf together and most of all for liver, kidney, and heart disease in dogs.

Dandelion should not be used in cases of bile duct obstruction or acute gallbladder inflammation. The high mineral content may affect the absorption of a certain class of antibiotics (quinolones). Dandelion leaf is particularly useful in animals that have a chronic problem with indigestion. If your dog has frequent gas and/or passes food that does not appear digested, apply a few drops of dandelion tincture on his/her tongue.

Dandelion is popular and is a safe but powerful diuretic and liver stimulant. Dandelion works with congestive heart failure, pulmonary edema, arthritis, gallbladder disease, and kidney stones. Drugs such as Lasix are often used to drain off excess fluid from the body and help the elimination of waste. Pharmaceutical diuretics are fast acting and very effective, but while they do a good job at reducing fluid buildup, they tend not to discriminate between what the body needs to keep and what it needs to lose. The body often loses too much potassium, a crucial heart and brain chemical, through urination. In this case, potassium must be supplemented throughout the therapy. Dandelion leaf on the other hand, contains its own rich source of potassium that the body can absorb.

While dandelion leaves are used as a diuretic, the root holds its own usefulness as a safe liver tonic. The liver is the primary filtering organ and responsible for removing toxins from the blood for elimination in the kidneys. And while dandelion leaf tea or tincture may do much toward relieving the symptoms through a nutritive/diuretic action, the root will work closer to the underlying causes. Dandelion does not further irritate an already inflamed condition. Dandelion root was shown to be effective in treating inflammatory diseases of the liver and the gall bladder including gallstones.

Devil's Claw
Used for reducing inflammation, especially with Osteoarthritis. There is a great range of dose with Devil's Claw. It's best to start with small amount and work up. Side effects if giving too much can include diarrhea as with all herbs and supplements although not common. Devil's Claw is used as an anti-inflammatory for arthritis. Devil's Claw is used for all types of muscle pain, and some forms of digestive upset – although it should not be used with ulcers. Devil's Claw has been used to treat loss of appetite, rheumatism, arthritis, fever, tendonitis, gastrointestinal problems, and liver and gallbladder problems. Devil's Claw is also used as a pain reliever (analgesic), sedative, and diuretic.

Dosage:
Small dogs: 250mg
Medium/Large dogs: 500mg
Giant dogs: Up to 1000mg

Cat's Claw
Cat's Claw is an immune system booster and contains natural cortisone. Cat's Claw may help create support for the intestinal and immune systems of the body, and may also create intestinal support with its ability to cleanse the entire intestinal tract. Cat's Claw may help with different stomach and bowel disorders, including colitis, irritable bowel syndrome, ulcers, and leaky gut syndrome. Cat's Claw is a natural anti-inflammatory and can help reduce inflammation within the body as well as joints. Cat's Claw also has been used in help treat cancers.

Do not give along with cortisone medications. Do not use Cat's Claw if your dog has Leukemia, bleeding disorders, autoimmune disease, or low blood pressure. Discontinue use two weeks before surgery.

White Willow Bark
White Willow Bark is similar to aspirin and should only be used on occasion when needed. You can try this in place of NSAIDs as this is in its natural form and is much safer than pain medications. Those with

tinnitus, peptic ulcers, seizure disorders, or bleeding disorders also should not use it. The side effects of willow bark include upset stomachs, itchiness, and rashes mostly in sensitive patients. If you have blood or kidney disorders, be particularly careful before using willow bark. There is no need to take willow bark on a regular basis as high doses can greatly increase your chances of experiencing side effects.

Grape Seed Extract
Grape Seed Extract is a powerful anti-inflammatory. Grape skin and the meat are toxic to dogs and can cause renal failure. Only the seeds and the oil of grape seeds are safe. Grape Seed extract is used in all illnesses causing inflammation including heart and arthritis along with cancer. Combining both Ubiquinol and Grape Seed Extract makes it a powerful cancer fighter. Also works with ulcerative colitis. Grape Seed Extract works extremely well with joint issues and inflammation anywhere in the body. Allergic reactions are rare but can occur such as tongue or face swelling, itching, nausea, and diarrhea. This is the case with many herbs although most of these are rare. If these occur, just stop using GSE. In case of allergic reactions such as face swelling, seek emergency treatment.

I use this with all five of my dogs without any issues. Use for up to 3 months then take a break from it for awhile before beginning use again. Organic is the only preferred selection so to avoid pesticides.

Use caution when using anti-coagulant, anti-platelet drugs or medications that are broken down by the liver. May interact with NSAIDs as with all anti-inflammatory herbs.

Echinacea
Echinacea has long been used for infections and as a blood purifier. Echinacea stimulates the immune system to help fight viral and bacterial infections. Echinacea is an immune stimulant that helps the body defend itself against viral infection more effectively.
Because of its powerful immune boosting ability, its best to only take Echinacea for a short period of time, usually from a few days to a few weeks, depending on your illness. This short period will activate your immune system.

Don't give echinacea in any form to a dog who has an auto-immune disease (lupus, thrombocytopenia, myasthenia gravis, thyroiditis).

Ginger Root
Ginger may be one of the most important plants used in herbal medicine. Ginger is one of the most prescribed herbs and is used in the treatment of colds for its ability to eliminate toxins and raise body heat.

Ginger Side Effects: Ginger is a blood thinner so if taking prescription blood thinners, have a bleeding disorder, or have gallbladder disease, don't take medicinal doses of ginger. Ginger can be used safely to treat a wide range of health problems, from simple nausea to arthritis. Ginger combines well with many herbs, improving taste and potency.

Avoid Ginger from countries such as China and India. That includes organic as well.

Amla
Amla fruit (Emblica officinalis), also known as Indian Gooseberry or Amalaki, is one of the richest sources of bioflavonoids and vitamin C. This plum-sized fruit is admired for its anti-aging and immune system-enhancing properties. Each Amla fruit contains up to 700mg of vitamin C.

It has been used for anemia, asthma, bleeding gums, diabetes, colds, chronic lung disease, hypertension, yeast infections, and cancer. It also increases lean body mass, accelerates the repair and regeneration of connective tissue, and enhances interferon and corticosteroid production. Amla also acts as an antacid and anti-tumorigenic agent. In addition, it increases protein synthesis and is useful in cases of hypoglycemia.

Amla powder is also rich in fiber, which helps support digestion and prevents constipation. Amla may also help reduce acidity in the gut, protect from gallbladder infections, treat diabetes, and reduce the risk for gastrointestinal cancer and cancer of the respiratory tract.

Dosage:
Small dogs: 500mg

Medium dogs: 750mg
Large dogs: 1000mg

Alfalfa
Alfalfa is an anti-inflammatory, anti-fungal, anti-cancer herb. For dogs that are anemic, Alfalfa is high in Vitamin K and is helpful for dogs with bleeding disorders which result from long-term use of medicines such as antibiotics. High amounts of Vitamin K has been linked to cases of Heinz-body anemia in dogs (and cats) when taken in large quantity.

Alfalfa works well for arthritis and cancer prevention. Also reduces overly acidic urine. Do not use in high amounts. Higher amounts can cause stomach upset and even bloat in larger dogs. Alfalfa may cause allergic reaction in pollen-sensitive pets. Purchase organic only as Alfalfa contains high amounts of pesticides.

Dosage:
Small dogs: 1/2 teaspoon daily
Medium dogs: 2/3 teaspoon daily
Large dogs: 1 teaspoon daily

Hawthorn
Hawthorn helps prevent and treat congestive heart failure in senior dogs (and people), and tones the hearts of younger dogs who have survived heartworm disease. Older dogs, especially those with cardiac or renal problems, can benefit from Hawthorn. Unlike most medications, tonic herbs do not suppress or replace natural functions in the body. Instead, they naturally help improve the body as a whole. Most tonic herbs do their work by providing special nutrients, enzymes that the body needs to bring overstressed organs and systems into functioning more appropriately. Hawthorn works over a period of time with daily use and improves the heart. Hawthorn helps support the heart in ways that no food or drug can. It helps to increase circulation and the transport of nutrients and oxygen throughout the body. Hawthorn has the ability to strengthen a weak or erratic heartbeat – such as that of elderly or energetically challenged dogs and this herb is very, very safe. In the hundreds of animal studies that have been conducted with this herb in the last 100 years, Hawthorn has shown

extremely low toxicity in every animal tested.
Hawthorn is useful in the daily care of any older dog, but especially those who suffer from chronic heart problems and that have a weakened heart to be able to help it to pump blood. Hawthorn is also useful in cases of renal failure, especially in early stages. When combined with Ginkgo Biloba, Hawthorn may be useful for getting more blood and oxygen into renal arteries and smaller vessels of the kidneys.

Boswellia
Boswellia has also been shown in preliminary research to be effective at reducing swelling around brain tumors. A study performed in 2004 shows that Boswellia is an herb that lives up to its reputation. Twenty-four dogs with chronic joint pain were administered a dose of Boswellia once a week for 6 weeks. After just a couple weeks, 71% of the dogs showed improvement. The research showed that improvement was gradual but Boswellia did seem to help reduce local pain and stiff gaits. Boswellia is one herb that seems to work well.

Camu Camu (Myrciaria dubia)
Camu Camu is high in vitamin C and has been shown to reduce inflammation, detoxify the body, and prevent viral infections. Camu Camu contains a huge amount of vitamin C. Camu Camu has one of the highest concentrations of vitamin C of any food source. Camu Camu has been known to prevent certain cognitive disorders such as Alzheimer's disease and dementia. It can also boost cognitive ability in younger people, increasing focus, memory, and concentration skills. Camu Camu is not known as an allergenic food, and can be taken in conjunction with other pharmaceuticals and supplements.

Hydrangea Root
A flower essence helps to naturally dissolve kidney stones and struvite crystals. A safe, natural alternative treatment. Used for kidney support, as a diuretic, eliminates swelling and fluid retention and increases the flow of urine. Will dissolve/remove bladder/struvite and kidney stones and relieve the pain they cause, and alleviate backache due to kidney issues. Hydrangea Root has been used to treat chronic rheumatoid arthritis and the swelling of arthritis (by reducing calcium deposits), gout, and edema. Hydrangea Root has also been used to help dissolve

bone spurs or calcification of muscles. It appears to help the body put calcium back into in the system. Hydrangea Root has an anti-inflammatory action that have a cortisone-like effect. This is useful for kidney infection and inflammation as well as for arthritis. It has also been used to break up lumps and tumors. It increases the production of urine (a diuretic) and also has a mild laxative effect. It may be combined with other herbs like Marshmallow. Specific breeds at highest risk for kidney and bladder stones include Miniature Schnauzers, Shih Tzu's, Bichon Frise, Cocker Spaniels, and Lhasa Apso's. Keep pH levels between 6-7 but no higher than 7. I recommend closer to the 7pH mark for cancer patients.

Hydrangea Root Capsule Dosage:
Kidney stones: Give for 6 - 8 weeks, then re-test
Struvite crystals: Give for 6 weeks, then re-test
Oxalate stones: Surgery may be required.

Dosage:
Up to 25 lbs: 1/2 capsule with food 3 times a day
25-50 lbs: 1 capsule with food 3 times a day
50-75 lbs: 1 1/2 capsules with food 3 times a day
75 lbs+: 2 capsules with food 3 times a day

Warning: Certain parts of hydrangeas are particularly dangerous and toxic to dogs. These parts are the buds and the leaves. Owners of dogs should make sure that their pets steer clear of hydrangeas, and make sure that the buds and leaves go nowhere near their mouths. Hydrangea Root is safe!

Ashwagandha
Ashwagandha has been used to promote health and longevity. Ashwagandha is admired for its anti-aging properties. It is used to enhance the immune system and treat anemia, inflammation, bacterial infection, and diarrhea. It is also thought to improve the quality of bodily tissues. Its herbal actions span a wide range from adaptogenic to sedative. Ashwagandha helps relieve general aches and pains. Ashwagandha is an excellent hematinic and contains high levels of iron and free amino acids such as glycine, valine, tyrosine, proline, and alanine. This herb has been shown to be safe for long-term use.

Ashwagandha has anti-inflammatory, diuretic, sedative, antibacterial, and anti-fungal activity. It also has anti-tumor uses in animals. Ashwagandha is used for anxiety and depression and helps relieve stress. Supports a healthy nervous system.

Dosage: (up to twice a day)
Small dogs: 500mg
Medium dogs: 1,000mg
Large dogs: 1,500mg

Quercetin
Flavonoids, such as Quercetin, are antioxidants. They scavenge particles in the body known as free radicals which damage cell membranes and cause cell death. They may reduce or even help prevent some of the damage free radicals cause. Quercetin prevents immune cells from releasing histamines, which are chemicals that cause allergic reactions. As a result, Quercetin may help reduce symptoms of allergies, including runny nose, watery eyes, hives, and swelling of the face and lips.

Scientists have considered Quercetin and other flavonoids contained in fruits and vegetables important in cancer prevention. People who eat more fruits and vegetables tend to have lower risk of certain types of cancer. Flavonoids have anti-cancer properties. Quercetin and other flavonoids have been shown in these studies to inhibit the growth of cancer cells from breast, colon, prostate, ovarian, endometrial, and lung tumors. A frequent intake of Quercetin-rich foods was associated with lower lung cancer risk. Quercetin supplements are available as pills or capsules. They are often packaged with Bromelain (an enzyme found in pineapple) because both are anti-inflammatories. Should only be used for short-term use.

Chlorella
Chlorella is blue-green algae like its cousin Spirulina. Chlorella's rich green color comes from a high concentration of chlorophyll. Chlorella contains a wide variety of B vitamins, vitamin C and E, amino acids and trace minerals. It contains more vitamin B-12 than liver. Chlorella is a great supplement to help boost the immune system and to help the

body detoxify as well from heavy metals. Helps in fighting cancer by building the immune system. Also lowers blood sugars and cholesterol.

Spirulina
Spirulina supplies beta carotene and chlorophyll and also contains a variety of vitamins including A, B-1, B-3, B-6 as well as vitamins C, D, E, and K. Spirulina has an Oxygen Radical Absorbance Capacity (ORAC) of over 24,000, which is four times the ORAC score of blueberries! The ORAC score measures the antioxidant concentration in foods.

Spirulina is reported to increase energy, restore immune system, has muscle building properties, and also may help avoid allergy attacks. Spirulina contains a wide range of minerals including calcium, manganese, iron, chromium, phosphorus, molybdenum, iodine, chloride, magnesium, sodium, zinc, potassium, selenium, germanium, copper, and boron. Amino acids play an important role in our body's ability to efficiently use these minerals - and Spirulina contains all nine essential amino acids! Spirulina easy to digest as well. It also is reported to have positive effects in treating radiation and arsenic poisoning.

Licorice Root (Glycyrrhiza uralensis)
This herb is an effective anti-inflammatory due to the presence of Glycyrrhizin, which stimulates the adrenals and makes it useful for treating Addison's disease. Due to its corticosteroid-like actions, licorice is effective in helping relieve pain and inflammation without the side effects from medications such as corticosteroids. If your dog has arthritis or skin problems such as eczema or atopic dermatitis; licorice is a good herb to use. Licorice Root also works on alleviating ulcers. It soothes and protects mucous membranes and is good for the gastrointestinal and upper respiratory tracts. Licorice Root can also treat liver toxicity and prevent many forms of liver disease.

Licorice Root does not interfere with corticosteroid drugs therefore licorice root can be used as a supportive adjunct as it has a strengthening effect which allows for lower doses of corticosteroids. Licorice root can also be used to wean the dog off of steroids safely.

This herb should not be given for periods longer than 2 weeks without a break in between. Do not give Licorice Root (Glycyrrhiza uralensis) to heart patients. Licorice Root can raise sugar levels in blood and should be used with caution in diabetic dogs.

If you must use for more than two weeks make sure that you add dandelion to the diet so that increased potassium requirement is met and elimination of excess sodium is enabled.

*Licorice can be processed to remove the glycyrrhiza, resulting in DGL (deglycyrrhizinated licorice), which does not appear to share the metabolic disadvantages of licorice and may be used in heart patients.

Marshmallow Root
Marshmallow Root is naturally high in mucilage, which allows it to provide soothing support for mucous membranes. This natural mucilage moistens membranes, especially in the bronchioles, mouth, and intestines. It's great for gastritis, ulcers, bladder, and kidney infections and can ease respiratory problems such as kennel cough. Marshmallow root can be used similarly to Slippery Elm for dogs that are weak and unable to eat many foods. Marshmallow herb frequently gets used for urinary problems such as cystitis, kidney stones, and UTIs. Besides being a demulcent specific to the urinary tract, it's also a diuretic. Marshmallow root is very safe but might impair absorption of medications if taken at the same time, so use an hour or so apart from any meds your dog takes.

Maqui Berry (The Super Berry)
Maqui Berry is a powerful botanical antioxidant due to its vast amount of anthocyanins, polyphenols and bioflavaoids. Contains 300% more anthocyanins and 150% more polyphenols than any other food.

Maqui Berry contains: Calcium, Iron, Magnesium, Phosphorus, Potassium, Zinc, Copper, Manganese, Selenium, vitamin C, Thiamin, Riboflavin, Niacin, Pantothenic Acid, vitamin B-6, Folate, Choline, Betaine, vitamin A (RAE), Beta carotene, vitamin A (IU), Lutein & Zeaxanthin, vitamin E, Beta Tocopherol, Gamma Tocopherol, Delta Tocopherol, vitamin K and including all your amino acids.

Maqui Berry may also help balance blood glucose levels. Maqui Berry is the king of all berries and offers the most nutrients available in one berry. It also has the highest quantity of antioxidants of any food on the planet and is a great immune booster. Can be used to treats colds and flu, helps control levels of cholesterol, fight sore throats and fever. Also, helps aid in digestion and may inhibit colon cancer cells. Giving Maqui Berry after meals may help with weight loss. Maqui Berry may also help in cardiovascular disease. These berries look much like blueberries but larger in size. You may add these berries into the diet as you would with any other berry or supplement.

Mushrooms (Beta-glucans)
Beta-glucans are chains of polysaccharides, and proteoglycans are proteins usually found in connective tissue. Mushrooms are great for building immunity, digestion, respiratory, cardiovascular, fighting off cancer cells, oxygenate the blood, fight off fatigue, detoxing, and even reduce inflammation in joints. Mushrooms improve skin and fur providing a clear skin and shiny coat. Mushrooms are an excellent source of antioxidants. Mushrooms also work against areas where there is a lot of oxidative stress especially in eye tissues, the liver and kidneys and red blood cells. The mycelium part of the mushroom that lies below the surface of the soil may hold the most nutritional benefits of mushrooms.

Some of the most common medicinal mushrooms are:
Shiitake (Lentinula edodes)
Reishi (Ganoderma lucidum)
Maitake (Grifola frondosa)
Lion's Mane (Hericium erinaceus)
Turkey Tail (Trametes versicolor)
Himematsutake (Agaricus blazei)
Cordyceps (Cordyceps militaris)
Chaga (Inonotus obliquus)

Other known medicinal mushrooms:
Polyporus umbellatus ("Lumpy Bracket")
King Trumpet (Pleurotus eryngii) also known as King Oyster
Oyster Mushroom (Pleurotus ostreatus)
Antrodia camphorata

Sanghwang (Phellinus linteus)

There are many mushrooms available but these are some of your more common ones. There is so much information pertaining to mushrooms, it would be impossible to put it all in this book. Many provide amino acids, vitamins, antioxidants, minerals and so much more.

Many non-believers say mushrooms can do nothing for you and doesn't even help cure cancer. Well here are my thoughts on this. Food is our medicine. Food is what heals us and makes us healthy and can provide lots of much needed nutrients not in our normal diets. While our soils are depleted on so many levels, buying organic helps retain more nutrients and avoid toxic chemicals. Every food provides certain nutrients. Each vegetable and fruit provides us with vitamins that meat or dairy may not be able to do. Every single thing we can consume as food can provide us with so much. It can build our immune systems in which in turn, will fight off cancer cells or any other illness. So the word "cure" may not be the right word for a food or mushroom or plant; it is bringing them all together to help cleanse your body, build the immune system, and fight off disease and illness. It is not one thing that cures anything. It all needs to come together. This is why a balanced healthy diet for your dog with clean organic supplemental foods such as mushrooms and Camu Camu or anything in its natural form, can and will help you heal a sick body. We catch colds because our immune systems are down. Immune systems become weakened from stress, toxins in our food, water, and air. We live in a sea of chemicals all around us that are man-made and not acceptable for our bodies. Our skin even absorbs chemicals like a sponge. This is why we must clean up our homes, our yards, and our surroundings to keep immune systems strong. So no, mushrooms won't cure cancer. Cannabis won't cure cancer. It takes an army of chemical-free food and water and many great supplemental additives into the diet to build a bigger and stronger army. I say this all the time when someone comes to me about their dog with joint issues and says, oh my dog is walking great now since I added CBD oil. But when I start digging and asking questions, that dog isn't just getting the CBD oil. It is getting other supplements as well. The CBD oil was just the icing on the cake that the dog needed. Yes, it helps with pain, yes it helps with inflammation but please don't limit yourself to one single supplement. You won't win in the long run.

I have two stories myself on my dogs with joint issues. It isn't one thing that FIXED them. It is a combination of a lot of things. It's that cherry on top that you are looking for. The one thing that finally makes a difference to what you are already doing. If by chance, someone happens to be feeding kibble and hasn't made any changes and then adds in mushrooms or CBD oil and their dog gets better, it's because that body is latching onto anything good coming into it and using it to the best of its ability. It may not continue to work for a long period because no other changes were made. It takes a combination for it to work and work well.

So when someone says to me, they don't believe this can cure cancer; it's because they haven't really learned what this means. You have to look at the whole picture, not just a piece of it. This is why the diet is so crucial in our health and our dog's lives. We must clean up the diet and provide our bodies the nutrients it is lacking. You cleaning up your home, throwing out the air fresheners and toxic dryer sheets and soaps, adding in HEPA air purifiers and removing chemicals as much as possible, will keep you and your pets healthy.

Use caution regarding use of echinacea, reishi, maitake, and astragalus for dogs with autoimmune issues.

Different combinations of herbs and supplements specific for illness/disease. Give at least 3-5 of each mixed. Buy organic if at all possible.

Herbs and supplements great for kidney and urinary support including struvite stones:
Uva Ursi
Hydrangea Root
Marshmallow Root
Goldenrod
Chanca Piedra (stone breaker)
Dandelion
Apple Cider Vinegar (raw, unfiltered)

Horsetail (use with caution when using other herbs)
Plantain (use with caution)
Olive Leaf
Mushrooms
Astragalus
Humic/Fulvic Acid
Organic Alfalfa (keep amounts low in large breeds)
IP-6
Pumpkin Seeds
Cranberry
L-Histidine (amino acid)
N-acetylcysteine (NAC)
Vitamin C (Magnesium Ascorbate)
Magnesium Citrate
D-Mannose (Avoid products containing xylitol)

Anti-inflammatory Herbs:
(Great for any type of infection in the body, joint issues as well as cancer.)
Devil's Claw
Cat's Claw
Boswellia
Turmeric
Yucca Root
Fever Few
White Willow Bark
Grape Seed Extract (Seeds Only)
Ginger
Organic Alfalfa

Kennel cough or cough, flu, sneezing, runny nose:
Fenugreek
Mullein
Vitamin C (Magnesium Ascorbate) to bowel tolerance or Camu Camu
Astragalus
Echinacea (short term use only) *(give to other dogs in same household for protection from ill dog)*
Organic Mushrooms
Grape Seed Extract (organic)

Diffuse the essential oils lavender and eucalyptus.
N-acetylcysteine (amino acid)
Licorice Root or Deglycrrhizinated Licorice Root (DGL) (small amounts and/or short term use) *(Do not use Licorice with heart disease although DGL may be much safer for heart patients)*
Manuka Honey
Slippery Elm mixed with water
Colloidal Silver (can also be diffused)

Thyroid support:
Astragalus
Siberian Ginseng (also known as Eleuthero Root)
Bladderwrack
Organic Ashwagandha Root
Gotu Kola (Can be toxic in large doses)
Licorice Root or Deglycrrhizinated Licorice Root (DGL) (small amounts and/or short term use unless you add in Dandelion with it.) *(Do not use Licorice with heart disease although DGL may be much safer for heart patients)*

Diabetes support:
Grape Seed Extract (organic)
Fenugreek
Gymnema Sylvestre
Turmeric
Golden Seal

Seizures:
Organic Cannabis Oil (CBD) (Full Spectrum-meaning all parts of plants used)
Passion Flower
Valerian
Chamomile
Blue Vervain
Skullcap
Vitamin E (daily)
B-complex vitamins
Magnesium
Taurine

Candida/Yeast:
Pau D'Arco
Golden Seal (do not give to puppies)
Garlic
Oregano Oil-(dilute topically/short-term use)
Apple Cider Vinegar (raw, unfiltered)
Probiotics/Digestive Enzymes
Organic Coconut Oil
Grapefruit Seed Extract
Olive Leaf
Saccharomyces boulardii (found in some probiotics)

Ear (yeast and infections)externally and internally applications:
Apple Cider Vinegar
Probiotics
Digestive enzymes
Add one drop of oregano oil to 1/2 oz of olive oil. Drop a small amount of the mixture into your dog's ear or soak it in a cotton ball and swab the earflap with it. Do this daily for 7 days. Calendula oil diluted with olive oil can also be used.

Infected anal glands:
Dilute 10 drops of Calendula oil into one cup of water for cuts and broken skin. Apply topically.
Give orally: Silicea 6c or 30c -use when your dog needs a little help to empty his glands. Can mix with filtered water and add to daily water bowl. Or, syringe it into the dog's mouth - twice a day for 7 days.

Dental (chronic tarter and bad breath):
Remove plague by adding this natural remedy Fragaria Vesca 6C to dog's water or food daily (3-5 pellets). Replace water daily.
Brush daily
Probiotic Rinse
Collodial Silver (brush and rinse)

Natural deworming (not including heartworm):
Diatomaceous Earth (may not kill tapeworms)
Organic Raw Pumpkin Seeds/Powder

Deep Detox (7-30 days): *(careful with this if your dog is coming of a commercial pet food diet. Save this for later after s/he has transitioned into a raw diet.)*
Activated Charcoal *(add powder into wet foods or capsules. Never give the dry powder to your dog as they can inhale and choke. Give this away from other supplements and medications if possible. For slow detox, 1 capsule per day for 3 - 5 days or smaller amounts daily for longer periods.)*
Greens Powder
Dandelion
Burdock Root
Milk Thistle
Apple Cider Vinegar
Coconut oil
Probiotics
Digestive Enzymes
Colostrum
Slippery Elm
Mushrooms
L-Glutamine (helps gut while detoxing)

Depression/Moodiness/Stress/Anxiety:
Relora
Siberian Ginseng (also known as Eleuthero Root)
Organic Ashwagandha
Organic Cannabis Oil (CBD)
Bacopa
SAMe (S-adenosylmethionine)

Dementia/Cognitive Dysfunction/Seizures:
Bacopa
MCT Oil/Coconut oil (reports that coconut oil has reversed the process)
Ginkgo Biloba (avoid with seizures)
Gotu Kola
Organic Cannabis Oil (CBD)
Turmeric
Fish oils
SAMe (S-adenosylmethionine)
7-HMRlignans from Norwegian Spruce Tree (Swanson sells it)

CBD Oil
Taurine
Rescue Remedy
B-Complex Vitamin
Vitamin E

Hormone balancer:
Dong Quai (Angelica sinensis)
Diindolylmethane (DIM) 10mg (crucifers like broccoli, cauliflower etc)
7-HMRlignans from Norwegian Spruce Tree (Swanson sells it)
DHEA (10-25mg)
SAMe (S-adenosylmethionine)
Wild Yam

Leaky Gut/ GI Tract Issues/Allergies/Acid Reflux/GERD:
Slippery Elm (also great for diarrhea)
L-Glutamine (can be used for ulcers)
Colostrum
Probiotics
Digestive Enzymes (higher doses)
L-Histidine (amino acid)
N-acetylcysteine (amino acid) *(also used for Tylenol toxicity)*
Bee Pollen
Licorice Root or Deglycrrhizinated Licorice Root (DGL) (small amounts and/or short term use) *(Do not use Licorice with heart disease although DGL may be much safer for heart patients)* (can be used for ulcers)
Cat's Claw
Oregon Grape
Calcium Carbonate (found in eggshells)
Amla

Heart:
D-Ribose
L-Carnitine
L Arginine
Hawthorn
COQ10/Ubiquinol
Pycnogenol

Astaxanthin
Magnesium Orotate
B complex
Fish oils
Vitamin E
Taurine
Dandelion Root
Turmeric
Boswellia
Selenium

Pancreas/Pancreatitis:
Cat's Claw
Digestive Enzymes (High in amylase, Lipase, pancreas, ox bile etc)
Probiotics (start 2 billion and work up)
Colostrum
Nigella sativa
Gamma-amino butyric acid (GABA)
Fenugreek
Raw Pancreas
Ancestral Grass Fed Beef Pancreas supplement

Liver/Fatty Liver Support:
Milk Thistle
Dandelion
Amla
Astragalus
Yellowdock Root
SAMe
Papaya
Vit E
Black Seed Oil
Ginger
Artichoke
Chicory Root
Silkworm Pupae

There are herbs you can use but will need to be used under the care of a holistic vet.

If dosage isn't listed under each supplement, use this chart for dosing:

Herb Dosage

Weight	Tincture	0 Capsule	Tea	Powder
5-10 lbs	2 drops	1/2 cap	1 tsp	1/4 tsp
10-20 lbs	4 drops	1 cap	2 tsp	1/4-1/2 tsp
20-30 lbs	6 drops	1 cap	1 TBSP	1/2 tsp
30-50 lbs	6 drops	2 caps	4 tsp	1/2-1 tsp
50-70 lbs	6-10 drops	2 caps	5 tsp	1 tsp
70-90 lbs	14-18 drops	3 caps	2 TBSP	1 1/2 tsp
90-110 lbs	18-22 drops	4 caps	3 TBSP	2 tsp
110-150 lbs	22-26 drops	4 caps	4 TBSP	2 1/2 tsp
150-180 lbs	26-30 drops	5 caps	5 TBSP	3 tsp

All herbs should be given 5 days on and 2 days off.

If your pet experiences unusual side effects, substitute with something else. Adverse reactions to the herbs recommended are unusual. But just like people, allergic reactions are possible. Do not give your dog softgels. They do not dissolve. Poke a hole and squeeze out.

Some herbs can be toxic in higher doses and should be used under a holistic vet's supervision. The ones listed here are safe unless a note with it says otherwise.

*Below is a list of which to **avoid** or only use under holistic veterinarian direction.*

Pennyroyal (toxic to liver)	Tea Tree Oil (undiluted correctly can cause death)	HOPS (toxic to greyhounds)	Comfrey (can cause liver damage)

Rue (can cause nausea and vomiting in high doses)	Wormwood (can irritate liver and kidneys)	White Willow Bark (avoid if taking NSAIDs)	Ma Huang (heart arrhythmias)
Tarragon (may slow blood blotting)			

Before using herbs, if your dog is on the following medications, consult with a holistic vet before giving:

- Steroids
- Aspirin
- Antibiotics
- Cardiac drugs
- Hormones (thyroxine)
- Diuretics (Furosemide, Diazide)
- Diabetic/hypoglycemic drugs (Insulin)
- Central Nervous System drugs (phenobarbital)
- Anti-inflammatories/NSAIDs (Rimadyl)
- Chemotherapy agents

For finding the best quality herbs out there, check out the Health Rangers (Mike Adams) products. A little pricey but I totally trust his products as they have been tested in his lab for purity. Always buy organic for full benefits. These are human supplements so check the ingredients to make sure they are safe for dogs. Grapes are in some of the products. Grape seeds only are safe for dogs.

*Avoid Turmeric, Ginger, and Garlic from countries such as China and India if at all possible. That includes organic as well.
If your dog has any type of kidney or liver disease or chronic illness, please check with your vet before giving any type of herbal supplements.*

Extra tips for using Colloidal Silver
- Spray hot spots, scrapes, cuts, burns, and infections to help heal

- Put into ear for earaches, ear mites, and yeasty ears.
- Helps with Cystitis and UTI's
- Add drops in eyes to help with pink eye, dry eyes, sty's, and other eye infections. (half distilled water and half CS)
- Brush teeth to prevent decay and bad breath (also spray in mouth daily)
- Spray in mouth on gums and teeth to help keep down tarter build up
- Reduces symptoms of flu, cold, respiratory
- Add to organic chemical-free shampoo to become a disinfectant
- Spray water bowl before filling with filtered water to help prevent mold and bacteria (purifies water also)

Recommended Dosing

Up to 10 lbs	1 tsp
11 - 25 lbs	1 1/3 tsp
26 - 40 lbs	2 tsp
41 - 55 lbs	2 1/2 tsp
56 - 80 lbs	3 tsp
81 - 100 lbs	3 1/2 tsp
101 - 150 lbs	4 tsp
151 - 200+lbs	4-5 tsp

Chapter 12
How To Prepare Your Dog For The Rabies Vaccine

This applies to adult dogs for the most part. Do not give the vitamins recommended in this chapter to puppies. If you are like me, you are dreading taking your dog again for another Rabies vaccine. Rabies vaccines are required by law every 3 years. I have seen many vets still want to only do 1-year vaccines and believe it or not, they do make both 1 and 3-year vaccines. If that's your vet, find a NEW vet. He is only in it for the money. I see way too many of these vets and it makes me furious. GREED is the key word here. And to say, it really isn't about making money off that vaccine but the fact he is getting you back in the door to spend more money or maybe because that vaccine might make your pet sick. This could go all kinds of directions but you get my point. They are not looking out for the best interest of your dog. Make sure you ask for the 3-year and Thimerosal-Free.

Some cities accept titers but that is a rarity. Also chronically ill dogs (Cancer, Autoimmune, seizure disorders etc) can get exceptions as well.

I've read a lot of articles where holistic vets tell you what to do after your dog has received a vaccine. I want to prepare you for before, during, and after.

These recommendations come from human reactions as well and are recommended by one of the top neurosurgeons in the world with about 30 years experience in medicine. So I am bringing you this list I put together to help your dog have the least amount of side effects if at all possible. Too many pets have died just from a Rabies vaccine so preparation is crucial.

Do NOT get the Rabies vaccine on same day as surgery. Do NOT get other vaccines on the same day. Wait 30 days to do surgery or receive another vaccine if absolutely needed. Do NOT give a vaccine to a sick or chronically ill, recently injured or any type of illness that has weakened the immune system to a pet.

Now with that said, you want to prepare for the Rabies vaccine. I only mention Rabies here but you can do this with all vaccines and I actually recommend that you do.

Preparing for the Rabies vaccine is key. By adding in supplements, keeping the food and water clean, removing toxins and chemicals from your home and yard and getting rid of flea and tick meds and heartworm meds, you can have a strong immune system in your dog. Adding in a little extra supplements is key to preparing for the Rabies and helping to reduce any reactions. Vaccines come with many health hazards so it's best to always prepare. You can start 2-4 weeks ahead of time depending on your dog's immune system and diet.

By doing this, you can add in vitamin C (Magnesium Ascorbate) to the diet (or better yet, the natural form-Camu Camu). Always know adding in vitamin C (Magnesium Ascorbate) can cause loose stools so work up slowly on the amounts. Start with small amounts.

Magnesium Ascorbate dosage:
Toy/Small dogs: 1/8 tsp to start
Med/Large dogs: 1/4 - 1/2 tsp to start

Camu Camu-follow herb chart

Then work up, increase this to 2 - 4 times a day in the highest amount possible without causing diarrhea. Yep there is a fine line there. You will know but go slow.

Adding in a little extra Selenium, Curcumin/Turmeric and Quercetin are great as well. Try to give these within an hour of getting the vaccine.

Vitamin E ("**d**" - Alpha Tocopherol) in a more natural form (not "**dl**" - Alpha Tocopherol) is critical in the diet along with preparing for a vaccine.

Astaxanthin is good at protecting against the toxic effects of the vaccine as well.

Zinc given daily for a couple days along within an hour before the vaccine will help stop the damaging effects. Make sure it is not mixed with copper or other substances. Zinc only. Only use this for several days then stop (day before, day of, day after). Zinc is very protective against vaccine toxicity.

Remember if you are purchasing human supplements; make sure there is only the one ingredient you are looking for in it.

The dosages on labels are usually based off of a 150 lb human. So for a 20 lb dog, provide a dash (1/8-1/4 capsule); 50 lb dog 1/4 - 1/2 of a capsule; 100+ lb dog - 1 full capsule.

Extra magnesium is also a great additive as well. So do the same as you do for the Zinc. Magnesium Malate or Citrate is recommended. Add in some celery and parsley to the diet several days before and day of if you like.

You should do these things up until the day of the vaccine. And it certainly won't hurt after the fact. Give good quality fish oils daily.

Also, give the homeopathic remedy **Lyssin** (also known as Hydrophobinum) **for the Rabies** vaccine. Lyssin 200c is best, but if you can't find it, 30c will work as well. It is recommended to do this a few days before, day of and a few days after. If you have a small dog or a dog that has had some mild reactions in the past, I would recommend using this for a couple of weeks, possibly a month. Dogs can show reactions for months after a vaccine so always keep a close eye out. (scratching, coughing, hair loss, seizures, lumps or hair loss at injection site, change in behavior etc).

Dosing:
3 pellets daily - small dogs
4 pellets daily - medium dogs
5 pellets daily - large dogs

For the **other vaccines use Thuja** homeopathic remedy with same dosing if you plan on getting them.

All the above can be done starting at least one week before, during, and at least a week after.

Make sure your dog gets plenty of sunshine during this time as well. If your dog isn't getting sunshine every day, then add a little vitamin D3 into the food for these several days of before, during, and after. A low dose depending on your dog's size is sufficient. Do not overdo this vitamin. It is fat-soluble, meaning your dog's body does not excrete it. It goes into the liver. Do not give this on a regular daily basis as part of the diet. Seek out a holistic vet for guidance on this vitamin if you plan on doing so. If softgels, poke hole or cut off tip and squirt onto foods. Or you can mix in with organic plain Kefir or Greek yogurt. Use this vitamin the day before, day of and day after, then stop giving it.

Alternative: You can use cod liver oil for these few days. Cod liver oil will be much safer but I do not recommend it for daily long-term use. Sardines are also high in vitamin D as well as Salmon and egg yolks.

*Do **not** give your dog mushrooms, whey protein, or beta-glucans during this process. Avoid all immune-stimulating supplements for at least 7 days before and after vaccine.

Avoid oils that suppress immunity and increase inflammation such as corn, safflower, sunflower, soybean, canola, and peanut oils.

Make sure your dog won't be under stress from travel (vacations) or guests in your home. Keep things calm and no stress for your dog for several weeks.

Ask your vet for the Thimerosal-Free Vaccine. Call ahead to make sure they carry it. If they don't, find a vet that does. Watch them draw up the vaccine in the room with you and watch them give it. If you can get a look or know the date on the vial, the older the serum the weaker it may be and less chance of a reaction. Especially for small dogs. I worry a lot about small dogs. They have to get the same amount as big dogs for these Rabies vaccines so it's seriously overdosing the small dogs and that's where the big problems come in. Maybe if you are buddy-buddy with your vet, ask for the oldest dated vial in the batch especially if your dog is small or has had past mild reactions. You need to know for yourself what's going in your dog so pay attention to everything going on around you. Now vets will probably charge you an office visit because you are seeing the vet, but isn't your dog's life worth it? I know mine is.

Once you completed this dreaded task of the vaccine, detox the liver also. Add in Milk Thistle the day of although I would use it for up to 30 days. Keep the food and water (filtered) clean, do not use any flea and tick meds AT ALL and avoid exposure to lawn chemicals such as fertilizers, bug and weed killers etc. Use Diatomaceous Earth instead.

Avoid air fresheners, candles, laundry soaps, bleach, dryer sheets, and shampoos to name a few in your home. All toxic! Use chemical-free products. Even Windex is toxic along with oven cleaners.

You can also apply a cold pack to injection area as soon as you get home from getting vaccine. Do that a couple times during the day. It helps to block the immune reaction. It's best to do it immediately after vaccine if you want to carry an ice pack with you, otherwise do it as soon as possible. Maybe have one handy in your vehicle.

The key here is to have a strong immune system. If your dog is on a kibble diet, you have a much bigger challenge to avoid severe reactions. But by doing the above mentioned, you can help reduce some of it.

* For any facial swelling, keep on hand the homeopathic remedy called **Apis**. Also great for insect bites and bee stings. Use **Sulphur** for red itchy skin as an added layer of protection.

Chapter 13
Leaving Your Pet at the Vet

Pet Parents taking their pets in for surgery or any type of illness, injury, routine teeth cleaning or even a spay/neuter, find out up front if your vet has a vet or vet tech on duty overnight after hours. Leaving your pet alone with a vet that leaves them alone at night can have its risks and can be deadly in certain situations. Even when it is routine and everything seems safe and non life-threatening, things can and have gone wrong.

Do not leave your pets overnight at your vets if they do not have someone with them 24 hours. A quick visit after hours by a vet tech or similar does not count. If your vet does not have 24-hour care around the clock, take your pet home. You can always bring them back to vet in the morning when someone is there. Clear this up before ever having surgery done or emergency care.

I know when two of my dogs had emergency surgery done, the on-call after hours vet said I could come get them in the morning. I said no, call me as soon as you are done and I will come get them and so I did. It was 2am.

Leaving your dog that is sick, injured, recuperating from surgery and that's had medications of any kind, should be monitored 24/7. And what about that nasty horrible food they feed your pet while there? You know the one with corn as the main ingredient? That's enough to definitely not leave your pet for any reason.

If your vet insists on your dog staying overnight, you can refuse. You can pick your pet up at the end of the day and take them home with special care instructions and watch them yourself. If an emergency arises, you can make a decision on what to do. You can call your vet if they handle on call emergencies or take them to an emergency clinic. Either way they have a better chance of survival with you being there instead of your pet being left in a crate all alone without being supervised at all times. If your vet refuses to let you take your pet home, find a new vet. In other words, find a vet that will agree <u>before</u> you ever take them in for any visit. It is your pet and your money. It is your choice to make. Not theirs.

If a human goes in for surgery, they get 24-hour care. In fact, those nurses just won't leave you alone to sleep. Your doctor won't release you either until you are well enough. But that human can walk out of that hospital at any time. No one is telling them no. No one is stopping them. Someone is with you at all times. So why is there no one taking care of pets after hours?

Why do vets keep a pet overnight if no one will be there? Its nuts!!!! Your pet is better off at home with you. If anything happens, you can handle the emergency. So prepare ahead of time if possible. Make a plan on what you will do if something goes wrong at home. Be ready to fly out the door if need be. No matter how routine things may be, things can always go wrong. This has happened more than once with pets staying overnight at a clinic that had no one present to care for them. There are reported deaths of pets dying for even routine care.

What if there was a fire? Or gas leak if the building has gas. So much can go wrong and out of your hands. Do not board your dog there if no one is at the clinic 24/7. If you have to leave your dog behind, find a friend or someone you know and trust that can keep your dog. Or hire a pet sitter. Its best if your pet is not locked up in a cage somewhere alone and probably scared without being able to move around.

I won't even recommend a boarding facility. If so, do they have cameras for you to watch 24/7? All boarding facilities should be wired with cameras in all areas. After all, don't many daycares for kids do this? If they don't, don't leave your kids there either.

We trust our vets whole-heartedly and we don't think anything could happen to our pets when in the care of professionals. This couldn't be further from the truth.

I cannot stress enough how important it is to educate yourself for your pet. Read books, get in a group to learn more. Be prepared.
Keep a first aid kit in your home and be prepared for emergencies as well. Keep emergency phone numbers on your frig. When you pick up your pet from the vet clinic at the end of the day, listen carefully to what your vet tells you for after care. Ask a lot of questions. Make sure you understand everything in case something goes wrong at home. Most of the time things go well but "just in case" be prepared. There is nothing more important than knowledge in saving a life. From knowing CPR, to handling broken limbs or poisoning.

Although we are never prepared for what may go wrong, we can help avoid fatalities when we have the knowledge and say-so on what goes on with our pets. Don't be bullied. Stand up for what is right! Don't trust your vet completely. Things can and do go wrong.

Speak with your vet that they will at least post a sign for all to see and read stating, "This clinic does not have on-staff employees after hours." That's the least vet clinics can do and you, as a pet parent, should not leave your pet otherwise. Know the risks involved. And stand up for your pets rights!

Chapter 14
Dog Parks: How Safe Are They?

Do you take your dog to a dog park? Are you all about safe fun days? This is my personal opinion on dog parks so go as you will. First off, dog parks are a great place to allow your dog to run OFF LEASH. I get that. But there are so many reasons **not** to go to a dog park.

1. Dogs that are sick may spread diseases especially in puppies. Vaccines or no vaccines, your dog can still get sick.
2. Your chances of a dogfight have increased dramatically. Be prepared financially along with possible lawsuits and even the worst, fatalities.

3. There have been reports of bad people throwing out poisonous treats, pieces of cheese with nails or razor blades in them.

4. Chemicals used to kill ticks, fleas, and bugs are on the grass and dirt. These toxins absorb into your dog's paws and/or skin and are dangerous (even deadly) to you and your pets. These chemicals do cause seizures, cancer etc.

If you really want to play with other dogs or socialize, call a dog friend up and meet at your house or theirs. Hang out in the backyard and play with the dogs. Install a sandbox for them to play in, an area with artificial turf that they may want to hang out on. How about a small pool for them to play in or a pool of plastic balls to roll around in. Make a doggie playground. You can do so much without visiting a public place where lots of things can and have gone wrong as well as reducing exposure to toxins.

    Dog parks are dangerous. I do NOT recommend them!

ENTER AT YOUR OWN RISK and the RISK OF YOUR OWN DOG!

Chapter 15
Safety Precautions When Walking Your Dog

When we as pet parents have the duty of walking our dog as we all should, we must also use our ears, eyes, and reflexes to stay alert and know how to handle other approaching animals especially loose ones. I am not a dog trainer. These are just my own common sense thoughts and what I see around me when walking my own dogs.

Most people walk their dogs during the day hours when people are out of their homes hanging out in the front yards or also walking their dogs. I myself walk my dogs late at night. I personally want to avoid humans as much as possible and I will explain later.

These are do's and don'ts when walking your dog and what to be aware of.

1. When you see an approaching pet parent walking their dog as well, either move to the other side of the street or go into the street away from the other approaching dogs. This is one I see that gets abused the most. Respect the other oncoming animals by allowing space.

2. Do not walk your dog on a retractable leash. I don't care if your dog is well behaved on it. It does not matter. You need to keep your dog close to you at all times. What if a loose animal approached your dog that was 15 feet away from you. How could you protect your dog? Reeling your dog back in won't work. I won't even mention anything about the retractables as I do use them in my front yard, but that's it.

3. Carry pepper spray and citronella spray on you when walking. Citronella for less aggressive dogs and animals, and pepper spray for an all out full-blown charging right-at-you animals. Carrying a taser gun doesn't keep them at a distance. You have very little chance to stop an interaction before it starts but can be used when they are already on you or your dog. A stick might help but where are you going to carry a stick while walking your dog?

4. Walk one dog at a time unless you can handle walking one calm well-trained and well-mannered dog and one not so well mannered. In a bad situation, you want to at least be able to give direction to one dog while you are holding on to the other. I would not recommend walking more than two dogs at a time unless you are an experienced dog handler or trainer. One is best however.

5. Do not wear headphones or talk on phone while walking your dog. This is like driving and texting. It just doesn't work in your favor. You won't be able to hear anything coming towards you in any direction. You won't be able to hear your dog growling.

6. STAY ALERT. Watch out for strange acting humans, wild animals and anything approaching you from the rear as well.

7. Carry your cell phone in your pocket in case you need to call 911. Like what if you step in a hole and break your foot or leg? You will need help. What if a loose animal attacks you or your dog, you will need to call for help. Keep your dogs under control though. Police have been known to shoot and ask questions later.

8. Let someone know where you are going and when to expect your return.

9. Do not walk your dog when it is hot or very cold outside. Before considering your walk, reach down and touch the pavement. If it is too hot to hold your hand on it for 20-30 seconds, it's too hot to walk your dog. I see this way too often. Same for cold. If it's warm out and you are taking a long long walk, carry some water for you and your dog. They even make fold-up portable water bowls you can stick in your pocket or clip on your belt. If you are walking your dog in below freezing temps, is it too cold for your feet or hands? If so, put some booties and a doggie coat on your dog. YES, they DO get cold like us humans. I normally won't walk my dogs below 50 degrees or above 75-80 degrees even at night not saying you shouldn't, just saying think before you do. And of course, this depends on the health and age of your dog. I am just saying, if your dog has heart issues, walking your dog in the heat will probably most likely kill it. That's my point here.

10. Don't let your dog poop in someone's yard. OK, when you gotta-go you gotta-go. So if your dog decides it needs to poop, keep it as close to the edge of the yard as possible closer to the street or the strip in-between sidewalks and the street. You get what I am saying. Keep your dog as far away from someone's house or yard as possible. Then pick up the poop with your poop bag and move on. I try to get my dogs to poop before we take a walk. Don't feed your dog then take a walk until they have pooped.

11. Do not walk your dog one hour before or one hour after feeding your dog. This can cause bloat or digestive issues including vomiting. Less common in raw fed dogs but don't push it.

12. Keep a close eye on your dog when walking. Don't let him eat things out of the grass. You don't know what may be lurking there. Poison could be in the grass or rotted chicken bones.

13. When returning from your walk, rinse off the dogs paws using apple cider vinegar and water or povidone iodine and water. It's best to dip feet into a pan of water, wash then remove and pat dry. This washes away pesticides and toxins from other grasses or even the chemicals dropped on the streets from cars. Your dog will lick their paws and you don't want them to lick those chemicals.

If you have a dog that is fearful, timid, hyper or reactive, it may be best to walk your dog after dark when children have gone inside. This way it keeps down the stress level of fearful dogs and doesn't allow reactive dogs to get overly excited. This is why I don't walk my dogs during the day. I avoid children at all costs. My dogs are not use to kids and have not been around them and I cannot say how they may react if a child did something to them or petted them wrong. So to PROTECT MY DOGS, I avoid daytime walks. If someone does ask me if they may pet my dog, I politely refuse for their child to pet my dogs. Because if something happens, it is my dog that will pay the price. I allowed their death sentence just because I was trying to be nice and not saying "no". I say no for the protection of my own dogs not counting any lawsuit that could happen. This is just not worth it to me. I don't know that child nor do I know if the parents have taught that child how to behave around a dog. For reactive/hyper or fearful dogs, you may want to try giving some CBD oil about 30 minutes to an hour before your walk.

If you have a dog that is a puller, put a harness on your dog instead of a collar. Harnesses can't choke or do damage to their esophagus and they can't slip out of them like they can a collar. Also, if your dog happens to get loose and run off, they won't be able to hang themselves if they get caught in a bad situation and hung up on something. They do make break away collars if you must.

This is for homeowners:
1. Don't throw your dog in the backyard and leave them there. Many times at night when it is really cool outside, I hear dogs barking as we

walk by. Even small dogs. WHY? Why are these dogs outside when it is so cold?

2. Keep your sidewalks clear of debris. ALL debris including tree limbs, trash, fallen acorns, leaves, fresh cut grass (unswept), portable basketball goals, motorcycles, and overgrown grass growing across the sidewalks from homeowners not taking care of their yards. I see grass growing together from one side of the sidewalk all the way across the other. Weeds 12+ inches tall in their yards. Trash piled up everywhere. Yep these are trashy uncaring lazy people and they live in every neighborhood including my own. How do people live like this? Sigh! Sorry but this just irks me!
Keeping sidewalks clear allows children; handicapped people in wheelchairs or alike and people walking their dogs to avoid the dangerous street.

3. Don't allow your dog to run loose in the front yard especially if they are hyper, reactive or are untrained. Even if it's midnight, there is someone always outside around you including wild animals. I had a Chihuahua charge us one night. The woman just stood there. Never said a word to her dog or me. I was hurdled over my dogs shielding them and had my hand out to keep the chi from attacking my dogs. I would rather get bit than my dogs. Then it might be "my word against hers case" against my bigger dogs. Now I have to avoid walking down in front of this house because of this woman that couldn't control her attacking dog so to protect mine.

4. Make sure your fence is secure and in good shape and good working order to help keep your dog contained and keep a lock on your gate so no one can open the gate or come inside. One night I was walking my dogs and as we passed by, a wood picket comes flying directly at my dog (within inches). Scared me to death as well as my dog. A large dog was on the other side of the fence and apparently this dog really wanted to come out of that fence at us and he knocked a picket out of the fence. What if he had of knocked out 2 or 3, just enough to come through that fence? This fence really needs replacing although the homeowner has only replaced a few pickets and zip tied some others.

5. If your dog won't stop barking, you need to do something about this. It's a city ordinance and is annoying for a dog to continuously bark. Some bark non-stop because they are bored or they just like to hear themselves bark. Get a bark collar or hire a trainer. Keep your dog inside most of the time. Give it one hour outside daily or 15 minute intervals. WALK YOUR DOG DAILY. But stop the barking. Whatever it takes. Be respectful to your neighbors. Certainly don't leave them outside during the day while you are away. You might just get a call from the police.

6. Keep all poisonous trees and plants out of harm's way. Check every single plant and tree to make sure it isn't poisonous to your pets. Most are.

7. Do not chain your dog. Chains cause aggressive dogs and it is cruel. Allow your dogs to roam freely within the confines of a fenced area. Give plenty of space with cover from the sun or any weather elements at all times. Make sure they have fresh filtered clean water daily. Social dogs are happy dogs and are not aggressive. Interact daily with your pets.

Ok there you have it. I said all the things you've wanted to say to others or maybe don't want to hear yourself. But these are safety guidelines and be respectful to others in keeping your dog safe, happy and for you as well.

Being overly protective or cautious keeps you and your pets out of court and keeps your dog from being euthanized if anything should go wrong, whether it is your dog's fault or not. In reality, it would be your fault if something bad happened to your dog by not taking steps to protect them at all costs.

First Aid Kit for Home Emergencies
(Use under guidance of veterinarian or poison control center in serious cases)

- Activated Charcoal (capsules) (for poisoning of toxins, food poisoning, ease vomiting and stomach cramps, upset stomach). Does **not** absorb - Cyanide, ethanol, ethylene glycol, iron, lithium, methanol, mineral acids and salts. Give 2-16 capsules or 1-6 tsp every 10-30 minutes. Seek emergency vet.
- Toxiban, CharcoAid, UAA Gel (contains Activated Charcoal)
- Vitamin K (rat poisoning-do not administer without professional guidance)
- Pro-Pectalin Gel, Imodium, Kaopectate, Slippery Elm, Bentonite Clay, Kaolin (Diarrhea)
- Arnica Montana (for shock and pain/bruising) Homeopathic
- CanineActiv (pain/inflammation for joint/sprain)
- Colloidal Silver (ears, cuts, eyes, teeth, skin)
- Gauze/Bandages/Tape
- Plastic wrap/bubble wrap/small boards for splints (bone breaks/sprains)
- Gas-x/Mylanta (Bloat-gives you a little bit of time to rush to hospital)
- Benadryl(severe reactions or use Epipen) and/or Quercetin (allergies/bee stings) (Also APIS, the homeopathic remedy)
- Rescue Remedy (fear, anxiety, calming, seizures)
- Hydrogen peroxide (3%) induce vomiting (do not apply to wounds or open sores) under guidance from vet or poison control
- Sterile Saline Solution (rinsing, irrigating and eye rinse)
- Mullein for coughs (also raw unfiltered honey)
- Rectal Thermometer
- CBD Oil (Seizures-rush to vet) (calming)
- Baking soda (make paste with water and apply to bee stings)
- Isopropyl (rubbing) alcohol (sterilizing)
- Povidone Iodine (Betadine) mix with water to dark tea color for rinsing or irrigating wounds or removing toxins from paws)

Remove Skunk Spray

In a plastic container, combine 1-quart hydrogen peroxide, 1/4 cup baking soda, and 1-2 teaspoons of liquid soap. Add lukewarm water if needed (for larger dogs). Mix ingredients well. The solution will fizz, as a chemical reaction is occurring. Use immediately - do not store. Do not soak your dog with water prior to bathing. Promptly begin cleansing the affected areas thoroughly, massaging the solution deep into your dog's coat. You may wish to use a sponge or washcloth.

Avoid getting the solution in the eyes, ears, or mouth. Allow the solution to remain on your dog for at least five minutes (longer if strong odor persists). Rinse your dog well with lukewarm water. Repeat steps 3-5 as necessary until odor is gone.

*Or keep on hand "**Nature's Miracle Skunk Odor Remover**"*

Treatment of Heat Exhaustion

If you believe your dog is suffering from heat exhaustion, seek veterinary care immediately even if your dog's condition does not seem serious. Cool water can be used to begin to decrease his body temperature during the trip to the veterinarian. Towels can be soaked in cool water and used to cover your dog. You can also place the towels between his legs and across his neck. Do not use cold water or ice. This may make the situation worse.

Emergency measures to cool the dog must begin at once. Move the dog out of the source of heat, preferably into an air-conditioned building. Take his rectal temperature every 10 minutes. Mild cases may be resolved by moving the dog into a cool environment.

If the rectal temperature is above 104°F, begin rapid cooling by spraying the dog with a garden hose or immersing him in a tub of cool water (not ice water) for up to two minutes. Alternatively, place the wet dog in front of an electric fan. Cool packs applied to the groin area may be helpful, as well as wiping his paws off with cool water. Monitor his rectal temperature and continue the cooling process until the rectal temperature falls below 103°F (39°C). At this point, stop the cooling process and dry the dog. Further cooling may induce hypothermia and shock.

Homemade Pedialyte (dehydration)
Mix together:
1-quart water
2 tablespoons sugar
1/2 teaspoon salt
or
1 liter of natural mineral water or filtered water
3 tablespoons sugar
1-teaspoon salt
1/2 teaspoon baking soda
The juice of half a lemon

Burns
Use cool water and rinse for 10-15 minutes and apply damp towels, rush to vet

For Bites and Wounds
Muzzle (in case dog is in pain and is snapping)
Snakebite: Carry dog if you can. Keep dog calm and not moving as much as possible. Rush to vet immediately. If you know which type of snake it was, this could be helpful in saving your dog's life as to which antidote or treatment to use. Don't go looking for it as you may be bitten as well and lose time in the process to save your dog.
~High-pressure rinse (using tap water) like with Waterpik or turkey baster for irrigating. Apply pressure to bleeding wounds. (Get to vet before the 4-hour window to reduce risk of infection)
You can use Ledum Palustre and/or Apis Mellifica pellets (homeopathic) twice a day for 2-3 days.~

Learn CPR
Never give OTC drugs such as Tylenol or Ibuprofen.

Pet Poison Hotline Number:
24/7 Animal Poison Control Center
855-764-7661
$59 USD per incident fee applies

Quick page reference to charts or solutions
Toothpaste and cleansing....................page 51
Quick Reference Feeding Chart...........page 60
Bone Broth Recipe...............................page 83
Herbal Dosing Chart..................pages 27, 253
List of Herbs for Diseases.................page 246

Find us at:
www.HolisticAndOrganixPetShoppe.com
www.CanineArthritisAndJoint.com

Disclaimer: The information herein is intended for informational, educational purposes only and is not a substitute for medical advice, diagnosis, or treatment. Do not attempt to self-diagnose or treat any health condition. You should always consult with a healthcare professional before starting any diet, exercise or supplementation program, before taking any medication, or if you have or suspect your pet may have a health problem. The Food and Drug Administration has not evaluated the information contained herein. The information presented here is not meant to replace your vets advice or prescribed medications, but only to suggest additional options to explore, based on your dog's health condition.

Limit of Liability/Disclaimer of Warranty: While the author has used her best efforts in preparing this book, she makes no representations or warranties with respect to the accuracy or completeness of the contents of this book. You should consult with a professional when appropriate. Author & publisher will not be liable for any loss of profit or any other commercial damages, including but not limited to special, incidental, consequential, or other damages.

Copyright © Debbie Daniel
9781793817389
Updated 6-23-2020
Revised Edition 2 - January 9th, 2019
All rights reserved. No part of this book may be reproduced, scanned, or distributed in any printed or electronic form without permission.

Printed in the United States of America
Cover designed by Debbie Daniel

Notes about the conventional veterinarian profession:

You may find in this book that I am pretty tough on veterinarians. And the reason is because they are our "go to" source. The middle man between Big Pharma, pet foods and our pets. I feel that a good supportive veterinarian is hard to find. Many are in a hurry, are all about the money or don't care enough to listen or help our pets. I hope veterinarians will wake up to the fact that this isn't acceptable and us pet parents are starting to stand up for our pets and demand better care that isn't guided by pharmaceutical companies and pet food companies or greed. So find a good vet that understands your needs and desires for your pets. And holistic vets may not be completely holistic. Learn the differences. Do they recommend optional vaccines? I understand vets may not always know about nutrition nor do they quite understand raw diets due to the talk traveling throughout the vet profession to advise against raw diets. But I hope that veterinarians in the future will have the desire to look outside these conventional means and learn how to integrate alternative methods as well. We need to keep the body healthy instead of waiting to treat a sick body.

Vets should recommend wellness exams instead of pushing vaccines for income purposes. Vets are crucial in emergencies and extreme illnesses and diagnosis, but mild illnesses (such as allergies etc) or wellness exams should not consist of vaccines or risky medications and garbage prescription pet foods. Veterinarians are not nutritionist's and most vet nutritionist's work for pet food companies. So it is crucial that vets support and learn about homemade diets. This is our future. A wellness exam can/should consist of yearly blood work (CBC), urinalysis, thyroid check, heartworm check, heart check, teeth inspection/cleaning if needed, x-rays if needed, as well as recommending joint supplements for all ages. An overall health wellness exam to help your pet live longer. Therefore, vets will have a client for life. A wellness exam can be a lot of money coming in if they will recommend this instead of vaccines to get you in the door. This is a win-win situation. If you have no choice but to visit a reactive versus a proactive veterinarian, you'll need to act as your pet's advocate. Don't ever be afraid to speak up on behalf of your dog.

Printed in Great Britain
by Amazon